ADAM AND EVOLUTION

ADAM AND

Maris Ross & David S. Jeans

EVOLUTION

Leslie Frewin of London

First published 1974 by
Leslie Frewin Publishers Limited,
Five Goodwin's Court,
Saint Martin's Lane,
London WC2N 4LL,
England.

This book is set in Garamond Bold
Printed and Bound by Weatherby Woolnough, Wellingborough,
England
ISBN 0 85632 075 7

CONTENTS

1

The Unrest of Man

IN EVERY SORT of culture since the beginnings of history man has endeavoured to account to himself for his origins. The mass of mythological and theological material is evidence that the human psyche has some deep-seated need to seek for explanations of the curious phenomenon of humanity. Perhaps the need is concerned primarily with man's destiny rather than the more academic matter of his creation, but since his nature and his origins might lend meaning to his existence, accounts of these matters have exercised an equal fascination upon him.

As different cultures have arisen, each has compiled its own version of the subject in a manner as compatible as possible with its own experience. As sophistication and knowledge widened, so new myths and theologies were demanded and inability to provide them may well be related to the subsequent death or decadence of the culture in which such failure occurred.

By the middle of the nineteenth century, both Catholic and Protestant theologies – which it may be contended were based not so much upon the Gospels themselves as upon the various churches' doctrinaire interpretation of them – had outlived their usefulness to Western man. That is to say his experience of his universe and immediate environment seemed to him increasingly inconsistent with traditional dogma.

At that time, science and the objective approach to problems had new things to say on many subjects. It had already eased and transformed peoples' way of life and promised much more in the future. Indeed, to the prevailing types of mind, it offered at least as much as the theologians had promised in earlier times but which, in the experience of many, they had dismally failed to deliver. Already a dichotomy was arising between those who sought to preserve the guidelines of the past and those who sought to explain circumstances in terms of formulated observations, experiment, and first-hand experience.

Beyond pointing out, to the discomfort of the Church, that the earth was demonstrably not the centre of the universe, science had said little as to the origins or significance of man himself. The traditionalists could still pronounce upon moral issues, behaviour, and fundamental truth without reference to any authority other than their own. The general acceptance of liberal ideas, new outlooks, and educational methods more consistent with the new scientific approach could still be repressed by clerics with a status and a philosophy to defend. The pressure for change was increasing. There was a growing hunger for new myths, new accounts, new explanations compatible with the new gods of scientific method. By the middle of the century a vacuum existed which the Western human psyche felt an urgent need to fill.

In 1859 Charles Darwin published *The Origin of Species* and the questing psyche received an answer. If the answer seemed chill to some, to others it had the paramount merit of coming from an authentic scientific source and at least on that account they were happy to accept it.

The Darwinist theory of evolution is based on two quite distinct propositions: firstly, the survival of the fittest, maintains that if any change takes place in the genes of any life-form so that new characteristics will be transmitted to the descendants of that individual, such descendants will survive more readily than other members of their species if this new characteristic affords them advantages in the particular environment in which they happen to find themselves; secondly, random mutation postulates that the changes which occur from time to time in the genes of individual

THE UNREST OF MAN

life-forms, take place purely as a matter of accident and chance – thus such changes may or may not be advantageous to survival, and on a chance basis the majority would be irrelevant or detrimental to it.

The proposition does not of course attempt to say anything regarding the origin of life itself but only how, given some initial living organism, different species of life may originate.

As these ideas became popularised in the controversy which for the subsequent thirty years ranged around them, attention was focused on the first of the two propositions – the idea of natural selection by the survival of the fittest and, at least in the minds of the non-specialist intelligentsia, it became synonymous with Darwinism. Today, over a hundred years later, the theory seems acceptable as self-evident to any relaxed schoolchild's thinking. At the time, however, this version of Darwinism rocked the clerics and some others, who found distasteful the implications that men had derived from a species of ape and had changed and improved very gradually by the process of natural selection.

They contested the theory on many grounds but since they emphasised the spectacular immediate implication, that mankind's father was not after all God but rather an ape, inevitably theirs was a lost battle. Things might have gone differently had they concentrated on the dubious speculation of the second part of the proposition, the theory of chance. As it was, less prejudiced people were content to see in the doctrine of the survival of the fittest comparatively simple and straightforward explanations as to how man had arisen. If they had religious beliefs they saw no need to disturb these unduly, simply because God had chosen this particular method of creating man; on the contrary the idea may have tended to reconcile some miraculous elements of the creation with everyday experience and to point to a time when more knowledge would remove the necessity for blind faith.

By the time the controversy had died down, the public had come to feel that recognition of an ape ancestry was a small price to pay for the advantages and blessings of science as against the miseries, futility and inconsistencies of theology. And, indeed, so far as it went the statement concerning natural selection was no doubt true and incontrovertible. After all the fittest survives not only in the field of biology, but also for instance in the economic world, and in any case the theory can, and has been, well demonstrated under controlled conditions. From there on, those with no immediate or special interest in the matter could assume that Darwin and the neo-Darwinist school which subsequently developed his original ideas, were right. In short the vindication of the first proposition concerning survival of the fittest was also accepted as substantiation of the second – regarding random mutation.

From the biologists' point of view Darwin formulated the operation by which nature can gradually, over millions of years, build up the vastly complicated structure of a wide variety of living species from a few original simple life-forms. With this authoritative assurance they felt free to proceed to develop their discipline in the light of objective method. Not only scientists but intellectuals generally would rejoice with Thomas Huxley that we could now dispense with the supernatural and press on unimpeded to realise the full potential of rational thought.

Perhaps it was the attractions afforded by the prospects of such freedom from traditional restraints which inhibited Huxley and other able scientists of the time from pointing out that survival of the fittest did not necessarily entail change by random mutation. Certainly they felt with justification that the dogmatic authority exercised by the Churches in so many cultural and educational matters must be discredited if rationality was to prevail. In the climate of the time it was difficult enough to uphold their end of the controversy: thus, to cavil with some part of Darwin's ideas might only undermine his image in the eyes of the world and discredit his theories in whole rather than in part.

Darwin was a man of science. If his thought was not entirely original, he supported it by meticulous and comprehensive field investigation. The scientific world at least was satisfied that here was no armchair naturalist, no philosopher trying to muscle in on sensational pseudo-scientific pronouncements but one who was genuinely concerned to observe and record facts and, apparently, to base his conclusions upon them. The general public was intrigued with work expressed in terms comprehensible to it which it was encouraged to believe was the authentic scientific account of man's origins – the first account alternative to the theological Adam and Eve. Henceforward it was reasonable and rational to believe that the age of myth was over. Now demonstrable truth was available to fulfil the age-old functions of the inaccessible, imaginative mystic.

With the tide flowing so satisfactorily in their direction could the guardians of scientific authenticity be blamed if they winked an eye? Science, then, we may suggest, was more concerned that Darwin should win his battle with the theologians than that the more dubious parts of his theories should be corrected. Looking back we can but congratulate the scientific world of that time for its good sense; any hair-splitting could only have confused the issue. The development of mankind and the growth of Western culture demanded the denial of traditional restraints. Their stranglehold could be broken and discredited only by such an antitheses as Darwin suggested, and Darwin's authority had at all costs to be upheld.

By the end of the century, science had succeeded in its challenge to the authority of the Churches. It could pursue its business unin-terrupted by denouncement of the righteousness of its conclusions and objectives. Yet, in some vague way, society, or a substantial part of it including many of the highest intellectual and moral integrity, were not convinced. The controversy was not so much resolved as allowed to die; thenceforward the protagonists, while not in fact reconciling their views, seemed to wish to appear to be reconciled.

Many scientists themselves continued to profess religious belief while pursuing a professional discipline which denies the possibility of the miraculous. Churchmen retreated on many issues and indeed seemed unduly concerned to explain the rationality of their views without however abandoning the fundamental faith in an historical authenticity of the direct intervention of a God – in the person of Jesus Christ – in the world's development. Both parties seemed to many to be more concerned with expediency than with the integrity of their convictions.

Universities continued to teach the inconsistent concepts of theology and physics, biology and psychiatry in watertight com-partments but nevertheless virtually under the same roof. Philosophers – whose business presumably was to mediate in the matter – appeared content to keep out of trouble and to attribute all divergent views to unresolvable problems of semantics. Academics in general devoted themselves to their own specialities and, at least until recently, carefully avoided cross-disciplinary studies.

As C G Jung* has remarked

> We have universities where the very thought of divine intervention is considered beneath dispute, but where theology is part of the curriculum. A research worker in natural science who thinks it positively obscene to attribute the smallest variation of an animal species to an act of divine arbitrariness may have in another compartment of his mind a full-blown Christian faith which he likes to parade on Sundays.

We find then a dichotomy in academic and intellectual life and we would suggest that, at the root of it, lies the Darwinist idea of random mutation. As a result, a sort of social schizophrenia has developed in which the state and our educational institutions speak with two voices – and seem to feel free to pontificate with either according to whichever happens to be best suited to the particular cause advocated at any particular moment. Those seeking guidance in the business of living encounter not one but two father figures, Science and the Church, saying different things.

It is suggested that we can blindly believe in an act of creation for divine purposes or accept an alternative dogma – that the jellyfish happened to develop by a chance series of random events, each in turn duly stabilised, and that events of this sort continued thereafter until at last fully-fashioned man occurred.

If the younger generation seems confused to their elders, is it entirely surprising? If it lacks respect for the Establishment, can it be blamed? If it reverts to interest in black magic, primitive religions, and the arcane, have we anything more positive to suggest?

For not only youth ask questions. A quality of curiosity is universal and, so long as the answers to our questions contain hope for the future of the individual and his species, we can derive enormous energy, courage, and inspiration to work to improve the lot of ourselves, our children, and our fellows. When, however, our

* *Civilization in Transition* (1964). Volume X of *The Collected Works of C G Jung*. Routledge & Kegan Paul.

enquiries produce the sort of evidence which is inimical to hope, destructive to the sort of ideals which since the evolution of consciousness we have cherished, then energy and inspiration may cease to flow and courage may fail. Dammed up, they seek other channels, other outlets, and take forms dissimilar from those the world has seen to date.

By the second half of the twentieth century, man in the sense of large numbers of people in politically sophisticated communities has educated himself sufficiently to be aware of the existence of arguments inconsistent with his earlier hopes. They are in fact directly contrary to any on which it is practicable to base ideals or a sense of progress and destiny. Although these arguments have been implicit in accepted scientific thinking for the past century, it is perhaps only since the 1960s that the effects of their implications have become apparent. The generation of this period, having been brought up to prize so much achieved in so many directions, discovered for itself with astonishment and dismay how little progress had been made in others. In particular, it sees no prospect from what has gone before, of achieving any way of living which could command its wholehearted esteem.

Before proceeding to review the idea of random mutation and on the accumulation of evidence against its probability, it is worth pausing to consider its extraordinary social importance.

We have already pointed out that man's place in relation to his environment and to the forces of nature has always been a matter of prime importance in every culture. In times gone by, priests held no less status than kings, and their authority derived from their accepted relative familiarity with these mysteries.

For 10,000 years of history some form of religion or taboo has functioned as an underpinning of the way of life in every civilisation. The derivatives of religion – the ideas which can in one way or another be associated with it – enabled kings, priests, dictators, and governments to establish and uphold authority. Ethical codes for governing the conduct of man and their relationships with one another were inspired and constructed around the implicit concept that everyone could play a part, however small, in some grand pattern which was taking place or soon to emerge.

Since the nineteenth century, the influence of the objective type of scientific approach has offered a seeming alternative authority from which fundamental guidance – on matters quite outside its ability to contribute – might be sought. It has suggested an order of life in which the rational faculty of mind is the final arbiter. Since happiness and emotional satisfaction are not subject to definition and measurement, its criteria are solely those of material needs and physical wellbeing. It may concede that man does not live by bread alone but it has no means of recognising, let alone for providing, spiritual wine.

The domination of the thought and development of Western culture for the last century by the scientific outlook demonstrates in part its ability to perform the function formerly carried out by religion. However, its continued success in this direction depends upon at least two conditions:

(a) its ability to win and conserve the respect of a wide spectrum of the populace by reflecting individual aspirations and experience, and

(b) its ability to widen the frontiers of experience as well as materialism – so as to contribute to the internal harmonies whereby different sections of society may pursue common goals.

To satisfy these conditions a viable scientific outlook must be seen to be true in the sense of conforming to experience, or to its own techniques of proving hypothesis by controlled experiment. It will inevitably fail in these conditions – or rather regress to an earlier mythological-type function – if it upholds, as axiomatic, propositions which can neither be demonstrated nor afford creative individuals a useful vehicle for their aspirations.

Only in recent years are we beginning to realise that science and even our rational faculty itself are only tools rather than a way of life. For like most tools, the misuse of science is highly dangerous, producing not only material wealth but also the nuclear bomb and pollution of the environment. Its inability to contribute to value judgments, and its constant tendency to confuse dogma with hypothesis, may have something to do with an upsurge in crime and violence, alcoholism, drug addiction, suicide, mental illness, and such manifestations as lead many to accept the idea that our society is sick.

Even its material contribution is qualified, considering we still lack the knowledge to cure the common cold, to run an economy without inflation, or to cultivate any spirit of harmony and unity between the groups in society who conceive their interests to be irreconcilable with those of others.

Herein lies the importance of Darwin's ideas and their subsequent development in neo-Darwinism for it is at this point, and with these theories, that life and science must ultimately deny each other. Existing lines of materialistic thought offer no prospect of further progress. Change, yes; progress, no. H G Wells*, a tireless exponent of the blessings of a scientific philosophy, admitted his defeat when he finally wrote of the man of our time: 'If his thinking has been sound, then this world is at the end of its tether. The end of everything we call life is close at hand and cannot be evaded . . . The more he scrutinised the realities around us, the more difficult it became to sketch out any Pattern of Things to Come.'

If humanity is indeed the outcome of the operation and accident of pure chance we must assume that as it was in the beginning so it will be in the future. If man is indeed a random creature he has no future inherent in him. There can be no purpose in his suffering, no significance in his form, no reality but pleasure, no pleasure but sensation, no prospect but struggle for survival in an increasingly over-populated, polluted world. At random we came; at random we would go.

If we must rule out the possibility that there may lie within us, influencing our thinking and motivation towards some positive ends, some inbuilt seeds or mechanism of our own survival, some instinct which may prompt us to make choices consistent with the survival of mankind, we must either abandon hope or cling to the slender possibility that we shall be able to think – and agree between ourselves – our way out of all the dangerous dilemmas that constantly threaten us.

If we are not to become victims of some mass type of anxiety psychosis, engendered by the necessity of thinking rather than growing, we need a sense of destiny or meaning which will always

* *Mind At The End Of Its Tether.* H G Wells (Now in print with the H G Wells Society). Quoted by permission of the Estate of H G Wells.

be denied us so long as the idea that we owe our existence to random mutation remains unchallenged.

The relevance of meaning to everyday life has been stressed by observers whose work provides direct experience of the consequences of the lack of it. Viktor Frankl*, Professor of Psychiatry and Neurology at the University of Vienna, for instance:

> I would like to say that reductionism today is a mask for nihilism. Contemporary nihilism no longer brandishes the word nothingness; today nihilism is camouflaged as nothing-but-ness . . .
>
> This situation accentuates a world-wide phenomenon that I consider a major challenge to psychiatry – I have called it the existential vacuum. More and more patients are crowding our clinics and consulting-rooms complaining of an inner emptiness, a sense of total and ultimate meaninglessness of their lives. One should not assume that this state of affairs is confined to our western civilisation . . . I was invited to lecture at the Karl Marx University in Leipzig, in Czechoslovakia and in Poland. During the question and answer period it transpired again and again that really the same problems are confronting our psychiatric colleagues in communist countries.
>
> To attempt a short explanation of the causes of this phenomenon, I would say that, in contrast to animals, man is not told by drives and instincts what he *must* do. Nor, in contrast to man in former times, is he any longer told by traditions and values what he *should* do. Sometimes he does not even know what he basically *wants* to do, but instead he just wants to do what other people are doing – which is conformism. Or else he just does what other people want him to do – which is totalitarianism. But in addition to conformism and totalitarianism we can observe a third side-effect of all the existential vacuum, and that is neuroticism. I am referring to a new type of neurosis that I have termed noogenic neurosis . . . (which) mainly results from the existential vacuum, from existential frustration . . . There is also agreement between various authors in various countries, that about twenty per cent of neuroses today are noogenic by nature and origin.
>
> We may define the existential vacuum as the frustration of what we may consider to be the most basic motivational force in man, and what we may call, by a deliberate over-simplification the will to meaning – in contrast to the Adlerians' will to power and to the Freudians' will to pleasure.

* *The Alpbach Symposium, Beyond Reductionism.* Edited by Arthur Koestler & J H Smythies. Hutchinson Publishing Group. 1969. Reprinted by permission of A D Peters and Company.

This thinking is echoed throughout the modern schools of existential psychology because they find the concept necessary to their work of restoring to active and fruitful lives those who have first sensed the impact of life without meaning.

Carl Gustav Jung, to whom credit should be given for first expounding the function which a sense of meaning plays in a healthy active psyche, included among his patients many highly intelligent and talented people who had achieved recognition and wealth before they were driven by inner conflicts to consult him. Nevertheless, even for those more naturally gifted than the majority of us, he concluded that some sense of function in an overall pattern, some sort of meaning in life, is a necessary condition of their continuing health and energies.

Not only psychologists but artists and philosophers too have stressed the urgency of a basis on which individuals may build some kind of *weltanschauung* compatible with accepted axioms of the culture of time. One may quote the despair of Chekhov's character in *The Three Sisters*:

> What is all this for? Why all this suffering? The answer will be known one day and then there will be no more mysteries left, but until then life must go on, we must work and work and think of nothing else . . . . Our faces will be forgotten and our voices and how many of us there were. But our sufferings will bring happiness to those who come after us, peace and joy will reign on earth, and there will be kind words and kind thoughts for us and our times.

Bertrand Russell* in his *History of Western Philosophy* thus set out some basic problems we need to recognise:

> Is the world divided into mind and matter, and, if so, what is mind and what is matter? Is mind subject to matter, or is it possessed of independent powers? Has the universe any unity or purpose? Is it evolving towards some goal? Are there really laws of nature, or do we believe in them only because of our innate love of order? Is man what he seems to the astronomer, a tiny lump of impure carbon and water, impotently crawling on a small and unimportant planet? Or is he what he appears to Hamlet? Is he perhaps both at once? Is there a way of living that is noble and another that is base, or are all the ways of

* *History of Western Philosophy*. Bertrand Russell. George Allen & Unwin. 1961.

17

living really futile? If there is a way of living that is noble, in what does it consist and how shall we achieve it? Must the good be eternal in order to deserve to be valued, or is it worth seeking even if the universe is inexorably moving towards death? Is there such a thing as wisdom, or is what seems such merely the ultimate refinement of folly? To such questions no answer can be found in the laboratory. Theologies have professed to give answers, all too definite; but their very definiteness causes modern minds to view them with suspicion. The study of these questions, if not the answering of them, is the business of philosophy.

Why, then, you may ask, waste time on such insoluble problems? To this one may answer as a historian, or as an individual facing the terror of cosmic loneliness.

These sad reflections contrast strangely with the pre-Darwinism Wordsworth's 'Bliss was it in that dawn to be alive, but to be young was very heaven.'

If reality consists of whatever concept is accepted in our place and time then before we become too depressed we might well follow the advice of the graffiti writer's scrawl: 'Do not adjust your mind – there is a fault with reality.'

Thus the root of the unrest of our day and the difference between present-day society and that of earlier times may well be the absence of that sense of purpose in life which sustained previous generations and which is, perhaps, an essential ingredient of human psychology. While the nature of a conviction of destiny, individual and universal, might not always have been clear and often was felt for entirely fallacious reasons, it nevertheless fulfilled a vital function. Life was worth while because a faith was upheld by some who could be regarded with respect. If their actions implied that one day sense would be made out of suffering, the rest of us could accept our lot with resignation. Somewhere, somehow there was some useful function served by our existence. Let us not be persuaded to abandon that hope too readily by a pseudo-scientific dogma which has outworn its usefulness. So much future happiness and wellbeing depends upon demonstrating the inconsistencies of Darwinism that no possibility of doing so, compatible with honesty, can be passed up.

For to deny Darwin is not, as his contemporary supporters seem to have supposed, to deny his thesis that man like other life-forms is subject to rules which govern the evolution of plant and animal life generally. Darwin maintained there was no cause to consider man a unique life-form, while his opponents quoted scripture to argue that he was wrong. In fact, like many original minds he was probably right in his main contention but for the wrong reasons. His main concern was after all to demonstrate by direct field observation the way in which successive generations of creatures adapt to their surroundings. The voluminous data he compiled for this purpose was however irrelevant to the reasons why individual members of a species may be born with characteristics different from those of their forebears. In fact he offered no evidence on this point but merely assumed that new characteristics occurred accidentally, purely at random, becoming established features of the species if they were useful in the ecological system in which they developed.

To challenge Darwinism is merely to suggest that the mutations and change which undoubtedly occur in the course of evolution are not so random as one might first suppose. The cells of a growing acorn or hatching egg do not orientate themselves at random. They follow some order either inherent in them or dictated to them by some archetypal pattern. Chance plays no part. They are bound inexorably to the orderly and remorseless progression of events. Their free will, if any, is strictly limited to the capacity and versatility of their various roles. A force inherent in them directs the cells of an acorn to organise themselves to form an oak tree and the cells of an egg to form a chicken. May it not then be supposed that even elementary life-forms contain some programme which determines not only how they will develop, but also predisposes the mutation to change not at random but in certain more specific directions?

Recognition of these possibilities is not likely to re-establish discredited doctrines of the Church but may make room for the development of ideas transcending those of the past, of the type which Sir Alister Hardy has called 'Natural Theology'. Exciting possibilities will open up which are likely to transform our culture and its ideals in every department of life.

We are not entitled to brush aside existing evolutionary theory because we find its conclusions depressing or because we consider it incompatible with any more positive directional hypothesis. We should therefore examine it as it is currently taught; noting, in passing, that it has no practical validity nor outcome in the modern world except as material for teaching, for demonstrating how scientific thought, which has proved true in other fields, could possibly apply also in this one.

Neo-Darwinists hold that variations in species arise from the chance mutation of genes: a random genetic change happens in a life-form, one mutation among many variations. The mutation is a change in chromosomal genes during the reduplication of the genetic DNA code which forms the make-up of that particular creature. The change has been likened to a secretary's typing error of one letter in a string while copying a master-list. Thereafter natural selection takes over, sifting out for survival the mutations most suited to the particular climate and circumstances in which they find themselves. The unsuitable die out. A high proportion of aborted foetuses have been found to be abnormal and this appears to be nature's way of getting rid of the abnormality. All the time, the growing part is encouraging the mutations in a species' gene pool that are most beneficial, and discarding the unfit.

As an account of a method of undirected yet progressive change, this is plausible enough when considering the case of the simplest life-forms consisting of a few cells only. It leaves a great deal unanswered when it is applied to higher forms of life, with their several thousand functional organs, each with its own complex structure and distinct, highly specialised purpose. Every minute part of the heart, liver, spleen, kidneys, ears, different sorts of joints, lungs, as well as blood, skin, hair, teeth, and nails, has a thousand specific characteristics. These did not evolve separately, one by one, in creatures otherwise whole and functioning. They had to form simultaneously in concert with one another. In building a computer or even in cooking a meal, one of the problems which arises concerns the co-ordination of the preparation of the various parts of the whole – an art which, in industry, requires specialist techniques in themselves, quite apart from the overall design problems. To believe it can happen by chance not only once but over and over again, entails belief in a time-span so enormous as to predate the earth itself. The human brain is said to consist of 12,000,000,000,000 cells. Presumably each has its function and its usefulness has lent its possessors some advantages in the battle for survival. Yet for each single function to arise even in successive generations a very large number of individuals in each of these generations would be necessary, and the number of generations requiring up to twenty years each to mature would involve a period exceeding the five thousand million years which geologists place on the age of the earth. In short the arithmetic of the idea of random mutation simply does not come out right.

Darwin said, when arguing the case for the formation of an eye by this means, 'Let this process go on for millions of years; and during each year on millions of individuals of many kinds; and may we not believe that a living optical instrument might thus be formed superior to one of glass?' However, the number of years available was not so great as all that and we know that the number of individuals of any species living at any one time was often strictly limited – the earth was not always inhabited so densely as at present. Darwin himself remarked doubtfully this theory 'seems, I freely confess, absurd to the highest degree'.

It has been suggested that if enough monkeys banged away long enough on enough typewriters eventually one of them would produce the works of Shakespeare. In practice this would not happen because there would not be enough monkeys, nor enough typewriters, nor enough paper for the purpose. In other words the theory of random mutation demands not only an infinity of time but also an infinity of resources to stabilise each stage of a progressive advance.

Besides the difficulties of time and resources, there are three others which cannot easily be explained away.

Firstly, random processes are observed in various branches of physics to lead to the breakdown of ordered and differentiated forms and consequent reversion of material to its basic elements. This is to say that the difficulty of writing Shakespeare would be enhanced by the disintegration of the monkeys and their typewriters in the process of doing so. Complex life-forms would not only have to happen but they would also have to overcome an infinite number of natural hazards which, in the process, would be likely to happen fortuitously and related in no way to the general process of evolution.

Secondly, the individual members of some species undergo change, beneficial to their individual longevity, in the latter half of their natural life-span – that is to say after completion of that part of life during which they are most prolific. For example C G Jung has pointed out that not only women but men also undergo a change in middle life, usually in their early forties. The function of this change enables the individual to reorientate his energies so that he can not only confront the prospect of death with equanimity but also, in the meanwhile, can utilise his experience in his earlier years in a constructive manner which brings him satisfaction and a deep sense of fulfilment. Since in that period of prehistory when man evolved, his life-span rarely exceeded forty years, it is not easy to understand how such characteristics would ever establish themselves.

Thirdly, any organ, like a building, a bridge, or a machine, has, besides its immediately useful functioning parts, basic structures which have no survival value except to support the work of the organ as a whole. It is inconceivable that even the simplest organs came into being whole, as a result of a single random accident. Neither can it be imagined that the preliminary vestige of an organ would confer on its individual possessor marked survival advantages. In short the interim benefits of a developing but incomplete organ would surely be insufficient to encourage its further refinement by random processes and its survival value. A short-necked giraffe would have a difficult time indeed.

It is probably because of the apparent unimportance at first sight of evolutionary theory from the point of view of any practical application that the subject has been so astonishingly neglected by those most competent to examine it.

So far not many authorities have had the courage of Professor Sir Alister Hardy, a zoologist and biologist of the highest reputation in academic circles, who was moved to raise (in his Gifford Lectures) the exciting issues which it may become permissible – even fashionable – to consider once Darwinism is put in its right perspective. He suggested that evolution may well have been directed by some inherent selective pattern which steered activity so that more mutations of genes took place in certain specific channels than in others. If the creature concerned is well suited to survival in the circumstances towards which it feels an urge, it will tend to prefer those circumstances to former modes of existence. Thus, for instance, a water-bird would take to water first and evolve webbed feet, rather than the neo-Darwinist theory that creatures which happened to evolve webbed feet would take to water.

One of the characteristics of nature is its rhythm and pattern, from the seasons of the year down to a microscopic view of the cells that form life. Nothing seems to be haphazard. Even inert matter like particles of sand, when vibrated by rhythm, weave intricate patterns of circles with radiating lines.

A hypothesis that evolution takes place to a predetermined pattern might envision the influence of an archetypal life-form. Radiating out from this prototype would be all sorts of channels of life, moulds waiting to be filled, like the patterns created in the sand. When life began to grow and permutate, directional development took place, just as an acorn is destined to grow into an oak tree bearing enough acorns from which the rest of the forest can spring. Life-forms would all the time have an urge to push in some way to develop their organisation until they fulfilled what was required to flow into these moulds of predetermined life-forms. Survival would be governed by what fitted into the channels of the pattern, explaining perhaps more realistically than neo-Darwinism the general progression of evolution towards increasing organisation and differentiation rather than the increasing disorder of inanimate matter that forms a principle of physics.

A recent renewal of interest in evolutionary theory owes a great deal to men like Arthur Koestler, who need answers to the sort of phenomena of life which he describes in *The Roots of Coincidence*, and to imaginative scientists such as C H Waddington, Professor of Genetics at Edinburgh University, who tells us that we can shortly expect revolutionary changes in biological theory.

This is no place for a detailed account or appraisal of the proceedings of the 1968 Alpbach symposium and the Serbelloni symposia, first held in 1966 at the respective instigations of Koestler and Waddington. Perhaps these meetings made laymen aware for the

23

first time that scientists were by no means all convinced neo-Darwinists. However the implications of these proceedings have been little popularised and neither our intelligentsia nor the general public seem aware how revolutionary were the discussions nor how profound their eventual effect may be.

The symposia made evident that some imaginative yet nevertheless recognised scientists are beginning to be willing to admit the inconsistencies in maintaining the argument that creation depends on the occurrence of the one useful chance mutation at each stage in a necessary series of billions. Several now suggest evolution could take place in accordance with a purposive system which is at present ill-defined and difficult to see. They argue that evolution by chance is no more likely than evolution predisposed, by some causes or mechanisms as yet unidentified, to flow into certain specific channels. The crux of the matter is whether mutations take place on a purely random basis or whether they in fact take place by some sort of curious process which directs that more mutations take place in certain directions than in others.

There is a certain amount of evidence to this effect. For example, the Tasmanian wolf and the Siberian wolf, which supposedly evolved independently over eight hundred million years, are just one example of species from different land masses that resemble each other very closely. If these were the result of survivals of chance mutations, why so alike?

Again, a laboratory experiment suggests that flies have a pre-disposition to evolve in a particular shape. Experiments produced stocks of the fruit-fly *Drosophila* which, by mutation, lacked eyes or antennae. By neo-Darwinist theory, these flies should have continued to develop randomly and been discarded if the absence of eyes and antennae did not suit their environment. Instead, by inbreeding, they somehow reassorted their genes so that their eyes and antennae reappeared. Rather than random development or extinction, evolution returned them to the shape and mould of the fruit-fly.

The flavour of some of the papers presented at the symposia can be sampled by this extract from that of Professor Ludwig Von Bertalanffy* of the State University of New York:

* *The Alpbach Symposium, Beyond Reductionism.* Edited by Arthur Koestler & J H Smythies. Hutchinson Publishing Group. 1969. Reprinted by permission of A D Peters and Company.

Many pertinent questions (concerning Darwin's work) have been left unanswered and swept under the carpet. I for one, in spite of all the benefits drawn from genetics and the mathematical theory of selection, am still at a loss to understand why it is of selective advantage for the eels of the Comacchio to travel perilously to the Sargasso Sea, or why Ascaris has to emigrate all round the host's body instead of comfortably settling in the intestine where it belongs; or what was the survival value of a multiple stomach for a cow when a horse, also vegetarian and of comparable size, does very well with a simple stomach; or why certain insects had to develop those admirable mimicries and protective colorations when the common cabbage butterfly is far more abundant with its conspicuous white wings. One cannot reject these and innumerable similar questions as incompetent; if the selectionist explanation works well in some cases, a selectionist explanation cannot be refused in others.

In current theory, a speculative 'may have been' or 'must have been' - expressions occurring innumerable times in selectionist literature - is accepted in lieu of an explanation which cannot be provided. For example, paleontologists give ingenious reasons why such and such a shape of tooth or bone or reconstructed muscle was advantageous to a carnivore, tree-climber or runner, but it must remain subjective opinion what selective value to attribute to a sabre tooth or the rudiments of an eye millions of years ago.

This is at the bottom of the question, recently discussed anew – namely, whether the principle of selection is a tautology. It is in the sense that the selectionist explanation is always a construction a posteriori. Every surviving form, structure or behaviour – however bizarre, unnecessarily complex or outright crazy it might appear – must, ipso facto, have been viable or of some 'selective advantage', for otherwise it would not have survived. But this is no proof that it was a product of selection.

As with history, a part of the fascination of evolutionary theory is due to the light it may throw upon our future. To understand where man is going, he must first understand where he has come from and how the dynamics of past problems still effect him today. Only to a limited extent is man a rational animal; his instinctive actions, motivations, and the driving force of his beliefs and hopes, determine his future at least as much as his seeking for satisfaction of the immediate needs of which he is conscious.

Already we know a good deal about the human psyche but we do not know enough. We need to know – or at least to speculate – more about its origins, about the characteristics which enabled it to survive, for example, and the dynamics of the forces which affected its development in its early stages until it began to possess the attributes which we have begun to observe in it today.

Present-day psychology – the discipline most concerned with the psyche – pays little enough attention to social anthropology and none to the dynamics of evolution. Neo-Darwinists might conceivably provide an account of the development of physical characteristics but it certainly does not tell us about even that small portion of our inner subjective world with which we are already familiar.

With the aid of such concepts we might deduce something of the effects on our future of those forces which have shaped us in the past. Just as the fossil expert can take a few fragments and draw an accurate picture of what the whole animal looked like, we might be enabled to surmise much more about the nature of man, and the relation of his present state to his ultimate potential development. We are unlikely to find the courage to attempt this study so long as we believe the matter to be determined by the accidents of random mutation.

To formulate a working hypothesis we might do well to take a fresh look at some fundamental assumptions which we tend to accept as axiomatic. For instance, should we assume that we are already a fully evolved and stabilised species? If this is not the case then we may certainly attribute many of our difficulties to our growing pains. We might find a constructive 'meaning' in life in an attempt to live in a manner consistent with the operation of those forces which shaped us in the past and which would inevitably continue to shape us today whether or not we are aware of them. In the end the objectivity of science might not appear so inconsistent with the symbolic truths of mythology and religion.

2

Evolving
Man

IN RECENT YEARS a good deal of stress has been laid upon the animal characteristics of man. This has perhaps been a healthy exercise counteracting some of the remnants of Victorian sentimentality which credited him with unique and even noble qualities. No doubt man is a unique creature in that we know of no equivalent species, but today most of us would be reluctant to consider him wholly 'noble'.

Nevertheless, while recognising that he shares much in common with other animals, man has about him a quality quite different not in degree – such as his intelligence which is perhaps better yet similar – but in kind. This quality, difficult to define, is generally described as consciousness.

Authorities tell us that true man with a brain similar to ours and capacity for self-awareness first appeared on earth only in the last fifty thousand years. In terms of the change which takes place in a single year in our own age, fifty thousand years seems an incredibly long time. In relation to the two or three million years during which hominoid types were existent, a mere fifty thousand years is the shortest of evolutionary epochs.

In this time, the impact of evolution has shifted from physical development to the evolution of man's mind and, parallel to mental development, the evolution of a society which might represent the culmination of the co-operation of minds. It is in this area that man must look to see what evolution holds for him which is relevant and new.

One is apt all too easily to assume that once man had become capable of using reason, he proceeded to take over from nature the direction of his own destiny. This assumption is in all probability very far from the truth. Had man known where to look and what questions to raise, he might at best have seen the direction in which natural forces were impelling him. He could, and still does, use reason to foresee and avoid some of the more terrible of the natural catastrophes; yet he has proved himself helpless to avert some of the equally appalling causes of suffering devised by his own kind. Thus even after he acquired consciousness and the capacity to exercise reason, a very long time elapsed before he could use them to modify his former behaviour patterns and only today are we beginning to realise their limitations for prescribing our way of life and directing our future development.

So far as we can establish, the way of life of *Homo Sapiens* changed little in the first four-fifths of his existence from the way of his predecessors. The reasons why early man, potentially as intelligent as his twentieth-century descendant, lived for forty thousand years in unchanging primitive conditions before he began to introduce the elements of civilisation, are vitally important to us today because we are still subject to them, although to a lesser extent.

First of all, we propose to look at the nature of consciousness, this quality of difference between man and other creatures; then the problems which had to be overcome if progress was – and still is – to be achieved in society and individual lives; and, finally, the extent to which these problems moulded the evolving mind of man.

In the twentieth century, we have come to hold our conscious faculties in great reverence and respect. Only in moments of great despair do we hope or consider the possibility of help of any other kind or from any other source. We have been taught, and continue to teach, our young, that to achieve anything desirable one must go about the matter in a systematic 'sensible' manner, applying the criterion of conscious reason at each stage. The method requires a very high degree of self-discipline and a considerable capacity for inhibiting inclinations of other aspects of our nature. The frequent successes of the method, particularly as regards specific short-term projects, have blinded us to its very serious limitations. We need to go back fifty thousand years to see these in operation.

*   *   *

The essential difference between the mind of man and that of other creatures appears to lie in its faculty of self-awareness and all that this implies.

Animals feel pain but do not act as if they are aware of suffering in the sense of anticipating pain, frustration, hopelessness, and futility. They can be conditioned to associate certain sensory perceptions with pain or pleasure and, to this extent, will anticipate these things when stimulated to do so. Man also is easily conditioned in this manner and we know from direct experience that the process causes us to react strongly with fear, anger, or joy when stimulated by the appropriate signal.

But man can also trigger off expectation in quite a different way; that is, by use of his reason. Seeing the agony of another hurt in a street accident or wounded in war, he is likely to go into a state of shock himself. Told that torture will be inflicted upon him in the near future, he will immediately go into an agony of anticipated suffering. Mercifully, animals display no signs of reacting in this way.

Anticipation of pain, with its attendant liability to suffering, is a side effect of the quality of consciousness and self-awareness which distinguishes the mental mechanism of man from other types. Appalling as the effects of suffering may be, its action – as we shall discuss later – may be essential for the development of the species to drive man on towards an ultimate destiny. In the meanwhile, its impact at least provides a corrective to any inclination to complacency or stasis.

If anticipation of pain is one aspect of human consciousness, the essential feature of this consciousness is a detailed memory with the power of recall and selection from it, regardless of whether immediate objects or sensations are likely to remind the subject of

29

what he is recalling. Animals, on the other hand, react in general as if they remember only what is associated with their immediate sense perceptions. Again, man can project his mind forward as well as backward. He can expect, hope, and speculate. He can make plans and implement them, whereas animals do not appear to have this ability.

If it is true that animals lack thought in the human sense of selecting and dwelling on experience drawn from memory while endeavouring to relate it to other circumstances so as to solve an immediate problem, then they live entirely by inherited instincts and intuitive faculties. Such unconscious mental activity compels them to react and behave in accordance with well-established, predictable patterns. It enables them to survive well in suitable conditions but commonly restricts their activities to a very limited range characteristic of their particular species. The mental mechanism of birds enables them to navigate over long distances on migratory flights, returning unerringly to the same places every year. But the birds have no choice in the matter. They must return to their particular nesting-sites. If the habitat in the meantime changes so that it no longer suits them, individual birds may have little ability to adapt and establish themselves elsewhere.

Young animals fostered by different species display confusion later on as to which of the species they belong to. Ducks reared by hens continue to behave like hens and even attempt to mate with them while ignoring their own kind. If brought up by hand, they may behave towards their human foster parent as they would towards a natural one.

From this and much similar evidence, we may reasonably deduce that unconscious processes govern the activities of animals. An appropriate response to danger, discomfort, or satisfaction is automatically evoked in them but they cannot relate past experience to new circumstances. In short, they lack man's conscious faculty for adaptation based upon memory recall, selection, and assessment. They are unable to reflect, to define their problems and desires, and to identify themselves as apart from, or in relation to, other objects and creatures.

However, such an inability does not incapacitate any life-form from functioning fully and effectively in appropriate surroundings. A gibbon swinging from one treetop to another will not be helped by a detached knowledge of the act it is performing. On the contrary, awareness of its fate if it missed the next handhold would distract it so much as to make it almost certainly do so.

The creature that immediately preceded man was evidently governed – as indeed are many of us for a part of our activity even today – by precisely the same sort of unconscious mind which enables animals to perform their daily round. Its range of activities and adaptability was as limited as those of other creatures but effectively preserved its existence in the manner other animals endure today.

At some point, however, and without any conscious effort on its part, the creature gained a new dimension of mind: consciousness in the human sense of the word. If at first it did not observe or speculate about itself, it was capable of doing so by its newly acquired faculty of self-awareness which no animal since shows any sign of possessing. This new creature could differentiate between what happened to it and what it could cause to happen, at least to some extent. It was able to pause, reflect and draw conclusions on what it was doing and what it wanted. Man, a self-perceiving animal, had arrived.

The implications of his new-found talent of consciousness were vast and would eventually enable him to overrun the earth, visit the moon, and, at least by remote control, explore some of the planets. These aspects of consciousness cause us to believe too readily that, from then onwards, natural evolution played little part in man's development. In this we should be utterly wrong. For excellent reasons which we shall presently examine, the evolution of man and society was – and still largely is – pressurised and shaped by the action of a natural system of dynamics over which he has little conscious control.

We do not know, of course, exactly how man arrived at self-awareness, how he was affected by the change in him, and whether it took place very gradually in a few individuals or relatively overnight to many. Possibly Neanderthal man, who was not true man, had a form of self-awareness because skeletons have been found buried with food and flint weapons beside them. The first art forms of true man betoken a being with self-awareness quite highly developed. His efforts so early on to depict himself and other animals in cave art and chalk figures cut into the hills probably arose in the course of seeking his identity, of trying to stand outside himself and define the relationship between himself and other forms of life. It is interesting, too, to note that his subsequent reaction towards his own identity, as· he began to recognise it, was to worship it. Images of himself were regarded as those of gods and reverenced, particularly for their sexual qualities, since the cycle of reproduction was a wondrous mystery. Man's identification of himself as a whole physical being was probably just as great a feat as his present endeavour to identify himself at more subtle levels.

When man gained consciousness, he was already living in accordance with some unconscious precepts of behaviour that accorded with his gregarious nature and protected him from extinction. We may reasonably surmise he carried on in small hunting tribes and behaved very much as he must have done previously when he relied solely on instinct without any power to imagine the effect he could have, if he wished, on his surroundings. The possession of a thinking faculty might have afforded awareness of things previously accepted instinctively but would not enable them readily to be changed. Systematic thinking is a comparatively late development in man's experience and for at least four-fifths of his existence had no place in directing his affairs. Instead, the requirements of survival imposed on man unwritten laws to which he had to conform, just as a swarm of bees or a herd of beasts is governed by characteristic habit patterns. The first steps in the evolution of society were not the work of rational man with specific desires or objectives in mind but the crude product of natural man.

He carried on as before possibly for three reasons: first, thinking, which seems to us to take place so naturally, nevertheless has a technique of its own which needs time and practice if it is to be used effectively. The selection and rejection of facts, impressions, sensations, and emotions from a memory store, and the relating of these one to another in all sorts of ways, is a vastly more sophisticated business than it might appear after fifty thousand years of practice;

second, he needed to communicate with others who could also think so that the best of their thoughts or ideas could be stored and handed on to future generations; third, since man is a gregarious animal and can do little singlehanded and almost nothing without the consent, acceptance, and assistance of his fellows, he had not only to be able to communicate his ideas but win acceptance of them before he could put them into practice.

It is no wonder therefore that so great a time-span was to elapse before man began to apply reason to his undertakings – and we have still made little more than a beginning with this art.

* * *

A systematic study has yet to be made of the fundamental dynamics of human society. Too much attention has been directed instead towards the comparatively narrow field of economies to the neglect of the larger framework within which such systems operate.

For our present purpose, we are concerned with two out of four of the more obvious principles fundamental to society and forming the major dynamics of human behaviour. In health, individual or political, a balance will be struck between the needs of the individual and the needs of his society; and, in progress, between his past and future. In sickness, too great an emphasis on one or other will be found. These dynamics do no less than decree the parameters of individual welfare and effective political action.

The first of these two dynamics arises from the gregarious nature of man. Early man was more adaptable than other animals in the sense of more intelligently reactive to unfamiliar circumstances than they would have been. But physically he was less potent in any one field than the animals he encountered. In isolation he was no match for them and to protect himself it was expedient to live with groups of his fellows. To survive in such conditions, his consciousness had, above all, to conform to the characteristics imposed by tribal survival. Those solitary individuals disposed to go it alone would – if in a minority – appear so ill disposed that they would be cast out. If in a majority, their tribe would split up to go its separate ways. To feel an interest in one's neighbour, consideration for and a willing-ness to work with him, is not therefore some altruistic ideal but the result of thousands of years of mind-conditioning.

Early man, then, was motivated in two different directions. On the one hand he had to look after himself, to take full and ungrudging responsibility for himself and his own needs, material and emotional. In the first years of childhood he had particularly to be motivated by the most selfish of interests to ensure he got as much as possible of every material comfort to assist his physical growth and survival. At this stage he felt no extension of his personality to a mate or offspring. It was right – and probably still is – that the child should be the essence of self-seeking egotism. The success of the community, then as now, depended upon the physical wellbeing of the units comprising it. At this stage, the individual's contribution to that community was his or her own physical development.

On the other hand, as the child began to attain physical maturity, the inclination to promote individual welfare would become modified at least in some respects by the necessity to make conces-sions to the tribe which were against immediate self interest but essential to ensure tribal survival. Individual drive motivations would have to be subordinated even to the point of jeopardising self-preservation, in order to collaborate with others in pulling down larger or fiercer animals and to protect the community in inter-tribal warfare. Primitive man was constantly called upon to sacrifice him-self for his tribe in combat. This he presumably undertook without question, as many citizens are still prepared today to fight for their country or cause in a war from which they are unlikely to benefit individually. It is paradoxical that man's nobler instincts are the result of the continuing necessity for thousands of years to fight his own species for survival. The historical anachronism of this sort of conduct is not always recognised where it persists today.

The most successful tribes would be those whose members were willing to sacrifice their own safety, their comfort, and, if necessary, their lives when outside forces opposed them. Such were the tribes surviving longest and those ones therefore from which present day man derives his inherited characteristics.

Individual courage was likely to have been recognised as a

superior quality to be emulated. Presumably such recognition was one of the earliest forms of non-materialistic satisfaction. In a materialistic age, we can still recognise non-materialistic elements within ourselves to which we must conform or suffer frustration. It is worth noting that concern for the community and unselfishness have origins not in any ethical idealism but in the stern conditions of survival. Any disturbance in the balance of such qualities – such as may be occurring today – is likely to distort the serenity of relationships between individuals and peoples. Such imbalance is among the more important factors in man's unrest.

The second of the dynamics of survival concerns rates of progress. For centuries it has been so difficult to organise change in societies and their institutions that we have had no occasion to give serious thought to the dangers it may bring to stability – a quality at least as important as progress. In the twentieth century, when large corporate organisations are subjected to deliberate planned reorganisation, we have better opportunity to study the less beneficial effects of ill-considered change on stability.

The growth and stability of society is ever dependent on a practical, workable balance between stasis and change. Progress must not be confused with the latter. It occurs only where change is balanced against conservation of what has been effective in the past, thereby providing a secure anchor against disruption. The path of progress lies between the turmoil of an overdose of change and the stagnation of activities carried on endlessly in the manner and methods of forefathers.

*   *   *

Consciousness gave man the choice of varying his ways. However, realisation of and ability to handle the choice had to germinate slowly. Individuals who did not possess prudence towards the unknown could quickly eliminate themselves. In the absence of any facility to study or record facts, successful experiments had to be repeated many times over before their results became recognised and incorporated into normal behavioural patterns. In the meantime, progress was a matter of trial and error, with infinitely more chance of error at each stage than the few alternative successive possibilities. Even when success is achieved in one direction, formidable side effects may appear in others. Early man's survival depended upon caution regarding the adoption of new practices. Thus, although he had the ability to exercise choice and to modify his circumstances to accord with his comfort and welfare, it is not surprising that he learnt that change was a serious matter involving big disadvantages. Those to whom it appeared attractive often died young. Wherever innovations occurred, they were probably resorted to because of dire necessity. Only with the advent of the scientific approach could change be undertaken with comparative safety – only comparative because ecologists now tell us change embodies more perils than we can anticipate or science predict.

But change is necessary if progress is to be achieved and, since man's evolution into a stable species does not yet appear to be complete, progress will continue to be necessary until some satisfactory form of stable life is attained at last. The history of mankind is largely a history of the devices he has unconsciously adopted to control the rate at which change can be digested at the different stages of development. It is interesting at the same time to notice the parallel between the needs felt by each individual for new and more stimulating interests and occupations at the different stages of his life and the needs of society as a whole at its different epochs.

The first device to protect tribal man from unwise innovations was the cult of taboo. Certain objects or practices associated with danger or discomfort were labelled as forbidden or taboo. By this means the necessity for maintaining existing behaviour and habits could be communicated to the young. Much of these systems would have been patent nonsense because primitive man's associations of cause and effect were not selective. He attributed both true and false causes to the discomforts he sought to avoid. But on the whole, the taboos were compatible with survival and proved over a period of time as practical. The primitive communities that flourished owed their health to the fact that on the whole their habitual practices tallied with health.

Had man departed too soon from taboo, the species would have died out. For he could not reason which taboos were necessary for survival and which were not; and he could not drop them by trial and error since he would soon have made the error, for example, of eating tainted meat. Yet had he clung overlong to taboo, he would have stagnated when its rigid framework eventually became too constricting for the further evolution of mind. Some inbuilt demand of consciousness pushed man on to a more pliant system. Taboo's shortcoming was that its inflexible code prohibited but never provided a reason for the prohibition. Taboo virtually precluded thinking. One might speculate that the taboo placed upon the eating of pork by some Asiatic peoples was a practical prohibition based on experience over the years of trichinosis in hot climates. But even today this basic practicality is not taught as a reason for the taboo.

Taboo served an essential purpose in that it gave man the first intellectual concepts with which to grapple with his environment. Objects and conduct had to be described before they could be forbidden. And once conceived, attitudes towards them could be modified – but not too directly. The challenge to taboo came in a roundabout and gradual manner.

Progress arose from the hunger of man's mind. Consciousness had brought him many advantages but enormous problems followed in its wake. It had made him aware of certain questions. In so far as his observations answered those which arose concerning his immediate environment, he would have felt secure. He could exercise some conscious control over the circumstances. If he ate green apples, he perceived and remembered that he felt pain and realised that such instances could be avoided in future. Yet the world was full of far greater and more terrible events which not only befell him today but, as he was now conscious of the future, might also befall him tomorrow. The visitations of death and disease upon his tribe, climatic changes which threatened his food supply, the earthquakes and storms, arose from causes on which he could not possibly speculate under his system of taboos.

Experience shows that mind will not tolerate a vacuum. Where mind cannot find a cause, it will invent one, and, if it cannot invent a realistic one, it will settle for one less satisfactory. One may ask why man should be troubled by the desire for answers and can only accept that it is implied in the nature of consciousness. Man has always felt

37

the need for security against the anxieties arising out of his awareness of the future. His explorative urges and curiosity are closely connected with this need. Since his cave days, he has tried to discover the formula which explains his place in the universe and gives him a place with other men. Without this knowledge or the illusion of having it, he feels an outcast and at the mercy of any whim of fate.

The immediate device open to primitive man to account for the forces of nature was to endow them with a living quality and personal characteristics similar to his own. He weaved myths around them which sought to interpret their action in terms of his own motivations. They were the early gods; and having constructed them, man believed he could placate them. For, all the time, he was projecting into the future and seeking how he might avoid the dangers which he realised potentially existed for him. He replaced the hit-and-miss methods of taboo with the more subtle means of personification and propitiation.

When the sun, the thunder, and the lightning were personified as deities which, like humans, could become angry, man could then speculate as to the reasons for their annoyance and what might appease them. Over a long period of time, he projected his likes, dislikes, and other characteristics on to what had formerly been the inexplicable in his life. He peopled the world with a multitude of good and evil spirits which he believed responsible for everything that happened. Thus was evolved an explanation of the past, present, and future. Man devised from this explanation patterns of behaviour that he supposed might procure safety from catastrophes that he feared might strike at any time. The spirits, for instance, could be induced to favour him if sacrifices were made to them or ritual ways of borrowing their powers discovered.

The myths led to a flexibility in keeping with man's growing experience and need to accept variance in his ways of living. Those who were gifted at inventing stories and appeared most successful at promoting fertility and good fortune became the priests and wise men of the community and played the leading role in amending the taboo structures. In so far as any quality other than physical strength enabled one man to rule the community rather than another, these mythmakers would supply it.

Their inventions would have been shaped to answer in the best terms available at that time the fundamental questions that man had started to ask. Their myths arose out of their imagination, and to the extent that imagination is intuitive and intuition is valid, their stories were not wholly without foundation. The myths were probably far truer than the authors had any right to expect although they were dressed up in symbolic language whose practical interpretation was – and often is – not immediately obvious. The fact that old wives' and witch-doctors' remedies are often effective and their fortune-telling sometimes in accordance with subsequent developments should give us interest and even respect for the intuitive processes which produce them.

Some of primitive man's mythical personifications were consistent with his wellbeing but others, projections of his more destructive side, were less comfortable. Among the latter were demands for savage sacrifice and cruel atonement. As man's growing sense of values urged him to place things in their right fundamental perspective in terms of life, death, and human happiness, he started to emphasise the constructive myths and disregard the savage. With the exercise of value judgements, the transition from myths to fully-fledged religions began. The myths were gradually placed in order of their relevance to human life and codified into highly ethical systems of values that offered well-defined standards by which to govern family and community life. Suffice to say at this time that the interpretations of life and the ethical standards provided by the different formalised religions served to satisfy the practical and spiritual needs of the individual and society up to recent centuries.

Religion flourished at the expense of reason and often in conflict with it. Religion may be regarded as a product of man's feeling faculty, his sense of values. Reason may, we hope, be integrated with feeling, but it cannot long be subordinated to it, and society remained based upon religious doctrines until they became manifestly contrary to accumulating records and comparisons of experience. For centuries, mankind has tolerated glaring inconsistencies between the teaching of his various churches and the examples set by those who professed to follow them. The scandals of the Inquisition and

39

religious persecution generally could be overlooked but, in the end, had to be paid for.

However, the loss of faith was not due so much to any intellectual judgment passed on the record of the churches but to the growing inability of the ordinary man to apply the doctrines of the church to his daily life. Religion is expressed in analogies and anecdotal parables, so that their statement affords no explanation consistent with normal experience. Since many of the events described in the scriptures of all religions were considered to be scientifically unlikely, much of the dogma based on interpretations of scripture stories was felt to be unworkable. The dogma prescribed the rules for living. Yet strive as they might, few could find it in their hearts to love a recalcitrant neighbour or honour an erring parent. Henry VIII defied dogma, but no apparent retribution followed. Others felt free to take up his challenge without fear of divine disfavour.

With the breakdown of dogma, conscious examination and selection of beliefs could begin. Society set out to attempt to govern itself by laws made in the light of reason rather than religion, for it appeared at the time that reason could supply the structure which religion could no longer support.

The Roman and Greek civilisations had fostered early – and extraordinarily advanced – concepts that the shape of society might be made to conform to the conclusions of so-called rational thinking. But the benefits of the stimulation they afforded were available only to a minority who had the leisure time for experimental logic but little opportunity to apply it in practice to the government of communities founded on slave labour.

Reliance on reason had to wait many centuries for the growth of free states and the education of their citizens. A further condition for the abandonment of dogma was the provision of some intellectual account of the origins of mankind and this was not forthcoming until the Darwinian explanation became available.

Man began to codify his ideals intellectually, to consider what he would like to be, and to construct what seemed to him logical principles by which he might plan the conduct of society. He conceived ideals to which he thought society should conform, though he did not always take into consideration whether it was possible for society to do so. He had invented the concept of 'it-ought-to-be', based on imagining a relationship between matter and abstract principles such as people and equality.

However the age of reason is much less reasonable than is first supposed. In fact it might be called the age of pseudo-reason. For reason is little recognised as the frequent disguise for rationalisation of unconscious motivations and attitudes which are cloaked as much from their holders as from their beholders. In our everyday lives, we often tell ourselves we are doing something for a particular reason, only to discover we are driven by some other, completely unconnected motivation. Too often man is unable to agree on what is reasonable or logical. And this is hardly surprising, considering that the motivations of each individual may not be the products of his rational thought at all but, as we shall illustrate, the results of unconscious drives which differ from person to person.

In rebelling against the subordination of reason to feeling, man went to the other extreme, subordinating feeling to reason. An enduring answer to his needs is likely to be one which transcends both religious dogma and rational demonstration.

Meanwhile, the problems with which we are faced are of two types: material and emotional. The former might yield to the devices of logic but the latter can be remedied only by quite different means. Rational processes can be employed only where one has reliable facts on which to base them; and facts are only available to a limited extent in connection with human affairs.

Science, far from fulfilling the hopes of providing the facts, has only demonstrated its inability to do so. In its widest sense, science is little more than a routine technique for verifying imaginative hypotheses by assessing their implications in terms of the observable or measurable facts. This procedure has led to rapid innovation and material progress in the Western world. Scientific method has been one of the most successful of man's attempts to organise his thinking. It has enabled the men of the greatest ability to teach lesser mortals how to get results with a minimum of inspiration. If they follow the prescribed methodology, they have little scope to distort the results. 'Truth' can be unveiled even by the most shortsighted who cannot see such except they verify its presence by tests and proofs.

Yet so many of the important experiences and qualities in life cannot be measured, tested, and proved to conform to laws governing the behaviour of matter in this way. One person's relationship with another cannot be judged in scientific terms. Happiness cannot be defined, let alone measured, by science. It obeys no definable laws and cannot be prescribed by them. However many facts are collected about states of anxiety, they may be only a tiny fraction of those needed to be taken into consideration to seek a solution, and even they are too many to be held in any one mind at a time for logical examination.

Logic is not, however, the only means by which problems are solved. The intuitive flash of inspiration works in a different way and often more effectively. Perhaps the difference lies in the distinction between wisdom and intelligence. Intelligence can work only on the facts present, arbitrarily ranking them as right or wrong, useful or useless. Computers operate on similar principles but it is doubtful if they can be made to achieve wisdom – the exercise of a larger maturity and flexibility of mind.

Examples of the solution of problems by means other than routine logic have been recounted throughout history and vested with a peculiar sense of satisfaction. One recalls the problem of Archimedes when he was called upon to report on the amount of pure gold in the King's crown. He knew of course that it depended on the weight of the metal relative to its volume – but how to establish the volume of an intricately constructed object without first melting it down? When he got into his bath and saw the water rise as it was displaced by the volume of his own body, he knew he had the answer and his cry of 'Eureka!' as he rushed away in his bath towel to put the idea into practice has echoed down two thousand years to celebrate an instance of an inspirational brain function. The history of science in the last three hundred years abounds with stories of problems solved by insight – sometimes even, as in the case of von Kekulé, by dreams – rather than by the exercise of mundane plodding logic.

One may try it out for oneself. Put six matchsticks on a table and try arranging them so as to form four equal triangles. No amount of knowledge about formal logic, or even about the facts of triangles, match-sticks or geometry will help as much as the freedom of mind to work in three dimensions.

Problem solving by inspiration has obvious advantages. But the difficulties of getting away from ingrained habits of the logical approach are considerable, both for the individual and for society.

At the present time, we find man frustrated in his achievements because he has trusted the convincing appearance of his logic without regard to its limitations. Since the same sort of frustrations occur to some degree across the civilised world wherever man's style of living is compatible with present-day knowledge, we can conclude that his unrest arises out of the inhibitions which living in accordance with that knowledge puts upon him.

We find that in man's attempt to govern his society by logic, the dynamics of society are not being observed despite their vital bearing on the situation and the unrest produced by the imbalance between individual interests and the community and between stasis and change.

Modern society teaches its members to be rational. It gives no place to helping others without a rational cause. It implies that any method – at least within the current code of law – which promote self-interest are not only acceptable but praiseworthy. The modern state has tended to relieve individuals of the inherent instinct to contribute voluntarily to the common need by taxing them and redistributing the proceeds as if this entirely fulfilled their obligation to the community, leaving them free to please themselves. However, such token payment fails to satisfy the age-old emotional need of the individual to do something for others, and in consequence he suffers an uneasy emptiness. If man now discards the ability to balance his individual self-advancement with his contribution to the community's wellbeing, he offends against elements of his basic nature evolved over thousands of years. Its elimination is as offensive to his nature as if, at the other extreme, he entirely subordinated himself to the welfare of the community in a bee-like colony where the individual counted for nothing.

Progress has become confused with a self-perpetuating interest in technological and revolutionary change, regardless of whether the innovations are beneficial or can be absorbed by the community. The failure of social institutions to keep pace with these changes and the needs of the time is leading to their abandonment rather than to the maintenance of their constructive aspects and the lopping off of outdated aspects. Yet if they are abolished too fast, the same sort of disaster can overtake 1970s' man as happened to previous communities that tried to digest too much change at once without precedent or guidelines. Desmond Morris* says in *The Naked Ape*:

> We can see plenty of examples of the too rigid and too rash cultures around the world today. The small, backward societies, completely dominated by their heavy burden of taboos and ancient customs, are cases of the former. The same societies, when converted and 'aided' by advanced cultures, rapidly become examples of the latter. The sudden overdose of social novelty and exploratory excitement swamps the stabilising forces of ancestral imitation and tips the scales too far the other way. The result is cultural turmoil and disintegration.

Meanwhile, man is trying to operate in a vacuum of uncertainty because his dependence on his rational faculty disqualifies his previous answers to the fundamental questions about himself and his destiny, but fails to provide him with new ones.

In summary, the root of society's turbulence can be recognised as the completion of an evolutionary phase. The present period is one where old inspirations have been exhausted and new ones have not yet appeared. The same upheavals are now apparent as marked the previous transitions from taboo to myth, from religion to pseudo-reason. Yet this time the scale of the symptoms is probably more alarming because the population explosion has limited opportunities for recovery from error.

They take on a more constructive light, however, when viewed as manifestations that the process of evolution itself may be undergoing a change. The growing pains of man are not about to bring his decline but the growth inherent in his nature from the beginning. Man cannot make society evolve faster than its own potential any more than he can make the sun rise before its time. He can ease the transition by identifying and accepting its fundamental direction; or he can lengthen it at the cost of appalling suffering by frustrating

* *The Naked Ape.* Desmond Morris. Jonathan Cape Ltd. 1967.

44

life's potential for a while until counteracting forces build up to overwhelm his opposition.

The restlessness of our time indicates a pressing need for a new structure to society which would provide a direction and purpose to life more satisfying and stabilising than the confusion at the moment.

By the present time, man has tried out what are apparently the only four possible styles of consciousness in different forms of society. He employed perception to win his livelihood from nature in his most primitive days; intuition to conjure up his myths; a sense of values to formalise the more important myths into religions; thinking to codify intellectually what he believed his ideals to be and the methods by which they might be achieved. It is interesting to speculate that the orientation of society around each of the four in turn has served the purposes of unconscious impulse to develop and practise them in the mind one after the other. Since their individual possibilities are explored and exhausted, reversion to a system of society based on any one of them would be intolerable.

The remaining way ahead appears to be a structure of life which incorporates the best features of all four principles but transcends any one of them. Such a synthesis would be in harmony with the facts of the material world; would take into account the potentialities of the situation; would rate its elements in order of their relative importance; and constellate them in a pattern consistent with achieving a defined objective.

There are grounds for believing such a structure and meaning can be found, but society cannot find the inspiration to embark on its construction until the present barriers – the limitations of mind – are understood.

3

Predictable
Man

MANY OF TODAY'S problems and the directions in which change is taking place reflect the limitations of consciousness and the necessarily slow rate at which human attitudes adapt to external requirements. This is not surprising when we reflect that man has spent most of his existence in circumstances that changed little and shaped his conduct in ways from which, even today in vastly different conditions, he finds it difficult to escape.

During that long period of time when environment strictly limited the practice of intellect to dealing with a small range of typical situations, mental habit patterns came into being. The solving of recurring types of problems by applying well-proved thought patterns worked upon the mind of man as water, running over rock, carves out channels along which it may more readily flow and from which it has difficulty in escaping. Thus when early mind had adapted itself to dealing with a particular type of problem in a way which was at least sufficient to ensure survival, then change of that method was likely to bring about more perils than benefits.

In the present day both our reactions and our view of the world have elements originating in the forces and pressures which moulded our ancestors. We still too easily follow the water-course of archaic habit patterns unless and until we become aware both intellectually and emotionally of ourselves and our origins, and in so doing become free to conform to, or deviate from, our fundamental roots without damage to them.

For this reason, it is worth considering in some detail how the attitudes of primitive man, which presumably governed his decisions and behaviour, were moulded by the requirements of survival. Space prevents the presentation of anything more than a composite picture of the mode of life to which he was subjected and the sort of decisions he had to make. The description may be typical of prehistory's day-to-day life but possibly never literally accurate in all respects as regards any one time or geographical place.

First we know that early man was omnivorous – an eater of vegetation or of meat when he could get it. Since his first weapons were small and ineffective, he was more often in danger from bears, wolves, and the large cats than they were from him. His hunting was largely a matter of watching and following the herds of deer, bison, and wild horse across their pastures. Since they were stronger or more agile than himself, his livelihood depended more on his powers of perception, memory, and cunning in stalking his prey and pulling down stragglers. He must have been very able and sensitive to the signs, sounds, and smells of nature. He came to recognise and anticipate the habits of his prey, as he must also have learnt the lore of the smaller creatures and plant life on which his existence depended. Thus the male of the species was always interested, even fascinated, by the facts surrounding him and their significance. Today's child – particularly today's boy child – is still preoccupied by the things around him and the way they work, how animals behave and machinery operates. To us, the observation of nature is usually no more than a relief from more artificial pursuits; to the primitive it was the essence of his day-to-day task.

Since he was comparatively slow, sight was of particular use to him and he developed unusual ability to see and focus on minute detail and to distinguish colours. His cave-paintings bear witness to his vivid perception of animal form and the stirrings of his fledgling creativity to record that which was around him. His skill of hand and sense of touch grew with his making of implements that perhaps occupied part of the long dark winters when his touch told him more than he could see in the flickering firelight.

In the beginning, the number of families who lived and worked together in packs was no doubt quite small. A dozen active men and well-grown boys were enough to constitute an effective hunting-party or to beat off a night attack from other marauding men or beasts. Larger groups were difficult to organise and restrain. In all probability they occurred only when a leader of unusual strength, ferocity, or cunning – 'the old man' of the tribe – who could control and direct his band, arose.

The male's active life as the hunter was coupled with the active fight to retain or improve his position in the hierachy of his tribe. He had to be competitive, willing to challenge the stronger and dominate the weaker or less cunning than himself. The old man was, during his period of leadership, fittest in these respects. If he was to sleep soundly, he needed to chase away potentially competitive young males before they came to full strength. Unless he was exceptionally strong himself, he could tolerate only the young and the most subservient men around him. However, the hunting and fighting power of the tribe depended upon its size, so those tribes containing individuals likely to uphold the leadership of a chief throve best.

Like some modern examples of leaders, chiefs were probably not so intelligent or wise as adroit in the necessities of short-term survival. In character they were apt to be selfish, self-sufficient men who were dogmatic and intolerant of the needs of others. Proud of their strength and appreciative of admiration, they were no doubt ready and eager to look for the first signs of disrespect which could be considered a challenge and to make an example of such offenders.

The traits of their followers were different. Loyalty, the ability to accept and act under direction, subservience towards and dependence upon authority, became characteristics of the rank and file constituting the majority of the tribe. There must also have been a third type, those with the disposition of rebels who cared less for stability and the quiet, well-ordered life than for challenging the self-indulgence of the more powerful and, in the end, for the succession to leadership. The attitude of their more docile fellows towards them was necessarily ambivalent. They were to be disparaged, abused, and betrayed wherever their efforts were ill-conceived or unwise in the face of the wrath of authority. They were to be encouraged wherever authority was ineffective and unjust. If successful, they were to be flattered and served without question, so that they rapidly took on the original qualities of the deposed leader. The successful survival of communities demanded a relatively larger number of rebels than might seem strictly necessary because a sizeable proportion must have failed in their ambitions, only to be killed or driven out.

Stalking of herds indicates a nomadic life but two factors, climate and children, must have determined 'the establishment of bases. Fire and shelter aided the survival of tribes and, since fire was difficult to transport and rekindle, groups tended to occupy bases from which the hunting men would go on food-gathering expeditions. Water, too, was necessary. So the camp would be situated near a natural source. Camps themselves were important for the upbringing of children with more ease than while constantly wandering.

Both fire and children had to be tended and this was natural work for woman. In contrast to the active stance which was necessary to the male if he was to overcome the obstacles to his will presented by nature, the circumstances of feminine life developed an entirely different approach in the female towards achieving her ends – not, be it noted, inferior nor superior, only different from that of the male.

In a world where physical strength was the arbiter of will, she had little option but to adapt herself to the circumstances in any problem; that is to say, to take a passive course. She had a limited choice in the manner of her way of life. Sometimes her tribe might be overrun by another, in which case she became the spoils of war, to survive, if at all, as mate, slave, or both in a new environment. She always stayed in or near the tribal camp. Her daily tasks concerned the rearing of children and the menial jobs for the tribe – the gathering of firewood, the collecting of berries, the preparation of skins. She would give solicitous care to her mate should he be injured, because of her dependence on him for survival. But malingering would not be encouraged. On recovery he must be pushed out to resume his hunting and protective role. Any weakness caused her to react with niggling bad humour, the opposite of the tender care previously lavished upon him.

Over the range of animal life, *Homo Sapiens* was one of the few species whose functions – other than sexual – became so markedly divided between the sexes. The entirely dissimilar daily rounds pursued by the male and the female developed different propensities. She was less interested in nature and how things worked. If continuous squabbling and brawling was to be avoided in the day-long company of other women, children, and the sick, she flourished only if she could take a pleasurable interest in others and was sensitive to their moods.

At matable age, a girl's business was to attract the attention of the fittest male in the group – fittest in the sense of ability to contribute most to her and her children's survival. This was, and is, an unconscious mechanism. As we do not know where evolution is taking us, we may only theorise as to what we look for in people, what particular qualities make a man or woman more attractive to some than others. But presumably the factors which appeal most have a link with survival value for those individuals attracted to each other and their offspring. In those early days, physical fitness would presumably have been of prime survival importance.

Since groups were comparatively small, the chief's attention would have been easy to attract and no one could deny his wish when stimulated. But the number of women he could take was determined by the number, with their children, that the tribe could support and tolerate. If he took too many, the group would become disproportionate and impoverished. His jealous followers would be provoked into combining to challenge his authority.

Unless he was in his prime, selection by the chief was a mixed blessing. On average he was likely to be older than the majority. By the time he was deposed or died, the girl would find herself without a protector and her children still at a vulnerable age. The reigning leader was therefore to be avoided and an outwardly modest girl, however coquettish underneath, might hope to escape his attention. Her natural inclination would more likely draw her towards the rebel type in the group who might become chief at a later date. Those characteristics which distinguished him as such – courage, initiative, youth, and physical strength – would be those which would induce her to relax her camouflaging modesty when he was nearby.

Presumably the young man would couple with the girl whose characteristics appealed most – and the physical and other qualities to which he would react were evolution's way of determining the direction in which the development of the species was to go in future ages. Initially he would be driven by lust to take what stronger men were willing to leave for him and to what weaker men were unable to aspire to. Apart from encouraging some and avoiding others, a girl had no choice in the matter. Physical resistance would be acceptable and even commendable as evidence of energy and spirit and therefore a normal element in sexual gratification.

At first, primitive man must have been concerned chiefly with the satisfaction of needs and day-to-day survival. Intent on where his next meal was coming from, he had neither time nor inclination for detached speculation. He had little capacity for reasoning accurately or identifying the causes of the outside events which he encountered. His criteria were simple. Anything which threatened survival was likely to affect him in the form of pain, deprivation, or discomfort. These he lumped together as threatening, to be avoided, therefore bad. His preference was to accept whatever was comfortable and satisfying, therefore good. He had insufficient knowledge, experience, and communication with others to deal in any depth with the implications of his actions. He took everything at face value, pursued what seemed pleasant, and avoided the uncomfortable.

Gradually the development of language allowed his mind to grapple with more complex ideas. Formerly he had indulged himself in every way open to him and had no way of knowing or caring whether this was good for him or not. Now he explored the possibility of deferring today's pleasure for later and greater benefit. From being a hunter who immediately killed whatever game he came across, he herded the animals together for domestication. From eating whatever food grains he had in hand, he deprived himself of a certain amount in order to put enough aside to plant a new crop. He no longer scoffed his food. He waited and cooked it. He had learnt to distinguish between benefit now and security later, and the corollary of that lesson: decision and activity are not invariably linked. A decision to take no immediate action is just as much a decision, even though more often an unconscious one, as the deliberate resolution to effect a change.

Until the development of an extensive vocabulary, the children had no means of learning from their elders except by imitation. Even when spoken instructions could be formulated, the children were more likely to have been impressed by example than by verbal instruction. Tasks were learnt by imitation and conduct was regulated by taboo according to the necessities of community life. The way of life respectively appropriate to men and to women was learnt from observation of the behaviour of adults.

Since the brain of early man was as large and complex as our own, he would have been indistinguishable from us, had he been reared in similar circumstances. The difference between the men of our two epochs lay in the way the primitive used his mind. He could have had no concept of the process which we adopt every time we start to carry out some project outside the normal routine of daily life. First we imagine it, plan it; we may draw it or formulate it in words or merely think about it. Then we decide how we will go about putting it into effect and what obstacles we may encounter. Finally we perform the series of activities we have planned. If primitive man did not adopt such a procedure, it was not because he was incapable or stupid but because he had not yet learnt to use his mind in that particular and comparatively sophisticated way.

Since he could not yet plan his behaviour nor his way of life, early man followed the line of least resistance, which meant observing taboo and otherwise doing what came naturally.

As he became accustomed to dividing up objects and circumstances into good or bad according to whether he derived from them direct benefit or otherwise, so he imagined the forces of nature which he personified as spirits made an equivalent distinction. The forces that were good, by definition, were supposed to alleviate suffering while the evil forces increased it. In the terminology of modern psychology, he projected the workings of his own mind onto these spirits so that they seemed to him to have passions, inclinations, and motivations like his own – quite irrespective of the different circumstances of their disembodied or intangible nature. The ultimate

53

derivation could have been a god ('good' minus the one 'o') who was all merciful, all just and concerned with what was right and best for each individual's welfare, and a devil ('evil' plus 'd') who personified evil and injustice.

We have suggested the first tribes were small because of the leader's difficulties in maintaining his authority. However, larger groups were practicable if observation of taboo could be enforced. Thus where a witch-doctor or priest could get himself accepted as the guardian of taboo, tribes could grow and become sufficiently powerful to subordinate other tribes. And witch-doctors could elaborate on taboos until they became myths whose spirits took an interest and active participation in human affairs.

Stability of large tribes required a proper respect for authority and the leaders became duly invested with reverence and awe. No doubt they enhanced the myths to aid their status. To murder them offered no relief from their tyranny for they were buried with so much ritual and distinction to propitiate their souls that quite obviously they could, if offended, 'wake up' or return at any time to right any wrong done them.

Looking back over thousands of years, these patterns of behaviour appear so directly motivated that it is difficult to realise that they grew up infinitely slowly and were, in all probability, never seen for what they were by those who instigated and contributed to them.

The fact that chiefs and priests used for their own materialistic purposes the first indications of man's perception of powers outside himself to influence his affairs by no means implies that his convictions in this respect had no validity in their own right. Nor does it imply that such beliefs were simply a creation of those who wished to manipulate their fellows. We cannot, on this sort of evidence, reduce them to the 'nothing but' machinations of primitive politics. This is too often the point where the nihilism of the modern reductionist begins. But this is also where the first baby gets thrown out with the bath-water, for their conclusions do not necessarily follow from these circumstances. One may keep an open mind at this point, simply observing man's first intuitive perception of a god or gods, of a complex of phenomena determining his evolution, was as useful to the politicians of his time as his acquisitive inclinations and vanity are useful to the admen of today.

Be that as it may, primitive man used his new-found powers of consciousness not in accordance with their potential but as best he might in the circumstances in which he found himself. This style of cerebration continued for long generations without question of its effectiveness. Those tempted to challenge accepted patterns often died doing so. Thus we may expect that in confronting our difficulties today, both social and individual, we are all too prone to resort to predictable mechanisms which became inbuilt in the human mentality during this time.

As one of the more obvious examples, disagreement about all matters had to be solved by violence for the first four-fifths of man's existence because no other form of solution was available. A strong temptation therefore remains today to resolve arguments by force when other apparent methods have failed despite the obvious irrelevancy of violence to an intellectual process. One must be emancipated indeed to respond to situations and problems according to their rational content rather than their similarities with patterns of behaviour in pre-history. In the future, the attainment of an unbiased response may well be the objective of education rather than its present emphasis on the instillation of facts. But this sort of freedom will be won only when its nature and the need for it has been recognised. And man is conditioned by other factors besides his prehistorical background; and these must also be taken into account in the emancipating process.

*　　*　　*

In subsequent chapters we shall deal in some detail with the work of clinical psychology and its significance for our future. At this point we need to touch upon general aspects only briefly to illustrate the equivalent significance of pre-history for our life and times.

The theories of Freud and subsequent researchers concerning the conditioning of the individual by his upbringing and social environment have become widely known outside medical circles. Few methods intended for use in highly specific circumstances have had so much impact on the imagination of artists, writers, and, in the end, on the general reader's idea of man, the foundations of his mind and the way it works.

In spite of Freud's *Psychopathology of Everyday Life*, pioneers in psychiatric techniques were aware of the limitations of these ideas outside their original context of clinical work. Jung realised the ontological implications, the inferences as to the nature of things, but only in later life did he allow himself to indulge in speculating on them. Even so, he withstood the pressures of his followers to go further into philosophical and theological fields.

Possibly such pioneers were hesitant because of the scientific barrier imposed by neo-Darwinism; possibly because they had sufficient difficulty in winning acceptance for their methods. But more importantly and probably it was because they were well aware of the distinction between theories relating to individual development and disorientation and those relevant to man as a whole. It is essential that this distinction should be emphasised.

In general, clinical psychology is concerned with the deviation of the individual from the 'norm'. The doctor is not much concerned with the nature of that norm; for his part he must accept it. If all men are mad, it is not his business to wonder in relation to what standard and in what sense they are mad. If all men are sick, then 'sickness' is part of the human condition and the epithet becomes meaningless except in so far as it makes a distinction between man and some mythical creature who is imagined to be differently constituted. When, however, an individual (man or woman) becomes unable to carry on for whatever reason with the daily activities of the majority so that he is unable to attend to his own needs, then the case falls into a special category with which medicine is concerned. But the norm, the nature of man, is the province of the philosopher, the theologian, the ontologist, and of several other disciplines concerned with his attributes.

Had Freud been an ontologist, one may assume he would have extended his method to pay the same attention to the early formative experience of mankind as he gave, for his more specific purpose, to the early formative years of his individual patients.

In any study of behaviour, factors influencing the norm must have at least equal importance to those which create individual idiosyncrasies and, therefore, the work of the anthropologist is as important for our self-recognition as that of the psychiatrist.

* * *

Let us now return to early man to consider how the limitations of his way of life may still be with us; how atavistic in other words are many of our attitudes today.

The thousands of years lived in the most primitive conditions inevitably developed a polarity in man's thinking which he still uses indiscriminately in all directions. The habit of dividing every circumstance encountered into good or bad lasted for so long that the classification has become an inherent characteristic of his mentality. Without our realising it, our mind still flies automatically and predictably from one pole to the other, dividing everything that we come across into good or bad, right or wrong. Each perception, sensation, or thought-image is accepted and considered in several different ways but, at the same time, confusingly identified as:

Good (to be sought) or bad (to be avoided).
Right (correct) or wrong (false).
Right (permissible) or wrong (taboo).
Right (friendly, comfortable) or wrong (hostile, associated with pain).

The limitations of polarity are obvious. It ignores the dual aspect and relativity of all circumstances. In practice, facts are rarely wholly correct or wholly false and need lengthy qualification if they are to be stated as such. Even then, they will be right or wrong relative to their context. Again, that which is good in one instance may be bad in another. Good and bad are purely relative, never absolute. An influenza epidemic may be bad for the sufferers but profitable for the manufacturers of vaccine and medicines.

Even when aware of the limitations of classification, the individual mind nevertheless has a proclivity to see almost every matter as favourable or unfavourable by its particular standards. Such a method of thinking may have been sufficiently effective for the purposes of primitive man. Today it unduly simplifies the issues which arise in our more sophisticated society and relationships.

One can imagine some primitive philosopher to whom it occured to ask: 'What is beyond this vista of countryside around me? What is beyond the sea which stretches before me?' Using an all too familiar type of logic, he may understandably have concluded the answer could be only one of two: either the earth went on indefinitely, extending into some infinite sort of universe; or else at some point it abruptly finished in some sort of precipice beyond which there was nothing. Now of course we know the answer transcends this polarity type of 'either . . . or' thinking. To the man who first thought of the earth as a globe, the concept must have been shattering in its satisfactory simplicity, as indeed are so many solutions which arise when polarity concepts are suspended.

The Roman philosopher, Boethius is still remembered – and presumably in some circles respected – for his question: 'If God is, whence came evil things? If he is not, whence came good?' Today the essential silliness of trying to treat such questions by such methods is apparent. But evolution still has a long way to take us before we automatically use the type of thought which transcends opposites – unless, as we shall try to show in due course, ways may be found of assisting what would otherwise be a long and painful process determined by unconscious nature rather than conscious man.

In the previous chapter we pointed out two principles of choice to which primitive man became accustomed because of the dynamics of the circumstances of early communities. We suggested that, if he was to survive, his decisions over any appreciable period had to represent a balance between stasis and change and between his own interests and those of the fellow members of a group or tribe.

The conditions of prehistory illustrate two other dynamics of human behaviour involving the mind in polarity of decision in organising its activities:
(1) that of balancing short-term against long-term interests; postponement of present pleasures for security tomorrow; subordinating fear of the unknown future to courage sufficient for today. This requires a choice between satisfaction now or later wherever one cannot both have one's cake and eat it. Many have an impulse always to take what is here and now; others fear risk and store up for enjoyment in the future. The difference between rich and poor –

58

often assumed to lie in the realms of intelligence, ability, or opportunity – may also depend on a temperamental compulsion to make provision for tomorrow at the expense of today.

(2) that of adopting an active or a passive mode of approach to unsatisfactory circumstances. In fact, these are the only two methods of dealing with problems, obstacles, or uncomfortable situations. At their extreme, we have to decide whether 'to suffer the slings and arrows of outrageous fortune, or to take arms against a sea of troubles, and by opposing end them.' We have either to adapt our habits, attitude and way of life to circumstances which we do not like or we have to take action appropriate to change those circumstances in such a way that they become more acceptable to us. In primitive times, women had little option but to adopt the passive method. Men resorted to the active method whenever feasible. Eventually, the active method associated with force and cunning was refined in the Western cultures and became the basis of science. It is worth noting that many of the Eastern religions, now explored freely in the West, put great stress upon the equal efficacy of the passive method in obtaining an acceptable outcome. The Christianity of the Gospels also seems to have put more emphasis upon passive methods than one would suspect from the Pauline doctrines.

When we make decisions and choices, we do not see them in terms of these dynamics but usually as right or wrong, good or bad. And what is right or wrong, good or bad, for any one of us is usually different for someone else; hence the extreme difficulty in convincing others what is right and good in any particular instance.

We would suggest that the nature of any choice or decision can be considered in relation to these four dimensions, i.e. whether it represents a degree towards one or other extreme of change or stasis, self-interest or contribution, long or short term, passive or active solutions.

For all our scientific progress, we have not, generally speaking, either in our political decisions or in our daily life, learnt to transcend these extremes. Moreover, most of us do not even select that particular permutation of extremes which would be appropriate to the outcome we want. Too often the choice is made for us by the particular permutation that has become our habitual response on every occasion.

For instance, I win a prize of £100 in a lottery and decide I will give it (contribution) to a fund for promoting legislation (active) for the preservation of wild life (stasis) by the creation of nature reserves (long term). Nothing is wrong, of course, with this decision in itself. Yet if I examine other decisions and choices I make and they reveal a similar pattern of the dimensions of decision, then I may conclude I have less free will than I had thought. There may be less virtue in my altruism; less prudence in my anxiety to maintain the *status quo*; less courage in my willingness to take up an active role to achieve results; less patience in my long-term view of matters; less of all these qualitities than my actions would indicate and a greater degree of compulsive response pattern. To this extent, the sort of decision I make and the sort of behaviour I display is predictable, if not to myself, at least to those colleagues, friends, and enemies around me. I then find that I am responding to situations like a machine, like a computer, and therefore my advice, my relationships, and my wisdom are all suspect.

For many thousands of years, it was neither necessary nor desirable for man to change the habit pattern of his response to situations. Flexible attitudes were not and still are not today an essential characteristic of the working of consciousness. However, such an ability is desirable for adaptability and for solving situations in modern conditions. Nevertheless, as any member of a company board, political council, or church committee can testify, we – and of course particularly our neighbours – still approach problems with a predictable pattern of response.

It is a reasonable conjecture that this has its origins in a thousand generations of unchanging ways in prehistory and therefore our way of life today and responses in our personal work, relationships, and outlook are unduly atavistic. The measure of our rigidity and predictability irrespective of the changing circumstances to which we are invited to adapt ourselves, is uncertain but no doubt enough to be highly significant and relevant to the suffering of the human condition. History may well be an account of mankind's endeavours to widen his consciousness and break out from behind the formidable bars which have held it confined since its creation.

* * *

The specific effects of atavism merit more study and attention than they have been given. In the meantime we may emphasise their importance by a number of examples.

Among these the most significant is, perhaps, the emotional confusion which arises in us as we endeavour to adjust to the gradual change which civilisation brings to the prehistorical masculine and feminine roles. The trend of progress has removed the necessity for the original sharp distinctions and, in the last two hundred or three hundred years particularly, with the growth of rational thought, the modifications to the respective roles have speeded up. The male is no longer actively using his cunning or physical strength. Often he is professionally concerned with relationships. The female, assisted by labour-saving devices, can often look after her home almost in her spare time and devote her principal energies to a profession. Yet their former ways of life endured for countless centuries and the differentiation impressed itself into the nature of each sex. Basically and habitually, men and women continue to have a strong bias towards these different roles.

Modern man, at least in the first half of life, still takes readily to a competitive, aggressive role whether in intellectual, physical or general terms of achievement. Professional woman – however great her absorption in her occupation – still experiences the need for someone to depend upon, for a home and children, the soft comfort of the family circle. The active approach to problems still occurs to men as the 'natural', and sometimes the only, solution, while women more readily agree to adapt themselves to situations which might be difficult to change.

Woman has broken out of her historic role of domesticity to go out to work, where she is competing in what has hitherto been a man's world. In order to do her job effectively, she needs on occasion to take up a fairly active or aggressive stance which does not come easily to her.

The increasing need for a more restrained version of the active masculine role has created at least as many problems for men as its opposite has implied for women. Just as woman at work may have to refuse to assume her traditional passive adaptation, man finds from time to time that, especially in the large organisations typical of our time, adaptation is the best way of securing an objective.

In short, the logic of our social structure has not – and possibly rightly has not – made much concession for the difference of response inherent in the sexes. It may be that progress and evolution demand that the earlier sharp differentiation between the roles of the two sexes should be reduced. In the meanwhile the greater scope for self-expression, change, and development which modern life in the Western cultures affords is only to be grasped by those who can adapt freely.

But the happy freedom to be what circumstances require is achieved only by a minority. Those who remain prisoners of the past may act obsessively in accordance with what they believe is masculine or feminine behaviour, finding it, for instance, unacceptable for a man to pursue a passive course and unbecoming for a woman to adopt an active solution. Or they may become obsessively taken up with the opposite of their natural role because they think they ought to act so as a matter of enlightened procedure, thus losing touch with the roots of natural response. Rarely are they sufficiently emancipated to adopt active or passive attitudes as occasion rather than gender demands.

Thus for both sexes in their social activities and in those outside the home, traditional conduct consistent with prehistoric roles has decreasing importance. In sexual intercourse, in the domestic situation, and in intimate relationships between the sexes generally, the circumstances are different. In these matters inherent sexual differences are possibly as important as ever they were. *Vive le différence!* Let's not do without it – but the modern citizen may be forgiven his confusion if one set of attitudes is required in the office and another at home.

The enthusiastic advocates of sex education as a school subject treat it as a purely biological subject. So biased and simple an approach could be harmful, for, in the absence of appreciation of the full range of sexual distinction, one may project the characteristics of one's own sex upon the other – on the reasonable if false assumption that they are roughly similar. Yet since neither man nor woman has direct experience of the working of the mind of the other, neither can ever know, or at least be quite sure, exactly on what lines the other thinks. It is as irrelevant for two men to discuss the importance of children to women as for two women to try to assess the part a career plays in the life of a man.

When modern man attempts to repress his masculinity in dealing with his wife, or if he has become so confused about his masculine role that he misguidedly no longer believes in it, then both sides may become bewildered and emotionally unsatisfied. The woman may react emotionally to such conduct as if it were evidence of a lack of natural masculine dominance and decision which is attractive to her as a complement to her own femininity. The man may also be tempted to lean on the opinions of his wife or ask her to take on responsibilities which strictly he should be happy to shoulder. He may rationalise this as a consideration for her, but this again is to project upon her a part of the male mentality which demands this sort of consideration. The female does not easily accept his projection of his responsibilities; she welcomes his confidence in her but finds herself vaguely unhappy in this role. Primitive woman had need to pour scorn on the mate she considered weak in order to push him out to earn their livelihood. Solicitude turned quickly to nagging. The reaction of modern woman to any sign that she takes as weakness and diffidence in the male is not so far removed.

The wife is more likely to appreciate his conduct if, while remaining sufficiently kind and protective, he conforms to the original pattern of relationships and gives her the dominance or lead she expects and can emotionally accept. In her professional life, there is no reason why she should not have responsibility to make all her own decisions. But emotionally it is doubtful whether the average woman wants to have that same responsibility for every decision in her personal life. Experience indicates that in personal relationships it is difficult for men to treat women as like creatures while retaining their self-respect and in any case such treatment does not please women.

The whole trend of modern society has been to assume some sort of equality between a man and a woman. Equality there may be in that the characteristics of the sexes imply neither superiority nor inferiority. Man is not better or worse than woman. But their differences must be recognised for the roles to be seen in their correct perspective and for each to attract the other. The sexes need still to preserve and display their original characteristics to maintain satisfactory relationships – which are after all based upon emotional reaction rather than upon the objective requirements of professional situations.

This necessity relates not only to improved adult relationships but to children. As in primitive times, a child's significant learning of the basics of its existence is derived from observation and experience of example, as distinct from the intellectual process of scholasticism.

A child needs before all else to discover – or at least to feel it is on the way to discovering – its identity. The most important single element of its identity lies in its sex. What exactly is a man as distinct from a woman? How does a man behave? What would a woman do? In the child's mind, these generalised questions become: 'How does Dad do it? How does Dad talk to Mum?' and 'That's how Mum carries on.'

A growing child needs the example of the contrasting attitudes of activity and passivity, that is to say, the essence of what constitutes a man and a women. Lacking this example, the child will have the greatest difficulty in developing a proper sense of the identity of its sex and therefore its own identity, and will be unsure of its natural conduct in forming relationships and approaching problems. If the examples of the sexual roles are muddled by an aggressive, domineering mother or an unduly passive and weak father, so will the child's learning process also be muddled. Morris* says:

> The naked ape is a teaching ape. Much of what we do as adults is based on this imitative absorption during our childhood years. Frequently we imagine that we are behaving in a particular way because such behaviour accords with some abstract, lofty code of moral principles, when in reality all we are doing is obeying a deeply ingrained and long 'forgotten' set of purely imitative impressions. It is the unmodifiable obedience to these impressions that make it so hard for societies to change their customs and their 'beliefs'.

* *The Naked Ape.* Desmond Morris. Jonathan Cape Ltd. 1967.

To this we might add that individuals have equal difficulty in doing so.

Parents pass on not only by precept but more importantly by example a list of do's and don'ts, shoulds and should-nots, oughts and ought-not-to-bes. These latter-day taboos are often based not on natural behaviour but on artificial conduct temporarily necessary because of changing circumstances. But they are retained after their origins have been outdated, and a re-discovery of the natural conduct which preceded them followed by its modifications and adaptation would bring less stress and conflict.

As a part of the learning process, children make use of primitive man's projection mechanism. In order to gain understanding of their own human characteristics, they project them on to objects such as dolls and teddy bears and into make-believe games. In the normal course of events, the insight is achieved and the projection withdrawn. But mind, accustomed to using this mechanism since primitive times, continues to practise it in other forms in later life. In its most obvious manifestations, projection can be seen at work in pet-owners who talk to their animals as if they had conscious lives of their own. Similarly, mechanical objects such as airplanes and ships are fondly regarded as though they possessed human attributes.

Apart from the danger of illusion, recognition and escape from the projection mechanism is important in improvement of human communications. One human cannot talk to another except by assuming they are somewhat similar to each other and that therefore what one has to say will be meaningful to the other. However, unless the possibility of difference is recognised, one person is reduced to a mere reflection of the other and their separate identity and subtleties of personality are lost. Feelings and thoughts of the one are attributed to the other, who is expected to react as the first would react. If his views do not conform to one's idea of what is right, attempts are made to persuade or coerce him. No effort is made to understand his differing point of view. Should he refuse to change his opinion, he is considered to be at fault for not being other than he is.

Despite outstanding examples of the damage caused by moral pretences, certain conduct is still regarded as good and to be followed while other conduct is judged as bad and to be avoided without considering on what grounds the judgement is made.

Polarity of thinking is perpetuated not only by codes of morals but by political systems that fail to judge each situation on its merits. In Britain, the Conservative party is not right and the Labour party is not wrong, and vice versa. The validity of the philosophies depends upon the circumstances. Yet their arguments are carried to the country as if one party was always right, the other always wrong. Such polarity can be the basis of an intolerance which defeats progress and, at its worst, breeds wars.

Thus, and all too briefly, we have tried to illustrate how, in attempting to come to terms with life around him and in trying to answer the fundamental questions concerning his universe, man has always been bedevilled by the atavistic elements in his mentality. Perhaps when he succeeds in recognising his propensity in these matters and overcoming the mechanisms of polarity and projection which limit the viability of his mind, tremendous advances will be made beyond present concepts of science, religion, and human conduct.

4

Divided Man

I BELIEVE I can think. I am not always sure I know what I think, and I certainly know very little about how I think. Presumably some people think better – that is, more effectively – than others. But what is the criterion of 'effective' thinking anyway?

Perhaps it is effective when the thinker is enabled to achieve a desired objective, to draw up a plan which works. Or maybe when he gets on easily with other people. Or perhaps when he remembers easily the facts he needs – because remembering is part of the overall process of thinking. Or, again, it may be according to the clarity with which he can imagine pictures, scenes, colours, conversations, stories. I feel I am thinking clearly when ideas present themselves freshly and vividly, without undue confusion or contradiction. When this happens, I feel energetic and confident, even happy; otherwise I may be frustrated and confused, uncertain and insecure.

I know that on some days I get more satisfaction from my thinking than I do on others. I succeed in achieving a higher degree of quality. Some people, however, obviously get more pleasure from thinking than others. Is that fact due to some inborn characteristic which enables them to achieve such satisfaction more frequently? Has thinking anything to do with so-called intelligence, whatever that may be, or is it a matter of practice or learning? And if thinking, as apart from logic, can be studied and learnt, how would one go about it?

The sad fact is that, vitally important as thinking may be, very little is known on the subject. Since highly educated people do not impress one in this respect as having any advantage over others who are illiterate, it may be that existing education has little to do with improving the quality of individual thought, or does so only in some rather specialised directions.

In the attempt to explore the realms of thought, one probability at least seems relevant to the thesis of this book. I may suggest that whenever I operate my mind, or when it operates independently of my will (which often happens), words, ideas, and pictures occur within an existing structure of attitudes.

An attitude in this sense is an individual's habitual response to certain types of objects, persons, or circumstances – his willingness to accept or inclination to reject them. We have seen how, since the dawn of consciousness, mankind has tended to divide each object and experience into a subjective classification of good or bad. This universal predisposition gives rise to reactions of attitudes typical of each individual: positive if he likes something and regards it as favourable or negative if he is doubtful about it or actually hostile towards it. His associations with past experience recalled by what he is thinking obviously have much to do with determining his attitudes.

Besides their positive or negative quality, attitudes usually carry emotional and varying degrees of viability – that is to say, the subject's readiness to examine them in the light of conflicting feelings or evidence and modify them if he deems it desirable. A particular attitude may be so strong for an individual that ideas associated with it constantly intervene in the course of whatever has his immediate attention. Political attitudes, for instance, are often coloured with so much emotion that irrelevant subjects are readily linked with them.

A person in love finds ideas associated with the object of his or her affections constantly obtruding into every train of thought. Such cases are regarded with amused tolerance by friends and, in the normal course of events, this obsession settles down to assume more balanced proportions. But for a while the obsession has been like an illness in so far as it has incapacitated the sufferer from pursuing his or her normal way of life. Occasionally obsessions develop in directions other than towards matable members of the opposite sex. If they are as intense and continue indefinitely, then the sufferer is likely to be regarded as mentally disturbed.

No two people think exactly alike because classifications differ from one individual to another. Although people with similar backgrounds and experience may be found to have in common attitudes typical of their nationality, their profession, their religion, or their neighbourhood, their remaining responses will be widely conflicting. Public opinion polls reflect how extensively one person's attitudes differ from another's. One survey indicated twice as many adults in Britain followed their horoscopes as read or heard anything from the Bible. Even so, nine out of ten claimed to believe in God – forty five per cent thinking of him as a personal being who knows and cares, and forty three per cent regarding him or it as an impersonal creative force. Nine out of ten also thought one could lead a moral life without believing in God although they did not state from what, in such circumstances, the morality would be derived.

Many parts of an individual's structure of attitudes are likewise at variance with each other. As the song says, 'Everybody wants to go to Heaven – but nobody wants to die.' We do not have to look far into our own conduct to find countless inconsistencies not too readily admitted between our professed beliefs and our actions, and between the implications of one attitude and another.

Novels, plays, and films are largely about the conflicts of attitudes or idealogies which take place between nations, within communities and, more fascinatingly, within individuals. The dénouement points to the consequences of the conflict, whether tragic, comic, or happily solved.

In the previous chapter we pointed out how thousands of years of prehistoric living would be likely to leave us strongly disposed towards attitudes compatible with the conditions of those times, quite regardless of their applicability today. For instance, it still seems appropriate that men should propose to women rather than the reverse and that, quite apart from any immediate necessity of doing so, men should follow some bread-winning occupation while women attend to domestic arrangements. Women's lib movements rightly point out these attitudes have no foundation in logic. Nevertheless, they may be too deeply ingrained to be easily set aside.

The attitudes of an individual are formed also by two other factors: the customs and opinions of the community in which he is brought up; and conclusions drawn from his early personal experiences, particularly within the family circle. Even when one is in possession of all the facts, one can still draw false conclusions from events, and the meaning of experience as concluded by children must in the best of circumstances be suspect. Normally in the course of growing up, many false conclusions or attitudes are corrected. However, where experience has been so vivid as to amount to trauma, eradication may only come about in later life by conscious examination of the occurrence and its consequences.

Conflicts of attitude disturb one's way of life relatively little so long as one remains in the routine static channels of an unchanging job and a circle of friends. Suffering, however, is a part of the human condition and few are so protected as never to have known it, few so insensitive that they have not recognised its pressures. Sooner or later one comes face to face with a major reality of life – an emotional event, a broken marriage, tragedy in one of its numerous forms – and then the question of why such things happen occurs to the least philosophic of us with devastating force.

Security depends on a compatible set of attitudes. To the extent that events can be put into some sort of overall perspective, they become meaningful. The most wounding experience, if understood in relation to the overall principles of life, may be at least soothed by insights derived from it. But wherever conflicts of attitudes exist, anxiety and depression arise from the meaningless confusion experienced in the chaos of the happenings that have become one's life.

Throughout history, man has demanded an answer to the problem of suffering; always he has reached out in an endeavour to reconcile the joy and energies of living with the suffering of death, defeat, deprivation, denigration, and denial. Ever recurring questions are: Why did this have to happen to me? Why couldn't events have been different since they were so important to me? What do they mean?

The offer of an intellectual answer – by spoken word or book – is not enough. For an answer to make sense in terms of one's own life, one's successes and failures, and thus be accepted, it must be experienced emotionally as well as understood intelligibly.

Much of today's unrest is symptomatic of inconsistencies of attitudes as revealed in social and individual anxiety and frustration. Their nature and importance, however, are not generally recognised; nor is it generally felt that wherever subjective judgements of circumstances in terms of good and bad arise, solutions offered by the mind are unlikely to be rational.

The normal conscious way of extending our knowledge of any subject – including ourselves – is to break it down into its component parts and analyse the separate elements as easier to comprehend by themselves than when taken as a whole. The method has definite weaknesses but can contribute to our understanding. How, then, can we classify those attitudes which divide one man from another and even divide the will and motivations of any one man so that he is at war within himself?

The classic way considers qualities such as courage, loyalty, persistence, and the typical attitudes associated with them. On the other hand, in business undertakings, we find jobs no longer analysed and specified in terms of the qualities required to perform them but in terms of the tasks to be performed. The activity of living may be treated in this way to derive a classification of its parts. We cannot claim any fundamental validity for these distinctions; nevertheless, from a practical point of view they prove useful when considering the range of attitudes involved in living and the manner and localisation of conflict between them.

In this scheme, we suggest living involves four main groups of attitudes relating respectively to work, creativity, relationships, and religion – the last not so much as one's regard for any particular deity but in the wider sense of what, if anything, one believes in.

* * *

Work in the sense meant here is an activity pursued primarily for the sake of material reward and which, but for this return, would not be performed owing to the labour or fatigue entailed. This distin-

71

guishes work from activities undertaken primarily for other objectives but which nevertheless carry financial rewards that make work as such unnecessary. The arts, for instance, have an element of fascination which is the prime attraction for their followers. It is their good fortune that a means of livelihood is incidentally generated. Work, on the other hand, is that which is a necessary evil, something an individual would rather not do except for the fact that he feels compelled by materialistic or other similar influences.

Many people's attitudes to work are derived from the influence of parents and environment. Their work is thus chosen for them instead of the individual freely selecting what he wants to do with reference to his natural characteristics and interests. We are taught little specifically about work as such, in school or elsewhere, presumably because it is so widely accepted that one must work, as opposed to create, in order to earn a living. Other implications or possibilities are often dismissed as impractical or idealistic. We are taught about particular types and techniques of work, but not the essence of why one should work rather than steal. Almost nothing is said regarding the usefulness of the experience of work for its own sake.

Despite this lack of teaching, less trouble probably arises for the individual from inconsistent attitudes concerning work than in any of the three other areas. The means of livelihood is a pressing necessity on most of us and only those with realistic attitudes survive for long. Material requirements force the majority to be willing to devote time to an onerous, non-pleasurable pursuit in order to gain reward. For this a certain set of attitudes is to some degree necessary. The more balanced they are, the more prosperous and satisfied the individual is likely to be.

Probably the prime attitude of importance here is what has been described as leadership but is rarely well defined. Perhaps leadership is the ability to accomplish a task on one's own responsibility without looking towards somebody else to make good one's own deficiency. The responsible man or leader relies upon himself to do a job as best he can with the self-confidence that it will be done competently. This self-reliance marks out the difference between the man who is merely a cog in a large organisation and the man who heads it up. Someone somewhere along the line must take up ultimate responsibility for any continuing project and if 'top' people live better than the rest, they do so probably because they have the comparatively rare degree of courage and self-confidence to take responsibility for their own decisions.

Responsibility involves on the one hand the integrity to fulfil a task entrusted to us and, on the other, the ability to delegate and trust other people with work. This realm of co-operation demands a certain tolerance, faith, and respect for other people's ability, as well as one's own.

Work also involves a balance of domination and subordination. The former requires sufficient self-confidence to be able to give orders and sufficient humility not to assume that one's decision would have any value to employees in spheres outside the working situation. The latter requires sufficient subordination of one's ideas to be able to accept and carry out orders even where one disagrees with them. An attitude of respect for the other person's point of view allows that there may be reasons for orders of which one is unaware.

The types of activity which may be regarded as work are debatable. If the acquisition of material means is its sole objective, then fraud, theft and other activities normally classified or historically considered as immoral and possibly illegal may be considered to meet such a criterion. Inheritance, prize-winning, and gambling may also provide a living. Do they have much or anything in common with work, quite apart, as in the criminal instance, from the consequences of getting caught? One possibility suggests that in order to develop his abilities, man has to submit to the particular experiences in life which contribute to his growth, and work is one of them. To steal or win money, to drop out in any way from the obligations of the human condition, is to short-circuit one of the less pleasant disciplines encountered by man and, to that extent, to be less than man. Only by the whole experience of living can one become whole oneself. In the end, to refrain from any essential part of it is to be deprived of some of the qualities and abilities man engenders in himself by reason of the experiences he undergoes and through which, over the millennia, nature has equipped him to live.

Thus from this point of view, criminal acts are wrong regardless

73

of whether one gets caught or the consequences to the victim. Whatever the immediate benefit to the perpetrator, in the long term he stunts himself and conflict is likely to arise between his immature search for self-gratification at the community's expense and the inherent gregarious trait which needs expression in its contribution to the common welfare. Wherever such basic conflict persists, the personality is deprived of a sense of fulfilment.

With well-balanced attitudes to work, the possibility arises that even those in what are considered to be dull jobs may nevertheless find fascinating or constructive aspects to them. The operator on a mass-production line is generally regarded as carrying out a soulless occupation with a high degree of monotony. But those well-adapted in their attitudes may experience the repetitive element only as a part of the context in which a satisfying achievement of quality or quantity takes place.

*　　*　　*

Creativity arises from original perception and expression of relationships between objects and/or people which inspires new insight into their nature. The creative act sets in motion fresh sets of associated ideas as a stone flung into a pond radiates widening ripples.

Creativity breaks up the stereotyped views of tradition in which individuals have been educated or which are generally accepted by the community round them. As such, originality is more difficult to achieve than is usually supposed. For instance, a haphazard rearrangement of relationships in music or art in the hope of achieving something new is to imitate the creative rather than to achieve it. A great deal of confusion and disappointment follows such posturing by those who would like to take advantage of the extremely high valuation society puts upon the genuinely original.

Since originality will never arise from some established formula, how can the attitudes conducive to it be specified? Probably those minds which can truly be called creative have, at least within their chosen field, attitudes flexible enough to permit orientations of ideas, images, colours, or sounds to be freely changed around without hindrance from prejudice.

74

Creativity, unlike work, is not necessarily achieved by per-severance. One understands that those who attain it feel a fascination for their activity which would cause them to seek self-expression irrespective of financial reward. The attitudes of such artists must be finely balanced and, in consequence, are rare. There must be courage and self-sufficiency to stand alone against established viewpoints and hold an individual idea at least long enough to find means of expression. There must also be respect for what has gone before to improve on it. The motive for attempting to create must be one of pure interest in the subject, for, if it is confused with any wish for distinction, imitation of a proved success would be too tempting to avoid. Imitation proceeds from pre-association whereas originality stems from new association.

Everyone seems in some degree to seek actively to achieve something original, however slight, whether in the course of a hobby, or in their appearance, or even in conversation. The person who is completely predictable in these respects is the one whom we are all glad to avoid.

The individual who has originality of mind may find that the necessity for work is reduced or hardly arises because his creating provides his income. This, however, is a mixed blessing if he fails to develop the qualities engendered by work as such. Creativity in these circumstances is likely to become an indulgence.

Creativity is valued by society because it extends the horizons limiting human thought. The nature of reality may be much wider than what we normally perceive every day. When man became conscious, his first task was to use his mind to ensure his material existence. Therefore, if the sight of too much reality might distract his attention from the business of finding food and security, his perception might deliberately have levelled off at that consistent with, and just sufficient for, immediate survival. And so it may have persisted.

Much has been written about the opening of the doors of per-ception as if drugs had a peculiar power to induce creativity. While this does not seem to be true, certain drugs do temporarily – and often dangerously – liberate the mind from conventional views which normally limit perception of experience to what one knows by association or has been led to expect. This lifting of inhibiting factors may provide a temporary illusion of an exhilarating freedom from the reality of the familiar. It can be said of the drug movement that its motivating drive, however misleading or harmful, is the wish to experience new perception. Its adherents do not take drugs because they want to become managing directors or millionaires but because they want heightened awareness. This search for 'more' of life expresses the need, anxiety, and urgency for a wider aspiration of creativity generally and we may suppose that the attitudes of truly flexible man permit him to be creative in whatever field he is occupied.

*　　*　　*

Relationships include attitudes towards sex, towards the opposite sex, parents, children, friends, colleagues, people in general, and oneself. The dynamic equilibrium in this area is that which balances self-interest against understanding and concern for the other. Unlike work where the necessity for material existence forces the reconciliation between attitudes and needs, relationships do not undergo such immediate and extreme pressures. Perhaps for this reason, relationships are probably the most archaic and anachronistic of the categories of attitudes. To a great extent, they are dictated by rigorous conventions that suited society centuries ago and are out of step with modern conditions. The existing system of relationships in the West was largely built up in earlier times when the problems of living were very different. Life was much harder then, as it still is in many Eastern countries. The struggle to maintain sufficient food, shelter, and warmth took precedence over all else. There was insufficient opportunity to find out by trial and experiment what form relationships should or could take.

Traditional attitudes towards the family unit are so bred into us that today it is still difficult for married adults to have any degree of relationship with a member of the opposite sex without the risk of damage to the marriage. Convention limits man and wife to their own exclusive company even though their marriage might benefit from the increased insight gained if they widened their experience of people.

The entertainment industry has built up a myth of romantic possession whereby the key to all happiness is represented as the finding of a mate with whom one can live in perfect and exclusive accord for the remainder of one's life. The male engages in bread-winning, the female in housekeeping, childbearing, and generally taking charge of domestic arrangements. This mode of conduct is represented as right and natural. In fact, if a pair do not find romance's happy ending in a rather exclusive partnership, if the man is not fulfilled by a nice regular job, and if the wife is not content to stay home, then nobody should pretend surprise. But the myth is so strongly inculcated into us that any deviation from this accepted pattern is suspect. The man or woman who enters into a close relationship which is not exclusive, is viewed with serious doubt. The partner who tolerates so-called infidelity in the other is regarded as weak if he is a man, or downtrodden if she is a wife. The possessive spirit is often regarded, especially in Latin countries, as something admirable and as indicating the intensity of love. This sort of blatant jealousy might be better looked upon as immature self-interest arising from attitudes of insecurity and attempts to relieve doubts about oneself by demanding the other's continual attention. The profession of a love that seeks to justify a desire to possess the beloved, as if he or she was some material object, imposes expectations and obligations that the 'loved' one should reciprocate the 'love'; yet such an attitude is inconsistent with undemanding concern for the other's needs and happiness.

Even comparatively small changes of socially acceptable attitudes towards relationships may bring about far-reaching changes in civilisation. Much of literature, entertainment, thinking, and law is based upon and dominated by the concept that people by nature rather than habit live in pairs rather exclusively and have cause for complaint if one partner deviates sexually from a monogamous ethic. The concept may be correct, but who can tell so long as it remains unchallenged?

Balanced adjustment to relationships will surely come only when each individual feels free to discover and take responsibility for his own concept of them irrespective of the ideals or ethics pursued by parents, acquaintances, and society. This requires sufficient confidence and originality to overcome worries about oneself and to ignore outdated social pressures which approve of immature conduct and decry failure to conform. Freedom of the individual implies the ability to adopt conduct which feels right for him without reference to intellectual justifications and respectability's rules of oughts and ought-nots. So long as there is sincere concern for the other and responsibility for the outcome of one's actions, the ensuing relationships will be beneficial to both participants.

The huge range of attitudes towards relationships is experienced primarily between couples, secondly between them and their families, thirdly between them and their friends, fourthly between them and the community.

The main element, and possibly the most important in marriage, is acceptance of other people with all their difficulties, deficiences, and problems just as one hopes for tolerance and charity in one's own difficulties. Out of faith, hope, and charity, charity has been described as the most important. Charity in this sense might well mean tolerance towards the other, his mistakes, and the hurtful gestures which he inadvertently makes or cannot stop himself from making, just as oneself inadvertently hurts the other in turn. Seen as helplessly involved in their own problems, other people become more easily the object of 'charity' in this sense, or 'tolerance' in modern terminology. One learns and progresses from the encounters of a relationship, by observing both one's own and the other person's mistakes, one's own difficulties in adjustment and theirs. One may get hurt in the process of learning, but as one learns or realises the cause of the hurt, it is assuaged.

One wonders if parents are likely to be able to love their own child satisfactorily – i.e. provide it with the feelings or knowledge of basic security – unless they also love other children, in the sense of tolerating them and feeling sincere concern for their welfare. Parents who dote on their own child too often have high expectations of its future which betray more ambition than concern for the development of its nature. To bring up a child with love, a general attitude of loving disposition would seem essential. Nor can one be concerned for humanity generally if individual members are omitted. Some do-gooders profess sincere belief in performance of their charitable works to benefit society generally, while simultaneously they display intolerance towards individual members of it, including on occasion even their own family. What conflicting attitudes prompt such inconsistency?

In relationships with the community at large, or with individual friends in particular, it is the responsibility of the individual to adjust his attitudes so as to relate to – though not to imitate – the other. If he fails to do so, he alone must suffer the consequence, for while friends or even the community may endeavour to extend charity, unwarranted demands must be resisted and he who demands too much is likely to experience the unrelated state of isolation.

Failure to accept responsibility of this sort is, after all, to rate oneself superior to the other and to complain of attitudes all too human in the other, that is, their humanity, their criminality, their vulgarity, their politics, their conduct, and even their inconsistent attitudes.

What constellations of attitude then suggest that the remainder of humanity should not behave as seems fitting to the preacher? And, in spite of this realisation, how do the present authors take it upon themselves to suggest precepts of attitude? The dividing line is between observation of behaviour and formulation of precept is indeed a fine one. Who shall explore it without himself overstepping it?

*　　*　　*

Religion in the sense meant here is concerned with what we believe determines our destiny, whether indeed we have a destiny, and by implication the limits upon what we may or may not do. Thus an attitude towards a traditional deity is included, but so is the denial of any sort of god. Einstein said, 'If a man finds a satisfying answer to the question what is the meaning of his life, this man I would call religious.' The search for meaning is a continuous one.

The words 'eschatology', defined in the Concise Oxford Dictionary as 'Doctrine of death, judgment, heaven and hell', and 'ontogenesis', 'the origin and development of the individual being', are surely among those least used even in our highly educated society. Yet the attitudes of the individual towards their subject matter are virtually his policy of living. For those whose attitudes indicate that such a policy is unimportant, meaninglessness and trivia are presumably acceptable. But it is doubtful if their attitude to the importance of their own existence would be consistent with the joyful acceptance of inconsequentiality. This sort of consideration indicates how easily inconsistent attitudes flourish undetected in this field.

Two extreme positions may be identified. Those who are untroubled by the realisation that the limited span between birth and death is all we have available in which to experience the entire potential of what we call life, live in the anaesthesia of day-to-day trivia. At the other end of the scale, there are those overconscious that each day may be their last and, waiting always for what is to come, succeed only in missing what has already arrived.

Attitudes derived secondhand from doctrinaire religion provide some protection against the anxieties and insecurity which are the unfortunate side-effect of a conscious faculty that enables us to foresee and anticipate the possible discomforts of the future.

The price of entertaining these attitudes is considerable. For if a god who knows and cares about us tolerates the suffering and injustice to which we are only too accustomed and is nevertheless considered beneficent, what can we expect from other men, mere humans lacking divine attributes? And to gain the reassurance of traditional religion, acceptance of these fearful doubts about the nature of God's goodwill must be suppressed. Yet if we do not enquire about the nature and implication of suffering, we, not the deity, must accept responsibility for suffering. It is not by intellectual argument but by example that we may free ourselves from the bondage of pain which we have, in our resignation, come to look upon as the human condition. Yet that clarity of insight, those uncommitted attitudes which will enable it to be overcome, will not be easy to bear.

To maintain that traditional religious attitudes no longer fulfil their former roles is not to suggest that we can dispense with conscious attitudes towards the forces which have shaped, and continue to shape, both the species and the individual. The cost of having no faith is that of lacking any feeling that the interval between birth and death can be meaningfully filled. The evidence of the necessity for conviction is surely found in the God of Job, that frivolous, inconsequential creature least deserving of loyalty, which nevertheless provided the sense of security and comfort which enables us to conduct effectively our day-to-day affairs.

As Tolstoy makes clear, it is no easy matter to exist in an un-committed state:

> What will be the outcome of what I do today? Of what shall I do tomorrow? What will be the outcome of all my life? Why should I live? Why should I do anything? Is there in life any purpose which the inevitable death which awaits me does not undo and destroy?
>
> These questions are the simplest in the world. From the stupid child to the wisest of man, they are in the soul of every human being. Without an answer to them, it is impossible, as I experienced, for life to go on.
>
> 'But perhaps,' I often said to myself, 'there may be something I have failed to notice or to comprehend. It is not possible that this condition of despair should be natural to mankind.' And I sought for an explanation in all the branches of knowledge acquired by men. I questioned painfully and protractedly and with no idle curiosity. I sought, not with indolence, but labouriously and obstinately for days and nights together. I sought like a man who is lost and seeks to save himself – and I found nothing. I became convinced, moreover, that all those who before me had sought for an answer in the sciences have also found nothing. And not only this, but that they have recognised that the very thing which was leading me to despair – the meaningless absurdity of life – is the only incontestable knowledge accessible to man.

In the end Tolstoy could not sustain this tension: he settled with relief for something as unsatisfactory to the modern mind as that which he had earlier relinquished.

Since his endeavour, the urgency of the contrasts has become more acute. We still need to be able to take up attitudes in which belief does not conflict with experience – in which, on the contrary, the one supports and enriches the other. An attitude must be more than the outcome of an intellectual exercise if it is to fulfil its function. It must entail at least sufficient conviction that one may react to it as to an enlightening interpretation of one's own individual experience of living. As Somerset Maugham pointed out, it means nothing in the religious context if a man professes to believe in God unless he also behaves as if he does.

In the end, one is left with a feeling that the importance of ontogenetical matters is so great for the improvement of the quality of everyday life that consideration of them should not remain exclusively the province of the committed theologian.

*   *   *

The constellation of attitudes towards different aspects of living into separate categories has, at the risk of over-simplification, some advantages. If malformed attitudes ran across the board, the subject in each case would be disabled in every aspect of his life. He would be concurrently ineffective in every area of living and consequently unable to cope with any problems at all. In fact, contradictory attitudes do not effect all aspects of a life but are as if restricted within watertight compartments. Thus man's ineptitude in business does not mean his family life will also fail. Achievement can take place within one area quite independently of the others. Most people are reasonably balanced in one or two areas and operate comparatively effectively within these fields, whichever is their forte, though ignoring or incapacitated in the other aspects of life where inconsistencies exist. One constantly meets with cases of highly intelligent people who are capable of exercising the acutest skill in one part of their lives, yet behave like the crassest of idiots in some other sphere.

It is the number or strength of inconsistencies in attitude which marks out the difference between what is considered the sane and the insane man, the lucky and the unfortunate, the effective and the effete, the frustrated and the satisfied, the victorious and the defeated man.

One may well ask why, if an attitude is not logical, we do not put it right? But the correction is not easily made, as we shall next attempt to demonstrate. Man's mind, by which he is guided in his day-to-day decisions, is often not as logical, as sensible, as true to his interests, as he is tempted to believe. His attitudes form the framework within which logic operates and logic is their servant rather than their master.

5

Individual
Man

'COGITO, ERGO SUM,' said Descartes. 'I think, therefore, I am.'
Irreverently, and be it admitted in the context of his philosophy
quite irrelevantly, one is tempted to suggest the next step: What I am
is determined by what I think. If that is true, maybe the way is open
to find out something about myself. If I can establish what I think
– as apart from what Mary or John thinks – perhaps I shall begin to
discover my individuality; even, in the end, to find out who I am as
apart from what I am.

The real difference between me and my friend does not lie in the
respective length of our noses, the colour of our eyes and hair; nor
in our voices; nor even in the language and expressions we cus-
tomarily use. Those differences are readily identifiable and have
nothing to do with my – or his – essential personality. I may go grey
but remain the same person. Identical twins are sometimes almost
indistinguishable yet each has his or her unique individuality which
cannot be confused.

So, my physical characteristics are one element only in all of those
which differentiate me from other people. Neither does the difference
lie in what I think in the sense of the particular and comparatively
superficial ideas or opinions I happen to hold at any one moment.
They will inevitably change from time to time yet leave me still

83

identifiably me. I am not my ideas, but something like the first layer of my individuality begins to emerge with the style of my doubts, understandings, concepts, affirmations, denials, ethics, desires, and feelings. These surely are the stuff of which my individuality is constructed and from which my ideas emerge.

One man shouts and another man whispers. One is apologetic, another aggressive. Such mannerisms are consistent with his attitudes, and his attitudes are the fabric of his character – his characteristic approach to life, characteristic ways of reacting to events impinging upon him, to the approaches and attacks which make up his relations with others. If I need to know something of this personality I should surely look to its origins, to just how I came to think my particular set of thoughts. If my character did not spring into being fully furnished, how did it gradually take shape and what formed it?

So often the assumption is made in our society that one's view of life depends upon one's intelligence and ability to grasp what one has been taught. Yet in the reality of the matter, thoughts and feelings are well formed before ever they become the subject of intellectual education. Since we usually have reasons ready to support whatever we believe, we accept such belief as the result of some logical process. In fact our conduct and attitudes are shaped by what we happen to experience and deduce in our earliest formative years. On such foundations are beliefs formed; the supporting rationalisations follow on.

This sequence and the strength of conditioning experiences have been well demonstrated by the work of psychiatric practitioners. The classic case histories of schizophrenia and other mental disorientation which do not appear to have organic origins, illustrate how small a part logic plays in the way attitudes constellate and grow and how largely they are founded upon fortuitous experience. Perhaps because this process first became apparent in clinical work – and further, being associated with Freud's name, it was somehow believed to be part and parcel of his 'unwholesome' sexual theories – it was not considered proper for school curricula. Whatever the reason, the fact that we are conditioned rather than logical beings, that conditioning is a normal and necessary occurrence undergone by everyone, has

84

received surprisingly little recognition. In the absence of instruction on the matter, we are left to believe ourselves to be intellectual rather than experiential beings.

If man were entirely a rational creature, one might expect that, until old enough to accept or reject ideas for himself, a child would exist without commitment towards anything. Yet obviously one does not grow up in this way. No point arrives when one is free suddenly and deliberately to start to codify one's experience of the world around one and then to generalise about it.

Instead, the process, as one remembers it and as may be deduced from children's behaviour, is a gradual awareness of convictions about one's world and the people in it. One finds oneself reacting to circumstances in ways which seem, at least to oneself, perfectly natural. One has one's likes and dislikes, one's desires and denials which are compelling enough in their own right; whether they are expedient, ethical, rational or subject to any other other criterion is one's last concern – until, that is, they encounter opposition or some conflicting motivation to frustrate them. At that point, all too easily we account for ourselves with a judicious selection of evidence and argument having sufficient resemblance to reason to deceive at least oneself. Unfortunately such views and attitudes so genuinely believed to be based on logical grounds are not as rational as we imagine. The world is not as self-evident as it appears and there is every difference between the pseudo-reason of 'conviction support' and the detached examination of all the evidence available as well as its implications which, more correctly, we experience as the use of reason.

As logic machines, our minds are far from perfect and illogicality is not necessarily nor only a matter of intelligence or inability to associate cause and effect. On the contrary, illogicality is a willingness to condone the connection of events which have nothing to do with each other as if they were causal. Yet it must be emphasised that all this specious motivation and argument takes place within one's mind without the slightest intention to deceive either oneself or anyone else.

The Archbishop of Canterbury and the Pope are men of intelligence, integrity, and goodwill. The divergence of opinion which separates them does not arise from some inability on one side or the

85

other to take into account valid evidence in favour or in conflict with their views. But, like the rest of us, they are not as logical as possibly they suppose, and if their minds are better than those of most of us – in the sense of being more effective – it is because they accept their frailty. Humility is not only an attitude of respect for the other; it is also a willingness to accept and do the best with one's own limitations.

*   *   *

By the time the normal individual reaches adulthood, his views, motivations and reactions have been influenced and perhaps limited by three sorts of factors:

1. The mechanistic habits of mind already described as derived from the necessities of survival during the eons of prehistory.

2. The traditional beliefs and conventions of the localised community, difficult to challenge because so insidiously effective and accepted in so many directions, flavouring much with their implications.

3. The manner in which personal and highly individual experience in the earliest years of life leads on to an individual set of convictions and assumptions accepted as self-evident truth. At every turn, the subject must attempt to reconcile with these his desires, his actions, and his reasons.

Enlarging on the second and third of these factors, we may assume that a child starts life with no opinions and that such actions as he performs are unplanned and unconscious. As a baby he sends out signals concerning hunger and comfort. Consciousness proper involves associating incoming sense perceptions with memories of past experiences already in store. In the early stages the stores are virtually empty. There is no past as a guide to the present.

In the absence of experience, memories, and associations, one may imagine the infant mind existing in a blank, waxlike state ready to have the first impressions imprinted upon it. Once recorded, classified, and stored away in the vast mysterious recesses which even the smallest child's mental equipment has available to it, these impressions will be used to form the basis of future actions and responses to future situations.

Experience at any age – and some types of experiences more than others – is likely to be formative but during the first years of life is particularly relevant. Other than what is instinctive, the sum total of a child's knowledge can be derived only from his experience of what he sees, hears, feels, discovers can be done, and deduces from what is apparently approved and what is found to be punishable.

One can surmise that early impressions sink deeply and last a very long time if not throughout life, particularly since the child is often exposed in this period to experiences from which he forms generalisations without knowing how far his history is peculiar to him and how far true for others.

The child has few means of realising that anything suggested to him might not be true because his faculties of consciousness are too weak to exercise the powers of selection and rejection which will develop later. Since much of the information fed into his mind is in fact true and can be verified by experience, he is encouraged to accept also the proportion which is not well founded and which may colour or even warp his outlook and attitudes. Told that pepper tastes hot and ice feels cold, he can easily prove such statements. Other information, opinions, and impressions are not so simply checked. Many will be accepted in good faith. In the process of growing up, some will be tested, found wanting and corrected or discarded, but much will remain.

At no time is it practicable for the child to pause and examine the sum total of the content of his mind over again to see whether all the information is correct. He learns first, and adjusts everything else afterwards to conform to what he has learned, omitting to examine the consistency of the entire view which he has absorbed. The painful experiences bury themselves underground but, like cancer, spread out their harmful effects. Denigration of the dignity of the personality of the child may be particularly prejudicial to its need to relate to its true status in life. Once recorded, such impressions may not perhaps be indelible but certainly they will be most difficult to erase if for no other reason than the difficulty of recall for examination.

In childhood the capacity of the mind for conscious memory retention and recall is not yet working to any appreciable extent.

Even adults rarely remember every incident which happened to them the previous week, though under sufficient pressure they do have the power to recall, so the memory is still stored somewhere but below the level of immediate awareness. Adults are capable of recalling not only a particular experience the previous week or previous year but precise reasons for the conclusions, if any, which they drew. But the child's understanding of cause and effect is as primitive and uncritical as that of early man. The conclusions are often inaccurate and remembered without reference to the basic source material from which they are derived.

An individual vividly recollects some experiences from childhood but the memory of other important events and feelings of the utmost intensity have slipped below the level of awareness. Generalisations formed on insufficient or faulty evidence remain, but the reasons on which they are based are not consciously realised and therefore not available for re-examination.

In any storekeeping operation, and as indeed when constructing the memory banks of a computer, the method used for classifying and locating items to be put away is vital. Obviously the items are there to be used as and when required in the future. Therefore, they must be easily and readily available and this will be possible only if they are located in the store under some sort of system.

One may imagine two ways in which mind could perform this function:

First, the associative method whereby experience is lumped together with all those arising from a particular source. In infancy, sources of experience are likely to be Mummy, Daddy, food, and objects contributing or otherwise to comfort.

Secondly, the conceptual method whereby one may imagine that experience, insight, or sense perception is stored under the heading of its subject – whatever the particular individual mind conceives the subject of the experience to be.

In the early days, storage by the conceptual system is impossible since one presumes no concepts yet exist in the individual mind with which to classify them; thus the associative method is used exclusively. This type of elementary storage and recall certainly continues throughout life but probably to a decreasing extent as, later on, the second and more sophisticated arrangements come into use. Possibly both systems then exist side by side in a sort of cross-index similar to the author/subject catalogue used in libraries.

As the human embryo develops in the liquid-filled womb, it passes through stages which strangely resemble those of the human species itself in its development from the first cells in the primeval sea. It is tempting to suggest that, in parallel with this physical retracing, the mind of each individual goes after birth through several stages which also have some elements resembling the stages through which mankind passed as he evolved consciousness.

Thus the first conceptual arrangements likely to arise in the mind during its formative period will be based upon good and bad, right or wrong. Under each associative heading, one can imagine a simple two-bin storage-bank subdividing impressions into those to be accepted and those to be rejected. Although this 'two-bin system' may give trouble later in life because of its inflexibility, it is essential from the point of view of the welfare of the infant and the development of its ego. It provides the same sort of easy guide to safe conduct and short-term survival as the taboo system afforded primitive man. In spite of its limitations, the system is nevertheless effective enough to be used by many long after ceasing to be the only method available to them of determining their behaviour. Perhaps it would be an oversimplification to suggest that the process of maturing both in individuals and in mankind as a whole might consist of relaxation of this initial protective device, but in some respects the suggestion would be relevant.

In the meanwhile we may accept that the child's understanding is based solely on its particular individual and purely fortuitious experiences. The child has not the means of distinguishing between typical and unusual events. It has little possibility of rejecting or disregarding inconsistent perceptions. Constantly for hours, days, weeks, months, and even years, experiences are fed into his mind like data into a computer, to be used there to construct a peculiarly individual view of the life going on outside.

Three types of data which condition the child mind can be identified:

1. Direct sensory experience, including traumatic shock.

89

2. Example, particularly of parents, brothers, sisters, or other persons in regular contact with the child.

3. Instruction, such as parental advice, say-so, climate of opinion in the community, all of which get taken up without the critical screening exercised in later life.

The barest knowledge of accepted psychiatric theory is unnecessary to know that a child is affected by lack of love, a broken home, brutality or drunkennes on the part of the parents. David Stafford-Clark* writes in *Psychiatry Today*:

> In all communities the structure of the family and the relationship of the child with the parents, as well as their relationship with each other and with the society of which they form a part, is almost certainly the most important single influence upon the development of the personality and the liability to mental health or mental illness. The size of the family, its stability, and the security which the child can feel within its protection, the certainty of wholehearted acceptance and love, and the provision of consistent, tolerant, and responsible standards of behaviour, by example at least as much as by precept, all form a vital part of that essential shaping of an individual's character and possibilities which must take place during the first two decades of life; loss or separation of parents, for example, are among the most serious environmental threats to a child's security which can occur; but even more important than the actual loss or deprivation are the circumstances and emotional accompaniment to the experience and what follows. For example, a fatherless child or an orphan can still gain an underlying confidence, hope and inner stability, with the capacity to make personal adjustment to his loss and to subsequent experiences in life, if the disaster has been handled by the remaining parent or by those responsible for the child's subsequent upbringing with calmness, fortitude, and an abiding love. But where the separation has been the result of parental friction or accompanied by bitterness, hatred, and disillusionment, these feelings in their turn will influence not simply the child's immediate response but a great deal of his expectations and subsequent attitude to life and people as a whole.
>
> ... There are other more subtle but no less damaging ways of undermining the faith or happiness of such a child, and thereby comprising and threatening the emotional stability of the adult whom he will one day become. Sustained envy or bitterness on the part of the parents, jealousy or persecution within the family circle, or the

---

* *Psychiatry Today* (Pelican Original, Second Edition, 1963), Penguin Books Ltd. Copyright © David Stafford-Clark, 1963

deliberate distortion and betrayal of family life and ties often forming so obnoxious and degrading a feature of totalitarian systems, can all make their mark upon the inner life of the individual and upon his attitude to himself and his fellow men.

Any and every child needs to feel loved by his parents for his own sake, for if he is not acceptable in their eyes, then who in the world will he be acceptable to and where is his place and protection in the big, wide, frightening outside? The resulting insecurity from any feeling of lack of love, real or imagined, takes confidence away from the child to leave him a lonely, lost figure who cannot afford to love or put his faith in others. Out of self-protection, he must grow up self-centred. He lacks the confidence to face the problems of life or participate in a deep relationship. The effects can be life-long. Throughout life, his basic characteristics may be isolation, loneliness, doubt, distrust, bitterness, jealousy, self-pity, or selfishness. These traits cannot be foretold specifically but when they reveal themselves they can usually be traced back to the little frightened child who could not cope and should never have had to cope, in the beginning, on his own.

Regarded in this way, the psychiatrists' discovery that the origin of aberration in later life is not due to some poorly-functioning intellectual process but to the circumstances and upbringing of childhood, seems obvious enough. Indeed one begins to wonder how so many people ever succeed in making as much sense as they have out of so little and such circumscribed material. Obviously some corrective mechanism must be at work so that grossly misleading experience can be overlaid to some extent. Some events are more dramatic or otherwise startling than others, more vividly associated with pain or pleasure, and the conclusions unconsciously connected with these will be proportionately enduring. Trauma or near traumatic events of this type will be most deeply impressed and likely to lead to rigid adherence to attitudes of fear or desire and to defeat the processes of reason in this area.

*   *   *

One of the functions of my intellect is to enable me to satisfy my ever-increasing need to react effectively to my environment. Hence

91

my intellect compares new with past experience and selects as relevant – or 'right' or 'real' – that which seems consistent with what has gone before. At this point, I am less exposed to the effects of all experience and to some extent discriminative. If new experiences are sufficiently vivid or traumatic, they may swamp earlier associations on the same subject; if they are less strong but cannot be dismissed as irrelevant, I may be able to reconcile them with existing stores by rationalisation. I experience Daddy as a 'good' man, occasionally however as a drunken man who is rough, noisy, and very smelly. I conclude that good men are apt to get drunk occasionally; that men are rough, noisy, smelly, but often kind; that drunks are good to me when not drunk, apart from Uncle Tom who is never drunk but always sour.

Some experiences from childhood remain as vivid recollections but the memory of other important events and feelings of the utmost intensity slip below the level of awareness. Generalisations formed on insufficient or faulty evidence remain, but the reasons on which they are based are not consciously realised and therefore not available for re-examination.

As a small child, I scald myself spilling a cup of tea and am smacked by my habitually irascible parent. I do not experience sympathy, understanding of my hurt, nor tenderness and therefore do not expect them in the future on such occasions. I forget the trivial incident of that particular afternoon and the associations with others like it. I accept my dislike of tea as a personal idiosyncrasy as well as my generalisation from my parent's reaction that tenderness towards others is inappropriate. In such manner, an infinite number of conclusions about the essence of life come to be accepted all too easily and go unquestioned all too long.

Already even my superficial personality begins to split into two: the experimental being, the 'I am' founded upon what I have perceived to have happened to me, and the intellectual 'I am' of what I have concluded from my experiences. Throughout the rest of my life I shall be convinced – that is, I shall both know and act as if I know – only when I learn something both experientially and intellectually. This is a matter to which we will return since it is becoming increasingly important in our time.

92

Are we not in later life capable of perceiving our own inconsistencies and modifying them? There appear to be two obstacles which complicate the matter.

Firstly, even if one has access comparatively easily to the intellectual being so that one becomes aware of one's own idiosyncrasies, one will continue, in spite of oneself, to react as before unless one also experiences the idiosyncrasy emotionally. Thus the imprinting of early experience cannot be written off as false by any act of mere intelligence. It can be corrected only by a subsequent relevant experience of sufficient intensity to cause it to be discarded and at the same time, by knowledge of what is happening, by bringing it into the full light of conscious recall.

Knowledge

The second is the phenomenon of hypnotism about which unfortunately little is known. We may surmise that the receptivity of the child mind is similar to that of the adult who has been put into a hypnotic trance. Not everyone can be hypnotised – certainly at least not under experimental conditions. A large proportion are however subject to hypnotism and their suitability has nothing to do with their intelligence or their degree of faith in the process. Repeated experiments enable certain phenomena to be predicted with assurance so that we know what is likely to happen even if we do not know how it takes place.

hypnotism.

For instance, the hypnotised subject will accept information or instructions which in his normal state his perceptions would cause him to reject. He can be told that when he wakes he will see a person come into the room and sit on a chair – a chair that in fact is already occupied by someone. When the hypnotic subject comes out of the trance, his mind does allow him to see this non-existent person enter the room while drawing a complete blank over the real person who is already seated in the chair. Again, a non-smoker may be instructed to light up a cigarette as soon as he comes out of hypnosis, and he will do so. Not only that, but after a lifetime without touching a cigarette, his mind will construct a seemingly rational reason why he had accepted one. He may say he thought the other person in the room wanted to smoke and the reason for his action was as a courtesy to make them feel at ease.

If the adult mind is so open to hypnotic suggestion as to be able to produce these powerful and curious phenomena, the infant mind may well be even more susceptible. As a result, the accidents and incidents of childhood, the manner in which the individual grows up, impose upon him notions which influence his mind to such an extent that he can use only a part of his mental equipment and only a limited range of ideas and motives are acceptable to him. The power of these incidents derives from the fact their origins in the early life of the child are later on forgotten so that deductions made at the time resemble truth which is accepted unchallenged.

Dehypnotisation cannot be brought about by instruction, argument, the exercise of willpower or determination but only by reference to the original imprinting experience or the induced hypnotic suggestion.

Finally if it is not possible to do so in any other way, one might hope that contact with, and example of, other people would iron out one's conditioned idiosyncrasies. In fact this appears to occur to a limited extent only unless in controlled circumstances. I become aware that others do not share my views or my attitudes. I may accept the discrepancy or suppress my own individuality in respect of such matters but the realisation of difference in itself is unlikely to change my convictions. I am most likely to reconcile the difference in one of three ways:

1. I may dismiss the other's view as perversely stupid or blind because he cannot discern for himself what seems to me a universal truth.

2. I may believe the other capable of recognising the truth but deliberately ignoring or falsifying it to suit a purpose, or because of wishful thinking, or because he wants to deceive me.

3. I may accept the view of the other as superior to my own but one to which I cannot aspire myself because I have not his greater intelligence or capacity for insight.

In whatever of these three ways I may react to the other, I will rarely accept that my obvious truths are my own, may relate only to my individual experience, and for the most part are in fact neither universally obvious nor universally true.

If self-knowledge is desirable for the peace of the individual, it is to distinguish between attitudes derived from conditioning on

"Truths" are personal, not always universal.

which, unknown to us, we have based our views and those arising independently from within which represent the truly unique quality of each individual. The irrelevance of conclusions drawn by the immature mind may later lead to inner conflict and indecision regarding even the most important aspects of our lives, and this impedes us from embracing our personality and the way of life which is truly our own. In the absence of teaching on these matters, too often we discover in the hard way only in later life what it means to be true to oneself.

* * *

So far as character and individuality are concerned, the differing types of conditioning and the resulting individual attitudes may be more important in establishing the differences between one man and another than inherited physical or mental characteristics. For although the bodies of man might resemble each other, the differences between them – immediately apparent to their fellows – consist of those manifesting their attitudes and the manner and habits which arise from them.

Reverting to Descartes, I am therefore at least to some extent what I think and I think roughly in accordance with my experience. Such at any rate is what we might call my character simply to distinguish it from something else, a deeper stratum of individuality underlying this initial experiential structure.

If everything we have suggested so far is accepted without qualification, one could experience only a dull chill of disapointment. However drastic our circumstances, however humble our achievement, however modest our prospects, however ill-favoured our outward characteristics, most of us would prefer to be our own individual selves rather than entirely someone – anyone – else. We may envy another's looks, talents, intelligence, temperament, or possessions and wish we were as fortunate in this respect, but, if being that other meant negating our own personality, our own hopes, fears, and relationships, then most of us would probably decide that, for us, the advantages of being ourselves outweighed all the disadvantages. In other words, a person's individuality, while

95

accepted as a matter of course, is the thing most precious to him, second only perhaps to the security and happiness of those he loves.

Can so precious a thing as one's unique difference from all other beings, be merely the sum total of the fortuitous difference of conditioning and experience which one has undergone in formative years? Surely not; but if not, what then? If after all and in spite of Descartes' dictum, what I think and what I am are different – in other words if what I am is something more fundamental than the superficial content of my mind derived from sense perceptions in an immediate environment – what am I?

Again, although it is apparently difficult to dehypnotise, decondition, or otherwise free ourselves from the specific interpretation of early experience which we happen to have adopted, it can nevertheless be done. But what happens then? If attitudes are otherwise moulded into their essential shape by childhood conditioning, what happens when the influences which create a man's peculiarities in his formative years are stripped away? Is a great empty hole left where an attitude used to be? If so, wasn't some attitude – however bizarre it may have been – better than no attitude? And if the process is carried far enough, so that most or all of this initial conditioning is exposed for what it is and stripped away, of what do we consist then? If in short we are what we think, what are we if and when we succeed in stopping thinking?

Or is it that this proposition is in fact misleading? Are we each of us in our different ways something more fundamental than the loose collection of attitudes and notions which throng our minds?

And if we can only strip away that miscellaneity, a basic set of natural responses common to all men may be left. For natural man one is tempted to substitute 'rational man' but this would be misleading. A 'rational' man would be a monster of selfishness. He would have no spontaneity. Predictable and mechanical, he would act only when motivated by immediate and apparent stimuli and then presumably only when his self-protection, advancement, or benefit was involved. Natural man is motivated by many considerations besides his immediate interests. He has protective instincts for others; he is curious, constructive, and experimental. He plays without knowing why he plays and he obtains deep satisfaction and relaxation in certain things, situations, and objects which he considers beautiful. Poetry and painting, love and beauty, curiosity and experiment, are natural but not necessarily rational.

Men may not only be more alike in nature but the concept may hold true that all men are born different but nevertheless equal. Ability, if not personality, is generally assumed to be inborn or controlled by genetic and environmental factors because patent differences between individuals are evident. Yet, the idea of equality has been sensed for many centuries and has held great attraction. The founding fathers of socialism in its various forms tried to justify the concept by blaming inequality on the economic structure. They concluded that those brought up with affluence or privilege gained a lead on the less fortunate and that this inequality was cumulative, whereby the rich got richer and the poor got poorer. However, attempts to level off affluence have not produced any equality and tests show that ability differences exist both in those brought up in rich circumstances and in those from poor environments. The sort of equality envisaged by social thinkers of the past century will probably never work so long as it is interpreted in terms of wealth. However, the possibility remains that individuals have far greater potential for equality in their untapped resources than anything hitherto imagined. Hereditary differences there must always be and, in that respect, some will inevitably be more fortunate than others. But such differences may be relatively unimportant if the achievement of the dullest is raised to that of the greatest talent of earlier times. Perhaps the hope of the future lies in an adult education which aims to relax the fallacies, inhibitions, and restrictions imposed by conditioning, so that the inequality seen today between the effectiveness of individuals in society may be lessened and the gap between the successful and unsuccessful reduced.

In the meantime it is sufficient to point out that apparent individuality derived from initial particular experience, from teaching and ideas accepted at second hand, is no more than a protective shell necessary during the formative years.

Pending the development of the child's conscious faculty, life must go on and behaviour must be conducted along relatively harmless lines while the potentially rational mind matures sufficiently to take up its proper function.

Unfortunately, in the rigid conventionality of the pressurised civilisation we have built up, we are often deprived of the opportunity to break out from the protective shell to attain the birthright of this maturity. We can perhaps glimpse at what it would be like to do so from the example of those figures of genius which all humanity regards as 'great'.

They may not in every aspect or attitudinal area of life be free spirits but at least in their own field new, exciting, and stimulative thoughts have arisen unimpaired by the clichés of their time. The essence of their stature is their ability to exist without the comfort or security of assurance that whatever they maintain is consistent with the authority of what has gone before. The Taoist says that before a bowl can be filled it must be empty. We would suggest that before true individuality can be revealed the external protective layers lent to it for the purpose of its initial development must be recognised and set aside.

*　　*　　*

In our natural anxiety to give our children every possible chance of developing to their full potential, such ideas as those suggested here are open to abuse. The idea that superficial individuality arises from conditioning in the formative years might seem to imply that by avoiding such conditioning, true individuality would be enabled to show itself from the beginning. Any system which claimed to achieve this would be likely to be self-defeating. It would merely set before the child an example of artificial conduct, jarring with its atavistic roots, dictated by overanxiety and possibly excessive ambition to bring about some contrived, man-made concept of what an individual ought to be. By definition the outcome could not be original.

In any case, however much care might be lavished, conditioning arises not only from an individual's experience within his immediate circle but also from the various cultural or social customs and beliefs held by his particular community at the particular epoch of its development. These may be beliefs held by a majority of mankind or limited to the circumstances of one community only. Such communal conditioning affects later mental reactions to situations because the individual does not question whether the views that he holds are truly his own or accepted simply because they form part of the atmosphere in which he was brought up.

Whole communities are conditioned or biased against conduct that is different from their own. For example, the difference in outlook is extreme between the Eskimo who offers his wife as a mark of esteem to visiting guests, and those countries where such a relationship between wife and friend provides legal grounds for divorce. Those who grow up in a Christian community are conditioned by Christian concepts, regardless of whether they practise the Christian religion, and those who grow up in Hindu India are conditioned by the caste concept, whether or not they make caste distinctions. The views of those who grow up in South Africa must be influenced by the *apartheid* concept. The woman who wears a yashmak or lives in purdah must have a different outlook towards men from the woman who finds nothing unusual in conversing freely with them. Although such traditions grow up to be acceptable in a particular community, they condition the outlook of individuals in that community and are likely to produce strain from the point at which they depart from the mainstream of development. Such beliefs held in a community at any one era are different from and in addition to the universal factors dealt with previously which induce in all mankind such mental habits as, for instance, polarity of thought.

We know from the work of clinical psychologists that certain sorts of conditioning may have unduly enduring effects and moreover effects which are particularly inconsistent with the temporary requirements and the standards of the twentieth-century cultures of Western Europe and the Americas. A large part of the unrest of our time may be seen as rebellion against the too rigid assumptions upon which such standards are, by custom or expediency, based and the consequent unconscious endeavours of the human species to break down such artificial obstacles to its further evolution.

6

Compulsive Man

IF IT IS the inevitable state of man's mind to be conditioned by the requirements of racial survival, the environmental pressures of society, and the particular accidents of his upbringing, we may ask to what extent is one limited or disabled in this respect. We may suspect the effects are sufficiently serious to restrict one's whole way of life and sufficiently widespread to indicate that a majority, if not all, are subject to such distortion. The evidence is itself strong enough that when the beneficence of life and the human condition is in question we should ask, is it life and nature of which we complain or their distortion which we are confusing with life?

The symptoms of mental disorder are only an extreme example of the process which affects everyone to some degree. No one grows up in completely ideal circumstances. So no one is entirely free from conditioning problems.

The widespread adoption of such terms as 'square', 'uptight', and 'hang-up,' unknown even in the 1950s, implies a growing awareness of the artificiality of rigid attitudes and emotionally-charged standards of conduct which affect some aspects of all our lives. Acquaintance with neurotics and psychotics makes clear that their disabilities have a cramping, restricting effect upon their lives. We see their energies dissipated in overcoming non-existent obstacles

101

and, on the other side, we fail to persuade them to participate in activities which the rest of us enjoy or even find essential to our wellbeing.

We may not all be psychotic, that is, emotionally unable to accept the possibility of deficiency in ourselves, but most are ready to confess to some degree of neurosis. We regard ourselves as 'normal' or 'healthy' in so far as we can maintain fruitful relationships, earn our living, and cope with the routine problems of everyday life. Nevertheless, we may feel our talents are either undiscovered or not used to their fullest extent. We find ourselves frustrated by an inability to achieve aspirations, aims, or ambitions and we are left with the suspicion we could enjoy a bigger, wider life given greater freedom of action.

Inconsistent attitudes inevitably bring upon their owner results inconsistent with at least some of his or her desires. The inconsistencies are not, however, seen as such; more likely their reflection and consequences in the outside world are perceived as some quality of bewildering paradox with which the beholder cannot hope to come to terms. Nor is his compulsive or obsessional conduct which results from his attitudes experienced by the subject as such. Instead he finds himself to be the subject of 'bad luck', of appalling and quite unpredictable coincidence, the victim of the spite, ignorance, indifference, or stupidity of others. He may suffer from mental depression causing withdrawal of energy and interest, physical illness, or a feeling – usually quite unjustified – of personal inadequacy. His dissatisfactions may take the form of frustration at his job, envy of those who appear to lead more successful or glamorous lives, discontent with his sex life, boredom in marriage, and disillusion.

The causes are almost always felt to be outward circumstances beyond one's control. However, the conflicts one meets in life are not so much between oneself and another but between the inconsistent elements within oneself. In every case where a problem arouses an emotional response, that sense of depression, frustration, anger, worry, or fear is a sure indication of an inward conflict of attitude, unresolved and perpetuated while its origins in childhood misconceptions rest unseen. As these conflicts are hidden from immediate

102

consciousness, their possessor will normally have no idea what is happening within him, or why. To the outsider, his 'hang-ups' are obvious enough; from inside, the matter is obscure, difficult, and distressing. The subject will be aware only that things are not entirely going his way.

At this point we have arrived indeed at a gloomy picture of the life of a contemporary twentieth-century man. No wonder he is restless and unquiet. He is taught that, initially, he originated as the result of a random series of random changes in organic cells. Finally miraculous as the outcome of that random acitivity at first sight might appear, he is told in fact it is of little consequence. The impression that he is a free living, free thinking being is an illusion, the behaviourists maintain. He is, if he is to believe them, a sort of robot acting out a conditioning imposed upon him by his background and the individual idiosyncrasies of even the most loving parents.

What price now the romanticism of Wordsworth's blissful dawn, of youth's entry into heaven itself? The pendulum has surely swung to the furthest extreme from the vision of a new Jerusalem. Yet romanticism has flourished and likely will again. The pendulum swings backwards and forwards and, if it is now at its extreme, it will reverse all the faster in the other direction. Our hopes, dreams, and fantasies are something more than the smoke of a whimsey which obscures our view when conscious thought is allowed to stray from whatever project is in hand. Their presence and persistence indicate that, below the conscious level, some unconscious urge smoulders to give off these signals of its need for ventilation.

As our state of knowledge stands today, we have evidence from the work of the clinical psychiatrists that the operation of mind is determined by an imprinting process it undergoes in its formative years. With the emergence of the personality through the adolescent phase, the individual has normally developed a pattern, typical for him or her, of behavioural responses. In some respects the responses are likely to be in conflict so that some of what is accomplished by the one hand is, as it were, undone by the other. Nevertheless, the structure is, fortunately in the majority of cases, good enough to enable the subject to attend to his own needs and those of his family and to perform certain socially useful functions for which he is rewarded by society.

However, assuming one can go about one's daily life in a 'normal' way which is acceptable to colleagues and relatives, is that good enough for the aspiration appropriate to our time? Surely not. Life must be more than the business of fulfilling the expectations of others. If, in this age of technical facility, it is not bliss to be alive and to be young is very hell, then something must have changed. If circumstances are not to our liking we have two apparent choices: either change the circumstances; or change our attitude to them. Whatever has gone wrong, the scene is there to serve us. We and our descendants are not inevitable victims of circumstance. And having resolved that, where do we begin? Perhaps inside ourselves, perhaps with exploration of our compulsions which lead us either to accept or to rebel against the scene but not to overcome its limitations.

We have all been conditioned into outlooks and attitudes and to react in particular ways. The particular combination or permutation of attitudes and reactions is individual to each of us, resulting in an apparent – but, in reality, a pseudo – individuality. Underneath exists a more mysterious, more exciting because more unique, individual. In the meanwhile before that singularity is uncovered, however effectively we may operate within the social context of our time, we are governed at least to some and probably to a large extent by imprinted attitudes rather than any self-determined freedom.

If we find ourselves the lucky possessors of attitudes which enable us to perform socially useful functions, society will probably reward and even applaud us in a gratifying way. In so far as the token of this sort of success is more recognition or a higher income than the average, we may be encouraged to think of ourselves as superior in some way to 'normal' people, to think of our mental state as demonstrably 'healthy'.

But sometimes, success, whether artistic or materialistic, may be no more than a compensatory device whereby the individual repetitively or obsessively seeks status or recognition in consolation for what he was denied in his formative years by a parent or circumstances. Such behaviour patterns are brittle and their practitioners, far from displaying the relaxed adaptability which is the characteristic of mental maturity, are likely to succeed only in the context of the narrow circumstances in which their obsessional capabilities are accepted. The fact of their incidental wealth or recognition is irrelevant to any state of maturity they may have attained.

The rates of alcoholism, broken families, and suicides among the rich and famous are evidence that material success in itself offers no outlet. Many who have all the wealth, possessions, and luxurious surroundings that they can use, find in these things in the end only profound boredom and mental bankruptcy. Most of us, unfortunately, have to learn this particular lesson by harder ways than over-indulgence.

Obsessive concentration in one area as a compensation for other blocked outlets, may aid career aspirations but is detrimental to the possibility of enjoying life in other directions. The lives of popular celebrities provide little evidence that the achievement of their ambitions has brought them peace of mind and lasting satisfaction. The list of brilliant men who suffered mental anguish is endless. Their life-patterns reveal a frustrated struggle to escape almost, it can be said, from themselves. We are tempted to conclude that no popularly recognised leader in any specialised field is happier, on that account, than anyone else or has discovered a way of life that offers any hope for the majority to follow as an example. Fame and income, far from being the measure of mental health and success, may be largely the fortuitous results of particular conditioning over which we, in our true individuality, have had the minimum control.

In fact most of us, rich or poor, famous or neglected, talented or inept, find ourselves playing roles of one sort of another in accordance with expectations put upon us by families and society and, not least, which we find impelled to put upon ourselves. Some of us like and even glory in our roles; some of us wish they were more comfortable; few of us feel that we are free to take or leave the role that we have, and certainly not to change or substantially modify it. To this extent our lives live us.

During the conditioning period of our infancy, any sort of attitude or imprinting may be received with one exception: the ability to choose freely and determine our conduct, standards, and way of life for ourselves. The process essentially impels us to look towards, or to rebel from, particular experience and example. Hence imitation, or the avoidance of imitation, are alike suspect as compulsive and the antithesis of freedom. Given an example of freedom to follow, we shall find ourselves compulsively imitating it. Thus if we enact roles for ourselves, it is not because we are necessarily affected or dishonest but because, initially at least, we have not discovered any other way of conducting ourselves. The hippie movement, in its determination to avoid role-playing, cast away all known roles and succeeded in creating a new one – that of the hippie.

When compulsions are extreme, something can be done about them because they are so noticeable. When the degree is so moderate as to be merely inconvenient, it is likely to be overlooked. Most of the time, for most of us, the degree is in fact moderate only. We carry our minor aberrations, which constitute our prison, around with us.

The case study of John provides a composite example of the restricting results of conditioning. John's parents were Presbyterians, thoughtful, intelligent people who set some store upon citizenship and personal virtue. John himself responded well to their hopes of him. His angelic, fairhaired, blue-eyed innocence was supported by a demeanour of corresponding virtue; in sum, a model child fulfilling the worthy hopes of worthy parents and providing above all a wonderful recipient of their expectations of themselves and their theories about the upbringing of children.

Naturally enough John tried to support these expectations, ignoring and repressing those aspects of himself which cried out to learn, by direct experience rather than at second hand, the virtues – or vices – of virtue. Initially it was all too easy for him to cherish the illusion that he was different, perhaps better, than other people. What might be done by others, even what might be considered 'human', would not necessarily be seemly for him. He was 'above that sort of thing' – whatever 'that sort of thing' in his case might be. He accepted the concept of a world which contained especially virtuous persons – a minority which included himself. But human inclinations, however irrational, however 'uncivilised,' are not to be discarded so easily and certainly not by means of repression. Day-dreams and wishful thinking begin to absorb the energy that would otherwise go into self-expression. Sometimes John found himself vehemently condemning others: if only 'they' were as he believed himself to be, what a better place the world would be to live in. Few of us are so rational – and so inhuman – that we have not experienced such feelings at one time or another. Nor should we be so prudish as to condemn rather that to accept them in ourselves or in others.

Sometimes John found he could equally well participate in the deplored behaviour – at least in his day-dreams – so long as it could be associated with extenuating circumstances. A first-hand enjoyment of erotic experience would not conform to his parents' expectations. But one might associate with prostitutes if one's aim was to reform them. At the conscious level, it would be permissible, even praiseworthy, to risk the sacrifice of his place in society to bring salvation to others – and especially to females of a sort who inevitably had for him an obsessive fascination. The unconscious motive, however, is more likely to concern the exploration of the nature of uninhibited sex. Acting out his fantasy in the end, John succumbed to the temptation it held. The shock of finding that, after all, one is as others are, and that society has no special classes of merit to which one can claim membership, may end in suicide. In John's case, it ended with the sacrifice of the imprinted concepts about himself and a better understanding of the conditions of peace of mind and his potential for a balanced, normal – though not exemplary – life.

*   *   *

No amount of theorising is ever likely to convince anyone that he is anything other than – for the most part anyway – a rational being. Acceptance of the idea requires experiences of irrationalities in oneself. To begin with, then, where does one look for such experience?

Some types of compulsions and their consequences are much more common than others and the pioneers of clinical psychology tended to specialise in, perhaps even to overemphasise the importance of, the particular type which coincided with their individual experience.

Freud is popularly believed to have attributed much of our life-pattern and motivation to our sexual satisfactions and frustrations. Thus it is sometimes assumed that if one has capacity for uninhibited physical lovemaking there cannot be too much wrong. However, Freudian concepts are wider than this. It is not so much the ability to make love in a free manner which is commonly lacking but the ability to take up the attitudes appropriate to the particular relationships in which one becomes engaged. In relation to a woman, a man may be a father, a son, a husband, a friend, or a colleague. A woman, too, relates to any particular man as if she were his mother, his wife, his daughter, his colleague or an acquaintance.

If either adopts one of these roles which does not fit the facts of the outer reality, inconsistencies of attitudes and behaviour will, after a time, become apparent. The matter has little to do with age but rather with freedom to move into the attitudes and role appropriate to the situation and to do so in an experiential rather than an intellectual manner.

Many a woman has some attitude toward her lover or husband – at least in some important essentials – as if he were her father. Many a man has the protective feelings toward his wife which would be more appropriate towards his daughter and, possibly more often, has attitudes towards his wife which he has transferred directly and unmodified to her from his mother.

In descriptions of Freud's work it seems to us that too much attention is frequently directed to the improbable mechanisms of the Oedipus complex at the expense of underlining the implications of the sexual roles to which he was the first to draw attention.

The necessity for self-identification follows all of us throughout our lives. Few of us can resist talking about ourselves or wishing to know other people's opinions and feelings towards us. To each the subject of self – in one guise or another – is overwhelmingly fascinating. In consulting doctors, fortune-tellers, and vocational testers, and in reading horoscopes in popular papers, we seek something more than detached knowledge for an objective purpose.

The first clue to our identity is our sex. At least we feel we know which of two possibilities describes us. Boy or girl, man or woman, male or female. We possess the physical attributes of one or the other; so far so good. But what exactly is a man, and how exactly can his attributes be differentiated from those of a woman? Is it true that he is courageous and she is shrinking? We know and respect obvious exceptions to such apparently elementary assumptions so even that can be only relatively true for some. Then wherein does the essential difference lie?

We have suggested that the male role is to challenge and change circumstances he finds unsatisfactory and the female course to adapt to them and, in acceptance, to forget dissatisfaction. Something of the sort underlay the original pattern of society but the modern scene has become more complicated. Now the man must often adapt, and the woman is often called on to challenge and initiate change.

The essential differences easily become obscured, too, by a multitude of conditioning influences. An irritable mother who often refers to the father as an irresponsible brute may imprint this information on her child's mind. Consequently, if a boy, he may become afraid and timid of other men in later life, associating them with his mother's concept of man. If a girl, she may become reluctant to mix with men or distrustful of them. Deprived of the security deriving from trust in the opposite sex, feelings of paranoia, persecution, and exploitation may arise.

How in this changing scene is one to keep in touch with one's original sexual attitudes or if, having lost touch, regain it? It may sound foolish to say I do not know the difference between a boy and a girl, but do I? Can I really define that difference except in terms of who possesses what organs? My ideas on the matter, and therefore my behaviour, are likely to stem from the conduct and example set by my father as a typical male and those of my mother as a typical female. The fact that one or other or indeed both was not typical, was even highly singular, was not to be realised by me in my early formative years. Nor was the problem which it represented for me brought to my attention by the educational system later on. If I ever learn about it, it will be the hard way, as a result of my relationships with the opposite sex breaking down.

In the meantime it is difficult for me as a woman to accept easily and naturally that my femininity is mine by right and complete in itself, without gilding the lily, without achievement, contrivance, or role-playing, enough to attract men. As a man it is difficult perhaps for me to move with authority and assurance without the insignia of success, the fortune, the status, the diploma or degrees with which society has invested the role of the masculine leader.

If I am a woman I may find myself 'compelled' to seek reassurance in the hairdresser's or the dressmaker's. If I am a man I am 'compelled' to buy a bigger car than I need or can afford, to bed more women than I can appreciate, to get ulcers earning more money than I can spend. Such are some of the compulsions to which we are subject in an advanced civilisation and which we exploit (and by which we are exploited) in a commercially orientated one.

Sexual roles are not the only source of difficulty. Adler convincingly maintained that one's place in the family hierarchy gave rise to feelings of inferiority or superiority.

An older child will tend to grow up with a more responsible attitude, more prepared to look after the other members of the family and reconciled to others occupying the centre of attention because this sort of behaviour has become habitual in childhood. Attention by the parents to the later arrivals may be experienced by the older children as feelings of inferiority and displacement.

The youngest member of the family is apt to be more precocious and competitive because of his continual fight to keep up with the elder children who are naturally more advanced. The result in later life might be a competitive character but one who challenges habitually and compulsively without insight into the origins or objectives of its attitudes. Should the elder children suppress the youngest unduly and treat it as the baby of the family, the youngest may accept a place at the bottom of the pecking order, but more typically the elder is the one who declines to compete. The youngest, if spoiled and protected from taking responsibilities in childhood, may have an inability in later life to take up the responsibilities of adulthood.

The only child is even more likely than the youngest to be spoiled and pampered, resulting not only in overprotection so damaging in later life but also in timidity and anxiety should the parents have displayed overconcern. When the time comes to marry, such an individual may make heavy demands of his partners in so far as he has a continuing expectation for coddling on the lines set by his parents.

Obsessional inferiority – and compensating superiority – has of course other widespread causes so that at least to some degree it is found in all adults' attitudes and constitutes the most widespread of psychological difficulties. Most of us have failed to live up to some element of the expectations put upon us as we have understood them so that we have entertained doubts or felt unwanted or unloved.

Inferiority feelings also arise, for example, from doubts or confusions regarding one's sexual role. Simply to be a member of one sex is enough to attract members of the other; to have been led to believe that this attraction will occur only if the right image of oneself is produced and put across is enough to rob any personality of the basic self-confidence which, more than anything else, stimulates sexual attraction.

For self-protection, the personality compensates an area of inferiority with a feeling of superiority in another. Thus, the individual's judgement of lesser values of some aspect of himself is balanced out by an overvaluation somewhere else. For instance, a person who is self-centred because they believe that no one else cares for their self may compensate by ostensibly going to any amount of trouble to help others. Their highly valued 'good nature' stems from the type of compulsive, hypocritical need to disguise undisclosed selfishness, which has given 'do-gooding' a bad name in recent years. Someone whose views of themselves and others was damaged by insensitive treatment in childhood may compensate for their subsequent difficulties in relationships with a high valuation of intelligence or facts, objects, animals, anything non-human which cannot hurt them as they were once hurt.

Adler singled out physical attributes, or, more strictly speaking, one's parents' attitude towards physical attributes, as another principal cause of distortion in one's own self-picture. Thus it is not uncommon for the short man to compensate for his lack of inches with insistence on his status. We are familiar, too, with the good-natured giant who cannot find within himself any urge to assert himself.

The detailed explanations of the mechanics of each system are, when spelled out, to be distrusted in their simplicity. People are not machines but self-organising, self-correcting entities. On the other hand, systems as complex as Jung's analytical psychology are much more open-ended but less immediately useful in their vagueness. The relative merits of one theory as against another seem unimportant. They all contribute to and describe a common ground which is our concern here.

Certainly, love in the sense of tenderness, non-violation of feelings, and respect for the identity of the person, is of the first importance in the infant stage. Deprived of this or given duty-motivated substitutes, the child will react either with rebellious anger or overeagerness to please. In either case its effective individuality – its capacity for genius or at least for individual talent – will be swamped.

In combating the fears caused by insecurity, the child endeavours to adjust its behaviour to what it understands is most desired by its parents. Unloved as he perceived himself to be, he feels he must fulfil what he imagines they would like him to be in order to win the love and approval he needs. At that point the child ceases to be its natural self and pretends to be something other. The pretence can last a lifetime. As an adult, conscious knowledge of the origins of this pretended code of conduct is lost and normally stored beyond recollection. The assumed qualities of bravery, unselfishness, obedience, purity, honesty, are different from the genuine qualities of these particular modes of behaviour. As compulsive characteristics their opposite reactions, including fear, egotism, rebellion, lust, deception, are driven underground to manifest their presence in devious unconscious ways.

Parental concern is no substitute for relaxed love. Too often it carries with it an expectation derived from the transmittal of the parents' frustrated hopes or ambitions, an acting-out or extension of their own personalities rather than from the unique attributes of the child.

An infinite range of such parental ideas is put upon children as expectations which then become their compulsive life's work to fulfil. Not only career success but ethical standards and types of marriage partners can be dictated in this way. If the children do not conform to these wishes, they may feel a deep sense of guilt. Wherever an individual has strong rebellious, submissive, or guilty feelings, wherever they feel strongly that they ought or ought not to be doing something, these are the danger signals of early conditioning from which the subject cannot easily escape.

Thus certain general principles undoubtedly emerge from the theory and demonstrated therapy work of the analytical schools of psychology. They may be simply summarised in common sense terms: if a developing mentality is to arrive at a relatively realistic view of the culture of its time and to be able to relate to others in a natural way in later life, then as a child it needs love, affection, and the security of being able to rely on those attentions; it needs the examples of male and female conduct provided by its parents or their accepted substitutes and the example of a working relationship between the sexes. In fact these conditions are never totally fulfilled and as a result some degrees of inconsistent or compulsive behaviour results.

*   *   *

It is precisely an individual's ignorance of the fact that his attitudes are inconsistent and where the inconsistencies are to be found within him, which creates the difficulty of freeing himself so that his mind can function with something like its real potential. Nevertheless, in every individual there are certain areas of freedom. The hope of eventual integration lies in the expansion of these areas.

While it may be true to say that compulsive conduct is mainly due to conflicts of attitudes originating in childhood, it appears also to have the objective of widening these areas. Sometimes canalisation of energy takes a highly interesting, exciting, or pleasurable direction – though in the end even such positive compulsions may prove destructive to longer-term ends if they are misunderstood.

For example, the first line of explanations for the proverbial blindness of love which glosses over the faults of the other in a shining illusion of perfection is that such a strong unimpeded urge is necessary in order to bring together suitable physical types for reproduction. Perhaps reality might be too cold, too unromantic, and would not result in any union. So the oblivion of being in love perpetuates the species. However, if this was the whole of the matter, one would find attractive only those people best suited for

113

reproduction. Yet this does not always happen. Not everyone who attracts this sort of love is good-looking and fertile. Both men and women continue to fall in love after the age of potential parentage, as do the physically disabled. So the explanation for this phenomenon may well be more complex than that of the straight biological urge.

What the Greeks call *eros* is the fascination of one person for another. Its function, besides the promotion of sex relations, may be the bringing together of couples whose personalities are complementary in that each holds problems and attitudes which the other needs to experience for their own development and integration. Such blind fascination may exist because the one has need of intimate contact with this other to help the escape from illusions or to realise as their own qualities which are usually projected on to some other person. If life is forcing this advance, it may well do so by bringing the individual to confront and appreciate a type of mentality that is in some respects complementary to his own, and thus likely to bring about self-fulfilment. The potentiality of breaking down the illusion or realising the hidden values carries an enormous amount of energy which makes the fascination extraordinarily strong. Many marriages which look highly improbable from the outside become more probable if regarded in this light. However, when the illusion breaks down, so can the marriage unless the partners are ready both to give and take, to feel free to be what by nature they are, to accept that their experiences are universal ones and that marriage involves an understanding and experience of all its aspects.

In the absence of such concomitants as understanding and acceptance of the weaknesses of the other, love can be little more than a temporary state of fascination or obsession. Those suffering from it may be the first to deny its compulsive nature – or indeed the lack of any understanding or acceptance – but sadly and inevitably in the end events belie such protestation.

This example of normal but compulsive conduct which is unlikely to owe its origins to accident during the formative years, points to the probable existence of other similar types of motivation, perhaps less strong and therefore less obvious but nonetheless equally real. One may speculate that the natural way for individual man to conceptualise the nature of his personal problems and dilemmas is, in accordance with the oldest experiential basis of his being, to act them out. They are then exposed both to himself and to others near him so that by their reactions to his behaviour, he may correct or otherwise adapt inconsistent behaviour. To the intellectual – even to the intellectual side of the essentially experiential man – such acting out may seem immature or childish.

By definition the intellectual is one who may be accepted as wishing – and perhaps having the requisite ability – to conceptualise and express his problems in words rather than by communicating them non-verbally. The experiential man is happy to practise communication at the level of demonstration and experience. The disadvantage of the latter lies in the nature of acting out the communication in so far as it is much more likely to create an irrevocable situation than the use of words. On the other hand the intellectualising process of verbalisation may reduce the pressure of a problem without entailing the commitment which will eventually solve it.

However, even the most intellectual of us is unlikely to channel all his energies into verbalised concepts and the representation of problems by repetitious performance of their essentials in a variety of different circumstances is an underlying motive of such human conduct.

While one is endeavouring to carry out conscious aims with objectives which appear to one to be rational and consistent with one's desires or needs, another part of one's mind is subtly and remorselessly manoeuvring and manipulating.

Destructive as this may be to one's short term goals, the process essentially is one of healing. Just as the body automatically organises the supply of cells, blood, and tissue to heal a wound – without a moment's conscious contribution on the part of the sufferer – so mind organises its activities throughout life to bring about an ever-improving view of reality and one's relationship to it.

Thus, at any one time we may find we have two aims or motivations in many – though of course by no means all – of the activities we undertake. There are those obvious ambitions and needs we pursue and an unknown undercurrent to which we must also conform. The much abused term, 'integration of the personality', simply implies the alignment of these two separate sets of endeavour so that each assists rather than obstructs the other and energy is undivided.

Let it now be said that so far we have, to avoid confusion and complication, been guilty of loose use of the term unconscious. It has been used both in the sense of 'the unconscious' and as 'the subconscious'. We have come to the point however where a distinction between the two is necessary for the purpose of clarifying our present thesis – though not for developing the significance and comprehension of the terms for academic purposes.

The unconscious may be considered to consist of two separate 'organs', centres, activities, or systems. The subconscious contains all the personal memories and impressions produced on us in the course of conditioning, and it is from these experiences, now dropped beyond awareness, that the individual developed a pattern of behavioural responses typical for him or her. Having grown up with conditioning which enabled us to function in the original terms of our family and environment, we cannot suddenly dispense with it. But our subconscious is all the time eaten into by the second of the two systems, that of man's unconscious or instinctive appreciation of the relative nature of things.

*   *   *

Men and women might go through their entire lives suffering the disabling effects of conditioning and its stultifying effects on the assimilation of experience, were it not for the action of unconscious mechanisms. These result in phenomena recorded time and again in casebook histories and observable in the personal experience of us all to a limited extent. Life may be seen as a continuing process of growth; and mental growth, like the physical growth of the body, is a one-way and irreversible procedure. Mental energy is always diverted unconsciously to malconditioned areas to try to draw attention to repressed parts of the personality that are demanding to be brought to life. The life instinct continually attempts to push people into experiences and circumstances which may force them to identify their false impressions and take corrective action. If they cannot be tempted by rewards, they may be coerced by suffering.

116

This tendency towards greater freedom of mind goes on regardless of people's desire for it or awareness of its essential place in the pattern of their lives.

The curiosity which brings about experience needed to complement or correct convictions based upon half-truths is an essential ingredient of life. The inherent curiosity of mind apparent not only in man but in animals is the instrument of the development of the species, constantly probing, questioning, investigating, and in the end challenging and modifying the individual life-style. Koestler* writes, 'It is the driving power which makes the rat learn to find its way through the experimental maze without any obvious incentive being offered in the form of reward or punishment; and also the prime mover behind exploration and research.' It is probably most important that a child's thirst for knowledge should be satisfied as far as reasonably possible because his natural curiosity may become stultified if replies to his questions are denied or nonsense answers given. The child, lacking realistic-sounding answers from busy or embarrassed mentors, may become convinced that any attempt to exercise curiosity is a vain endeavour. Consequently his normal inquiring faculty, his originality of mind, may be hampered. We do not know, but we may suspect, that intelligence is associated with the ability to formulate meaningful questions about the nature of things and the confidence to expect and absorb answers.

The healing mechanism is all the time working underground in a variety of ways to try to dislodge the malformations of childhood. In the *Psychopathology of Everyday Life*, Freud drew attention to the extent to which the unconscious may contrive and use apparent accidents to further its own objectives. However disastrous a situation may appear, there is, irritatingly enough, often useful experience to be derived from it. But usually the subject has no conscious idea that this mechanism is at work – that he is being driven to bring to consciousness the roots and elements of problems created by inconsistent attitudes.

The healing operation can be seen in the manner in which people bring upon themselves that which they secretly fear most, perhaps to

* *The Act of Creation.* Arthur Koestler. Hutchinson Publishing Group. 1964. Reprinted by permission of A D Peters and Company.

117

demonstrate that some aspects of the fear are unfounded. This may be exceptionally hard to spot in one's own conduct though more easily discerned in others without really understanding what is happening. One notices only the friend who keeps running into extraordinary situations. At first one feels that he is unlucky, that fate has a succession of troubles in store for him. Later a pattern of repetitious events may emerge as if he had been compelled by some hypnotic force to experience the consequences of inconsistent attitudes until their nature dawned upon him. In the meanwhile he may feel 'driven' to follow courses of action – and to that extent feel he has no option in determining his own conduct and affairs. But he is unlikely to associate such circumstances as the inevitable outcome of his own attitudes and the enactment of his own problems.

Nevertheless, unconscious mechanisms seem to bring upon the individual every experience which he may need to cause him to pause and reconsider his attitudes. The immediate effect of this activity is to increase or intensify the effects of his prison of conditioning. He has only a partial opportunity to use his mental resources and all this available ability is preoccupied, whether he realises it or not, with trying to free the rest.

He may be seen, by the impartial observer, though certainly not by himself, to be making what is bad for him even worse so that by intensifying rather than alleviating a problem, it may in the end be highlighted and brought to the attention of his own consciousness for what it is – a self-created dilemma of inconsistent motives and attitudes. Freud, observing this phenomenon of individuals taking actions apparently in opposition to their own wellbeing, devised the improbable explanation of an inherent or instinctive death wish.

Quite obviously – and often necessarily – one tries to avoid situations which would correct conflicting attitudes if only one had the courage to sustain for long enough the tension they create. If the confrontation is too painful, we break off, so that old attitudes reassert themselves. This resistance to mental discomfort is a necessary subconscious mechanism to prevent an overdose of change which might destroy mental stability.

A foundation, however false, is better than no foundation at all and must be preserved from destruction for the personality-structure of the individual to survive. In order to preserve such mental integration as the subject may have, the changes of attitudes brought about by experience cannot exceed the pace at which adjustment can take place. A subconscious protective mechanism seeks to preserve the *status quo* through fear of what would happen should the carefully-built house of cards fall down, fear of being shut out in the cold, cold world with nowhere to go. Thus the value of much experience is lost until the right time comes for the digestion of the right element. Development is frustrated at a point where the drive for change equals our resistance to it. The action of these energies offsetting and constantly adjusting to each other constitutes a system of psychological dynamics.

The unconscious is a restless, shifting element and, like water, constantly leaks or breaks through so that the point of equilibrium between innovation and resistance is constantly moving, as reflected in moods and changing motives and desires. The subconscious endeavours to exercise its restraints with all the devices of rationalisation and projection, whilst the unconscious employs the will-o'-the-wisp of fascination, fantasy, and hallucination to lure the unadventurous into the deep waters of life in which it would have them develop an ability to survive.

Consciously the individual is unaware of this play of dynamics taking place within and it is effectively attended to, supervised and directed, as it were, by his unconscious and subconscious mind. In its endeavours to maintain stability, the subconscious will prompt the individual, usually through the immediate instruments of fear, dislike, disinclination, to resist all but the most gradual erosion of his life-style. Necessary as this mechanism is to the maintenance of stability and for the day-to-day attention to mundane bodily needs, such defence of security is sterile in that it does not allow for departure from a comparatively rigid behaviour structure. Unopposed it would result perhaps in individual comfort and stasis but would exclude the conversion of experience into learning and the development either of the individual or eventually of the species.

In the end, only the suffering and experience of living, interpreted positively, may force the individual to face the intense fear, anxiety, guilt, or painful memories which he felt as a child and which stunted his comprehension of the nature of 'whole' man. Such realisations might disclose unpleasant character traits within himself which, for his own self-defence, cannot be faced unless he can see from their childhood origins that he could not help himself and therefore can now forgive himself. Thus, for his own preservation he resists reviewing his attitudes since confrontation with such truth is always experienced as a threat to security. He will endeavour to distract his own attention, unknowingly make errors in thinking to make his misconceptions comply with observations or experience in other areas. He may compensate for his uncertainty with a display of overemphasised certainty. He may disclaim his involvement, make all manner of excuses, put up a shield to cover his inward disturbances. He may react emotionally as he once did as a child if forced into contact with sensitive spots.

Finding himself confronted by powerful feelings with no knowledge of their nature or origins, he will try to provide himself with some sort of explanation of them. He has several means open to him, including the development of imaginative, highly suspect theories, rationalisations, and projection of his problems on to other people. The defence mechanisms also take the forms of compensations, illusions, delusions, and withdrawal or strict canalisation of mental energy. These subconscious mechanisms hide an individual's inconsistencies of attitudes from himself in ways that frustrate or even cripple his life, yet shield him from the disintegration which might result if they were too suddenly withdrawn or eliminated.

Normally a behavioural quirk caused by malconditioning is mitigated by the ability of the mind to encapsulate the area affected and compensate for it to enable the personality to function at least adequately. If someone has an idiosyncrasy or particular obsession, he will usually attempt to hide it, at least as much from himself as from society at large. Often he will avoid a way of life which would make existence of the problem conspicuous. His mental mechanism will automatically compensate in some other way to make up for the inadequacy or imbalance, and so long as he can avoid coming into the open, his abnormality will not be apparent.

The immediate effect may therefore be avoidance of contact with areas of activity which would bring conflicts to light. Certain subjects which the individual does not want to discuss or recognise will be banished from his thinking. He might go through life turning a blind eye to experiences which would open his eyes to reality because of this self-protective censorship mechanism.

The subconscious therefore rationalises and projects; that is to say it distorts sense perception by both illusion and delusion so as to cause the subject to ignore certain facts, ideas, concepts, and perceptions and to overemphasise the importance of others, or indeed to invent, by means of hallucination, non-existent facts. Thus with the aid of such distortions he can reconcile intellectual concepts with conditioned or imprinted behaviour patterns.

Conditioning might lead to acts which could give their performer a feeling of guilt or self-accusation if they were acknowledged for what they were. When the act has been performed, a defence mechanism springs into motion which justifies the action by stringing together seemingly logical and convenient reasons for having taken such a course. Rationalisation thereby makes the act generally acceptable to the subject. In the same way a hypnotised subject will rationalise actions suggested to him under hypnosis by inventing circumstances to account for them.

The clinical psychologists have drawn attention to the propensity of mind to project or to attribute to others those traits within ourselves which are least acceptable to us. C G Jung remarked, 'A man's hatred is always concentrated upon that which makes him conscious of his bad qualities.'

It is a humbling and rather frightening experience when it first comes home to us that in condemning others we are in fact recognising and judging ourselves. However, the process is not all one way. We cannot truly appreciate nor esteem in others what we admire unless it is within ourselves also. The more fervently we feel about it the more capacity exists in us without perhaps the facility for its realisation. If the first type of experience is humbling, to listen to Beethoven's Ninth and to recognise that its grandeur relates also to something in oneself can only be exalting.

For the practical purpose of understanding the origins of conflict, hatred, and misunderstanding between even the most intelligent and perceptive of individuals, we may generalise to state that man

121

constantly deplores in others what he needs to accept himself. He has an overwhelming tendency to overlook or even deny a feeling, wish, or shortcoming in himself which he would not wish to recognise and to accuse someone else of it. The bad workman blames his tools instead of his own incompetence. The loser blames the world for misfortune of his own making. The latent homosexual condemns unduly loudly in others the inclinations he refuses to recognise in himself.

'Judge not, lest ye be judged', advises the New Testament.

In the second half of life as opportunities and energies are reduced, unfulfilled hopes and ambitions may become projected as well. If one cannot achieve them for oneself, the hope may arise that at least one's child or protégé can achieve a better life than one's own in respect of these matters. The temptation to ensure one's own perpetuation by means of another, even one's own child, is to violate his individuality and may impose a compulsion to fulfil a dream from which he may take a lifetime to escape.

Each of the mental devices of communication and direction which have now been identified has a distinct purpose, useful to some extent to preserve or direct the orientation and preservation of the individual yet prejudicial in their other effects. Thus they may not be regarded either as beneficial, to be encouraged, nor as detrimental, to be detected and exposed. They are an essential part of individual development. Even though they may be instrumental to compulsion, they are to be accepted and recognised. In others, they are to be tolerated and understood; in ourselves the possibility of their presence and action is to be expected and as far as possible allowed for. In a world where irrational ideas and conduct abound, only the markedly disorientated will suppose that he alone is rational; that the world consists of a foolish 'they' and a sensible 'I', however convincing our own theories may seem to our own compulsive selves.

* * *

Human reaction to individual experience falls into two categories:

1. The first arises from accurate observations of the origins of the experience and determines a response appropriate to the cause of the circumstances which is likely to further the desires of the subject

concerned. This might be called assimilated experience; it is accepted, understood, and incorporated into the factors which modify future behaviour patterns.

2. The second is that type of reaction whereby experience is misapprehended and virtually rejected. Such a reaction is usually different from that which would be recommended by an impartial witness to the events concerned and is not consistent with the outcome which the subject may consciously wish for. This type of rejected or repetitive experience usually has strong overtones both of fear and fascination for the subject as well as exercising some degree of compulsive influence upon him. It is termed repetitive because the subject, conditioned to ignore or misinterpret it, continually fails to incorporate its learning value into his future reactions. His life-pattern thenceforward seems designed and contrived to ensure a repetition of the essential elements of the rejected experience.

At least part of the motivation of unconscious activity seems to be directly concerned with increasing the proportion of assimilated experience to repetitive experience. In other words, the unconscious endeavours to free the subject from compulsions. One of its methods of doing this is to exaggerate gradually the extent and the absurdity of compulsive or obsessional behaviour until its nature, consequences and probable origins can no longer escape the attention of the subject and thereupon it ceases. At that point, he is free in respect of that particular matter and may respond to such circumstances in an effective way.

Since the beginning of history, man has observed these processes taking place within him – or more strictly speaking within other men, since they are so extremely difficult to identify in oneself. A large part of the doctrines of mysticism can be attributed to his inability to date to account for such procedures.

The Buddhist conception of the wheel of life and death may not symbolise physical rebirth or reincarnation as such. That is a matter of personal opinion, but it is certainly descriptive of the vicious circle where man brings upon himself the same problems again and again unless or until he realises that he can break free from his treadmill of conditioning and live – i.e. experience – anew. He really has little freedom until he overcomes the problems concerning his abilities to form satisfactory relationships, work on his own initiative, be original, and find answers to the basic questions of living. He is not even free to choose whom he loves, because he is driven into particular relationships through his compulsions. His unconscious mental energy appears to be directed expressly towards creating situations which might lead him to see the error of his attitudes.

It is hardly surprising that this complicated process has been observed only intuitively and in such analogous terms as, for example, those of reincarnation. A full treatment of compulsive conduct as the guiding communication medium and overriding director of conscious will is not possible in the space available here; nor in any case is it possible in our present state of knowledge. We must be content to summarise the matter simply by stating that compulsive conduct appears to arise from a conflict. On the one hand we find conscious endeavour to conform to expectations accepted in one form or another, positive or negative, and incorporated into an initial life-style or behavioural structure. On the other hand, there is an unconsciously-directed endeavour gradually to disregard such traditional or family influences so as to react to experience in a manner natural to man as a species and to the particular traits, characteristics, and inborn abilities of the person concerned.

For many years, man has debated to what extent he may have control over his destiny and to what extent his fortune is preordained. In fact free will would seem to be a matter of degree rather than an absolute quality. Every individual appears to have a certain area, however small, of free choice. To the extent that he can in the course of his lifetime use the fruits of his experience to widen this area and escape from preconditioned reactions, he will enlarge his free will.

In the meantime, mind, in its endeavours to get free, itself imposed a pattern of conduct on its owner which is paradoxically experienced as greater restriction. An unconscious mental mechanism within man dictates his activities and possibly even arranges matters in accordance with what by hindsight might be seen to be best for his long-term development. He really has little self-determination – except by inhibition to choose not to act – over his choice of relationships and some of the most minute events of his day-to-day life. In this respect even the most educated and sophisticated of people may be as puppets acting out the dictates of unconscious energies with which they have lost, or never had, ability to communicate.

Mental dishonesty – the manifestation of determinacy and conditioning – occurs not only as the motivation of overt action but is constantly present in intellectual processes. My view – and of course yours – and our arguments may well be biased towards a justification to our own satisfaction of our own compulsive patterns of behaviour and way of life. A humble approach towards even one's deepest convictions may therefore be healthy.

May we now distinguish the part which the prison of man's mind plays in the suffering and unrest of our time. Our affairs are neither planned nor administered according to any sort of logic but merely with that degree of truth and consistency which we can, at this stage of our development, adjust to accepting. If unrest is greater in one country, in one race, in one geographical area, in one faith, or in one individual than in another, look for the cause in the way that people or that person adapts to circumstances, change, and the need for the development towards the wholeness demanded by evolution.

7

Free
Man

THROUGHOUT THE HISTORY of man, no more persistent theme recurs than that of freedom. At different times it has had many different interpretations. All have had an impelling urgency.

Moses led the children of Israel out of the bondage of Egypt into the freedom of the Promised Land. The Roman slaves rebelled against their masters for their free status. The serfs of the Middle Ages rose up in Europe against their feudal lords, as in the English Peasants' Revolt of 1381. Parliamentarians rebelled against the constraints of monarchy, and colonies against imperial powers.

Authority has always had the problem of asserting and maintaining its dominance. The governed, the influenced, the followers, have always had to balance the advantages of submission against the urge for independence.

At one end of the scale, one thinks of the restless male member of a prehistoric tribe, low in the pecking order of its hierarchy, who preferred to wander off by himself into the bush to enjoy the freedom to survive or to die on his own terms. At the other end of the scale, one is fascinated by the ideal of twentieth-century youth to be free to express itself individually, each to be free to do his 'own thing'.

Perhaps because of the long tradition of tyrannies, oligarchies, and privilege, man continues for the most part to seek freedom in the modification of the 'establishment'. He is by no means free yet of some paranoid notion that someone or something external feels threatened by his aspiration and is directly concerned to deny it.

The idea that true freedom might lie in an individual capacity for self-determination is only just beginning to be accepted at the fringes of some circles of our culture. To many, its implications may appear threatening. The concept that some of my motivating attitudes – even those for which I am willing to take full responsibility – are nevertheless opposed by other of my own attitudes more than by any external authority or restriction, is a comparatively novel idea to the majority. Yet it is surely in this matter, if in any single element in life, that enduring and realistic freedom will be found. It is a quality which arises from recognition of one's strengths and paradoxically of one's own limitations and compulsions to conduct one's activities and relationships along predetermined lines, reflecting the conditioning of upbringing and social beliefs.

We have already suggested that man is neither free nor subject to determinism, but that each individual has an area of freedom in his personality which he can enlarge. It would seem that as he succeeds in doing so, the difference in outlook and motivation which takes place is more one of kind than of degree. It is doubtful whether this contention could ever be supported by any satisfactory evidence of a scientific type, but that is not to say it is negligible. We can suggest four separate lines of partial evidence which indicate that a change can take place during the process of coming to maturity so that, on release from the restrictions which have conditioned consciousness, mind thereafter works in quite a different way.

Firstly, the evidence of those who have recovered from mental illness. Many people who have undergone psycho-therapy are convinced that the insight they have gained into themselves and their own motives radically changed their whole way of life and opened up completely different viewpoints to them. Psycho-therapy, however, is usually undertaken for the purpose of overcoming a clinical disability and is not carried to its logical extreme. Evidence, therefore, is available about its effectiveness but not about the ultimate consequences if used to work on areas of irrationality other than those causing actual mental distress or disruption of day-to-day activities.

Secondly, the theological doctrine of original sin. In many religions, folklore, and myths, man is depicted or described as having been subject to a fall. At one time he lived in a golden age or Garden of Eden and was reputed to have been a better creature than he is now; but he fell from grace. It is an integral part of the religions which incorporate this belief that there is the possibility of redeeming man from original sin. The widespread persistence of this legend of a fall indicates that it may express a universal truth but in symbolic language. The myth could be taken to correspond closely with the birth and growth of a child with a mind that works perfectly well and objectively, but its initial conditioning then condemns or obscures its view of truth, and the way to redemption is the way of overcoming this. The destruction of an old world and the creation or rebirth of a new one is likewise a major theme recurring in different mythologies and might parallel figuratively the striving of man for a change from his conditioned way of life to a new state of mind. Thus, Adam and Eve living in a state of unconsciousness inhabit a world of bliss. As they eat from the tree of knowledge they share with the gods the quality of consciousness and the potentiality of self-recognition. The state of consciousness has a fascinating quality which cannot be renounced but also has disadvantages which must be endured. Of these disadvantages the most terrible is not that of pain – for this is shared with the lower orders of life – but the anticipation of pain or anguish, which is unique to the state of conscious self-awareness. Yet without anticipation, a search for the remedy to suffering would never be commenced. Thus, if man is destined to be driven to exert himself to discover his own soul and to transcend himself in the undertaking, he may do so only when, impelled by suffering, he has explored every aspect of consciousness and its potentialities. Then the answer to his identity, and to suffering as well, may be found where he might least expect it.

Thirdly, the consistency of the evidence of those who have undergone so-called 'religious' experience. Whether in fact these experiences are related to religion or are a demonstration of the existence of God is beside the point at this time but one to which we will return. Numinous experience is a readily identifiable phenomenon which has altered the lives of people. The faiths of those who come to this experience may vary enormously. They might be distinguished however from other non-religious beliefs by two characteristics: (1) they are rationalised as having an objective in the pleasing or placating of a real or imaginary 'god' or principle outside of, and apart from, the practitioner's own being; (2) they incorporate conformity to some code of behaviour or ethical concept which is considered to be good and efficacious in bringing the practitioner to a state of grace granted by the outside god, phenomenon, or field of energy, as a reward for 'good' conduct.

Fourthly, the development of insight by methods other than the religious as defined above. Those who have trained in various types of mental development such as yoga, who have exercised mind over matter in feats such as firewalking, or induced release from themselves in ritualistic dancing, testify that a different state of mind can be cultivated. This group of activities incorporates a series of exercises virtually for their own sake which have something in common with religion but do not share the suggestion that practitioners ought to act in a particular ethical way to gain heaven as their reward. Some Western interpreters of yoga, apparently anxious to retain the idea that any development has to be achieved by abstinence and ethical observance, appear to insist that all yoga practice has an ethical content. This is not necessarily true of all forms, yet they produce similar results.

These are examples of practices which people associate with changes which have taken place in their outlook and behaviour. They have in common that the types of change are not different in degree but mark something different in kind from previous attitudes and behaviour patterns. In this sense the change, and the way to freedom, may be said to be transcendental. For we might expect that mind would function basically in the same way, but much more effectively, on everyday problems if we could get rid of the less desirable consequences of initial experience and conditioning. It might well never occur to us, without direct experience of the matter, that a fully operational mind would no longer be similar in kind to other minds but quite different in outlook and motivation from what had gone before.

The fact that outlook and behaviour can undergo a change – experienced as an improvement – may in itself indicate that life normally offers something less to us than its full potential. But the descriptions used by those who have undergone this sort of change – who claims to have escaped, to have awoken, to have been reborn, to have overcome the limitations of the body, to have found enlightenment and at-oneness – leave even the most interested somewhat sceptical. The elaborate eulogies sound so far-fetched that they are difficult to accept. In many cases the proclaimed revelations are dubious for lack of substantiation. Authenticity can hardly be credited where subsequent conduct seems to fail to support the claim of a change, or to fulfil our expectations of the sort of change we personally would hope for.

A deep chasm exists between the two outlooks towards life, between the once-born and the twice-born. The essence of the experience undergone by the twice-born has remained down the ages incommunicable to the once-born and continues uncomprehended for several reasons.

If the experience was as real, stimulating, and absorbing as the sensation and feelings aroused, for instance, by sexual intercourse, it might be just as difficult to describe to anyone who had not undergone it directly for himself. It is virtually impossible to convey to a male or female virgin in any way which would be meaningful to them what they may discover for themselves. The right words, familiar images, and suitable analogies probably simply do not exist for communicating some types of experience which have little in common with other everyday events.

Religion, while exhorting its followers to seek the experience, has come to be associated over the centuries not with any attractive procedure but with a highly ethical content which has turned sour and negative. To say this is not to contest the validity of its content. It is to proclaim that imitation of virtue will produce an imitator rather than an innovator. Whatever or whoever Jesus Christ may have been, whether he was an historical personage or the hero of a legend, one thing in our concept of him he certainly was not. He was not an imitator. If Christianity has turned sour, one of the reasons is surely that so much of its doctrine is expressed in that supreme contradiction in terms, Thomas à Kempis' *Imitation of Christ*. How can we ever imitate a non-imitator? Virtue is a byproduct of character, rather than the reverse, as ethical adherents sometimes would seem to have us believe. Renunciation of the life of the world in the belief of imitating virtue may cut off that very experience of life through which progress may come. Austere religious practices over the centuries have largely prescribed denial and self-restraint, the pursuance of axiomatic precepts whose ultimate purpose is to lead to a heaven of doubtful authenticity and even more dubious attractions. Most healthy-minded people who have a good grasp of life usually achieve some degree of satisfaction in the numerous very real joys of the flesh. If a different view of life would involve a conversion excluding these, they do not want to become too closely involved. They feel quite naturally that revelation may be excellent for others but not for them while they have, by the standards of the world, succeeded in obtaining sensual and material advantages. These are sufficiently attractive to restrain them from putting themselves out unduly to seek a different state that is quite unknown to them. Why hurry the advent of revelation, at least before old age when advantage may be taken of what has anyway become a necessity? St Augustine prayed, 'Give me chastity and continence, only not yet.'

In short, the difficulties of communication are considerable and when the audience is, in spite of itself, understandably reluctant to listen, the undertaking is almost impossible.

A final reason remains why the experience is difficult to comprehend. However much one may try, one's mind is inclined in some degree to revert to its habit of polarity, particularly when grappling with unfamiliar problems or circumstances. One often tries to proceed in the familiar way of classifying the various elements in a situation as either 'this' or 'that'. Full appreciation of any description of a different state of mind would presumably involve seeing one's own circumstances in a new way, a third way, not in terms of any familiar state to be identified as this or that. We are back with the dilemma of the flat earth. Either the earth goes on indefinitely or stops suddenly in a precipice. No amount of argument will help a flat earth addict to the flash of inspiration revealing a sphere. But once given the clue, the idea will probably be grasped at once. This is probably true in this case. The idea cannot be conveyed in the abstract but its effects and therefore its essence may be communicated to each individual listener in terms of its significance to his own immediately personal circumstances, experiences, or dreams. 'I cannot describe God to you,' said one mystic, 'but follow me and you will see him for yourself.'

The snag about following the mystic is simply that it involves considerable sacrifice at the outset in exchange for something unknown and unfamiliar. How far does one know it will be worth while? One's experience of buying pigs in pokes has usually been bitter. Why should it be otherwise this time? The mystic, who spends all his time expounding how others should live, himself too often neglects the act of living.

Few 'well adjusted' or 'rich' people who have achieved an effective relationship with themselves and their aspirations are likely to put their stability at risk. Only when the need for change arises in the desperation of the outsider, the failure, the neurotic, the lonely, the lost, and the unhappy is the possibility considered as a last resort.

Thus we see that not only does one get caught up mentally with a particular view of life, but release from that original view presents all sorts of difficulties. Should freedom ever have been achieved in the past, it must have been only with the greatest difficulty, on rare occasions, and perhaps only to a partial extent.

But how important is this release? To what extent does the free world differ from the material world and how does the once-born, the person preoccupied with day-to-day affairs and the seeming realities surrounding him, differ from the reborn? Again, are there really people living among us who have achieved at least partial freedom, whose lives, whose very being, is different from ours, who do not share our problems, who are much more successful or happy than the normal run of mankind? And if there are, where are they? Who are they? Why do we not hear more of them? Why do they not come forward if they have achieved so much for themselves and help us to achieve something for mankind in running his affairs in a more enlightened manner? If reborn ones do indeed exist, why are our rulers, our politicians, so conspicuously once-born?

*   *   *

If man is not yet free; he has at least arrived at the stage where freedom of mind can be conceived, and when a concept can be formulated, it is usually comparatively close to realisation. Even if the particulars are wrong, a legitimate attempt can be made to deduce the shape and nature of that future.

The essence of the theory contained in this book is that, from the beginning of life, the aim of evolution has been the manifestation of mind working at its fullest potential and it is this which man instinctively seeks to realise. Man may, by now, have the mental equipment necessary. His habitual method of using it has been developed without a teacher, with no example of correct usage in front of him, and no source of guidance other than his own powers of perception, valuation, and reason acting upon unconscious promptings. The extraordinary faculty of conscious thought with which he found himself endowed has been subject to every sort of abuse and misuse in the course of experimentation. Imagine a modern piece of scientific apparatus, a car, for instance, presented to an educated and intelligent man of medieval times. How could he deduce the true function and purpose of all its parts, its dials, instruments, and controls? And if he ever discovered how to drive the car, could he guess its potential on the open road or its limitations in unsuitable circumstances? With the appearance of conscious mind, *homo sapiens* gained access to a far more complicated piece of equipment. Its purpose and mechanisms are not quite what they seemed to him at the first sampling of their powers. Man is here, present and correct, with all that he needs to fulfil his potential. But he has not yet fully explored the scope of his mental faculties or recognised how to act in accordance with his potential, taking due regard to the possibilities, limitations, and complexities involved.

It should follow that no individual can presume to help others to freedom unless he has achieved freedom within himself. But since no man may yet be free to put on and wear with dignity the mantle of his own freedom, may we suggest in the meantime the sort of behaviour which might be characteristic of a 'free' mind?

The free mind is one which is able to view its own relationships, activities, interests, and encounters in an impartial and entirely detached manner; one which perceives circumstances and people in a light undistorted by fear, greed, aggression, or expectations of similarities to previous experiences. It is freed from compulsions, from the sources of bias and prejudices. It no longer projects upon others its own weaknesses nor its own glories. It can tolerate a silence and accept the absence of an explanation where no probable explanation presents itself. It is willing and able to balance ideas and modes of approach which at first appear in conflict, and to weigh up contradictory probabilities and facts against each other without the intrusion of wishful thinking.

Mental faculties which have hitherto been blocked off may quite suddenly become consciously available, giving a more complete picture of life, a far greater understanding of other people, and an ability to communicate with them. The individual gains insight and answers which were hitherto denied him. He loses his old personality – his particularity – because essentially he becomes all personalities.

The free mind is essentially a charitable mind. It sees people whole, their failings and problems as they are, not the outcome of some personally-chosen wickedness but the result of circumstances beyond their control. As the free individual understands and accepts his own motives, almost simultaneously he may understand those of others, who are seen not as perverse, difficult or selfish, but as people who to some degree or other are afflicted by something outside their awareness, as if hypnotised or sleepwalking. In these circumstances, feelings of sympathy or concern may replace the more immature reaction of hostility or anger about individual shortcomings. At this point, the precept to love – and understand – thy neighbour begins to look more practicable. It is no longer like a bell, an empty but ringing exhortation, but thereafter a part of a tolerant, relaxed viewpoint.

The possession of a tolerant outlook is not to be confused with the sentimentality of pity. I may forgive a savage dog for biting me. No purpose is served by losing my temper over such an incident. But expediency may demand, for the health of the community, that the animal be destroyed. The contemporary idea of an understanding which implies indulgence towards individuals suffering from immaturity, at the expense of the remainder of the community, may be a purely sentimental one. The awareness of the probable origins of a vicious act on the part of an acquaintance and the ability to forgive him – in the sense of not wishing him ill or reacting with anger – does not mean he should be given the opportunity for repetition even though he may be unable to help his conduct. He has to experience the consequences of his actions so that he – and others like him in due course – may take responsibility for them. To deprive him of that experience by a sentimental forgiveness is to deny his individuality, to patronise and to denigrate him. Sooner or later he has to be convinced his conduct is unacceptable by the experience of its rejection, and sooner or later others must be protected from its effects. If the only means of which we are aware involve him in pain, hardship, ridicule, or a diminished living potential, it may be pretentious to reject their adoption.

This concept of freedom arises as and when the whole personality accepts the desirability of restricting that part of itself which may be identified as the ego. To succeed in doing so entails not only the will to limit the activities and attitudes of the ego but the knowledge and experience necessary to identify them and to relate to them as if they were not so much an impression of the whole but rather an expression of the needs of a part of the whole. As such they are neither to be denied nor encouraged. The alternatives of licence on the one hand and repression on the other are to be transcended in identification, recognition, and the establishment of a relationship.

Recognition acknowledges that urges which are anti-social or inconsistent with other needs of the personality nevertheless have a purpose and express a part of life which is oneself. Freedom consists in the establishment of a generous peace between these needs and these urges – a peace in which both can find full satisfaction.

Initially one cannot help but greet with disappointment the concept that the traditionally grandiose ideals of freedom for which men have fought and died, might amount to nothing more than freedom from compulsions. If such a shallow-sounding aim is the final aspiration of man's soul, many might complain that they are already free to think and do what they choose without gaining anything from it.

Yet this is to fail to appreciate the implications of what is involved. There is good reason to believe that the prison of our frustrated aspirations is something far more complex and, by the same token, freedom from it far more exciting, than anything one would at first have rational cause to suspect. An analogy might be drawn with a chicken hatching out from an egg or butterfly emerging from a chrysalis. Formerly their total energy was devoted to breaking out. Now they are free to wander at will. When this energy is free of its shackles, free of assumptions and preconceptions, its explorations may reveal many remarkable things and create equally wondrous situations. Whatever marvels have been seen to date, these may be only a small part of what may be expected in the future.

* * *

What is the evidence that freedom of mind might be the aim and ultimate objective of human endeavour?

In the legends of most countries and in the thinking of people individually, there is often a golden place, a golden person, a golden time, and a Garden of Eden. J B Priestley* wrote in *Man and Time*:

> This idea of an earlier time, an earthly paradise in which everything had been simple and good, has been one of our most persistent haunters. It is behind all the Arcadian shepherds and shepherdesses, the Strephons and Phyllises of literature. It is there in Rousseau's discovery of the Noble Savage. Young enthusiasts still set out for the South Seas looking for it. One of our most dauntless contemporary theorists, H. S. Bellamy, tells us that between the final disintegration of the old moon and the earth's capture of a new satellite, our present moon, there was a considerable moonless interval, without tides and sinister bright nights – a quiet but happy time that man remembers as the Golden Age.

Luckless expeditions have sought El Dorado, the supposed city of untold wealth. The survival of Latin as a scholastic language may be due to the attraction of its connexions with an apparently progressive

*J B Priestley's *Man and Time*. Copyright. 1964. Aldus Books, London.

or golden society that lived two thousand years ago. Not a few have had visions of restoring the glories of a bygone age. The seventeenth and eighteenth centuries are regarded nostalgically by many even today who wish to ignore the superstitions, stench, injustices, and discomforts of those times.

The teachings of Christianity, Buddhism, Taoism, and Islam concern at least in part the conduct of golden personalities. Whatever message underlies these teachings must have immense significance for mankind if we measure it in the reverence, time, money, energy, and building of churches and temples devoted down the centuries to their memory.

The question must arise whether man groped intuitively for concepts of his destiny and therefore expressed them in his myths and religions; yet the crude imagery of times long past is misleading today and out of date if propounded as literal truth. The symbols have to be treated as an ancient language which must be translated into modern idiom to be understood. All religions aim at a sort of salvation, but salvation from what and in order to become what? The implication is that, in the past, all nations and types of men sought to personify aspects of the blueprint of whole man as God in their religions. The gods of all religions, east and west, can be interpreted as concepts of the stages on the way to evolved man. God becomes not only the personification of the destination but the method of getting there: the beginning, the end product, and the becoming, like the Trinity, three in one and wholly indivisible. Religious laws, rituals, and interpretations of God's will would in this light be attempts to discern the nature and direction of man's destiny. The god who dictates our actions and gives rewards could be interpreted as advice or intuitive promptings, directions written in symbolic terms regarding the benefit to be derived from conduct appropriate to the destiny of man.

In this connexion, such concepts as the Taoist Man of Character, the Christian concept of Jesus Christ and the Buddha may be usefully compared with the object of discovering their individual contributions to a symbolic description of Ultimate Man. Some indications of his attitudes and way of life may be found in a similar comparison of the traditional accounts of Heaven, Nirvana and the Islamic paradise.

The Man of Character and the Christ personality are closely associated in that they seem to be operating with pure motivation. Their actions, as they are described, appear to represent direct intention rather than the product of compulsions.

If Christ did not exist in reality, it is said man would have had to invent him as an example of what he could become if he could realise the full potential of humanity. In the Bible, Christ is not only the son of God but the son of man, that is to say, the descendant of man, the reborn or reincarnated man whose old personality is dead and replaced by a new, free one. The outstanding characteristic of the Christ personality was his complete freedom from the accepted ideas of the day. In common with other great religious leaders, he conforms to the mystical description of avatar: an incarnation of God sent in human disguise to benefit man in time of need. Whether or not avatars had the qualities attributed to them, their value was that they had the sort of personality around which could be built myths that expressed the potential inherent in man.

If freedom of mind represents the goal of man's unconscious aspirations, how does this relate to those other goals which mankind has conceived and held in reverence so long: Heaven, Nirvana, and the Paradise of the Moslem? Are these concepts intuitive attempts to describe the ideals of free mind? At the time they were made, freedom in any shape or form was so remote for the common man that he could be forgiven if he failed to recognise it as his basic need and gaol.

Following a similar train of thought, can we find in the religious disciplines, the concepts of virtue, and the practices which various religious figures prescribed for their followers, anything which might be effective in helping the average modern individual to overcome the conditioning of his early years?

Heaven is the abode of God and, though promised to Christians as the reward for virtue, it was not Christ who defined virtue as rigid adherence to a set of rules. Christ, as we shall see, appears rather to have set an example of how man can become as God by crucifying his old personality.

Both Hindu and Buddist seek salvation in release from the bondage of Karma into an unconditioned concept of existence. This bondage is the recurrence of the inherited and unavoidable consequences of one's actions. The repetitive cycle may be equated with the chain of events or repetitive experience which is a result of mind-conditioning. Release into Nirvana is described as a state where desire, hatred, folly, and concern for the self cease, where one is freed from the human condition as we know it, and all change is transcended. This again corresponds closely with the idea of a mind that is able to assimilate experience and has become freed from compulsive reactions forced upon it by the exigencies of early conditioning.

The Taoist description of the Man of Character* can be interpreted as an advanced concept of freedom, although dating furthest back in time to origins in China side by side with its opposite, legalised slavery. Taoism recounts in parable form the attuning of oneself to the way things work and the discovery of one's true self in relation to that working:

> The Man of Character lives at home without exercising his mind and performs actions without worry. The notions of right and wrong and the praise and blame of others do not disturb him. When within the four seas all people can enjoy themselves, that is happiness for him; when all people are well provided, that is peace for him. Sorrowful in countenance, he looks like a baby who has lost his mother; appearing stupid, he goes about like one who has lost his way. He has plenty of money to spend, and does not know where it comes from. He drinks and eats just enough and does not know where the food comes from. This is the demeanour of the Man of Character.

A further description of the Pure Man* adds:

> Such men are free in mind and calm in demeanour with high foreheads. Sometimes disconsolate like autumn, and sometimes warm like spring, their joys and sorrows are in direct touch with the four seasons in harmony with all creation, and none know the limit thereof . . . The pure men of old appeared of towering stature and yet could not topple down. They behaved as though wanting in themselves, but without looking up to others. Living in unconstrained freedom, yet they did not try to show off. They appear to smile as if pleased, and to move only in natural response to their surroundings. Their serenity flowed from the store of goodness within. In social relationships, they kept to their inner character. Broad-minded, they

*The Wisdom of China. Edited by Lin Yutang. Michael Joseph Ltd.

appeared great; towering, they seemed beyond control. Continuously abiding, they seemed like doors kept shut; absent-minded, they seemed to forget speech.

Confusing as these verses sound, they do in essence depict a personality freed of conditioned responses and hidden motivations. They describe a personality who is emotionally secure, without egotistical tendencies, worries, or dissatisfactions, whose actions are not compulsive, who is not motivated by the sort of fear which, when stimulated, produce predictable self-defensive reactions.

Such a passive personality may appear bound to fall victim to the aggressive competition of modern experience, but ancient Taoism provides another parable to illustrate that the answer is neither the forcefulness of a Hitler nor the submissive quality sometimes, probably wrongly, associated with a gentle Jesus, meek and mild:

> Chishengtse used to raise fighting cocks for the king. After ten days had passed, the king asked if his cock was ready for a fight. 'Not yet,' he replied. 'The cock is still very impulsive and haughty.' After another ten days, the king asked again, and Chishengtse replied, 'Not yet. He still reacts to noises and shadows.' After another ten days had passed the king asked again and he replied, 'Not yet. His eyes still have an angry look, and he is full of fight.' Another ten days passed and he said, 'It is about ready. When he hears other cocks crow, he does not even react. You look at him, and he appears like a wooden cock. His character is whole now. No other cock will dare to fight him but will run away at first sight.

*　　*　　*

In modern times, concepts of freedom have been formulated in psychological terms by a number of authorities such as Jung, Karen Horney, Erich Fromm, Kurt Goldstein, Frieda Fromm-Reichmann, Abraham Maslow, and, more recently, Eric Howe and Carl Rogers. These and others such as Nietzsche offer ideas concerning life's ultimate goal which interestingly, have much in common. While hypotheses of this type are outside the realm of science, they are no more acceptable than the older church dogmas of man's origin and destiny unless and until they can be reconciled with neo-Darwinism – or an alternative theory of the workings of evolution.

141

To us, the most convincing and thorough treatment of the hypothetical possibilities is that running throughout the work of C G Jung. He concluded that the goal of psychic development was the maturing of the individual into wholeness as the contents of the subconscious are recognised and as a working relationship is established between the individual's consciousness and his access to a universal unconscious, to which Jung conceived that man, with other forms of life, owes his ultimate motivation. Jung* said: 'I use the term "individuation" to denote the process by which a person becomes a psychological "individual", that is, a separate, indivisible unity or "whole" . . . and, in so far as "in-dividuality" embraces our innermost, last and incomparable uniqueness, it also implies becoming one's own self.'

Part of Jung's thesis, contained in his now unfashionable *Psychological Types*, was that man unconsciously drives himself into circumstances likely to develop his conscious use of four mind faculties: sense perception, which establishes what is present in a situation; thinking, which gives meaning to what is perceived; feeling, which relates what is perceived to the motives and priorities of the individual in terms of its value for him; and intuition, which indicates the possibilities latent in the situation. These four faculties have already been mentioned as having come to the fore one after the other in the development of society during past ages. However, a synthesis of the four has not so far been achieved in the government of the affairs of man.

Jung sought to demonstrate that each individual has at least one or two of these faculties more strongly developed than the rest and could thereby be identified as having a particular permutation of conscious and unconscious mind factors. Of course no adult is the same as another, and no one can be pigeonholed under the headings of these four definitions. An individual's particular characteristics blur what would be in theory a pure thinker or a purely perceptive person. A study of the four broad categories, however, together with the outgoing and ingoing tendencies in each individual which Jung described as extravert and introvert, does aid understanding of the constituents of individuality. Different mind-types work in different

*Memories, Dreams, Reflections, C G Jung. Collins. 1963.

142

ways, and the conduct and ideas of each are often incomprehensible to the other as a result of failure to visualise how the other looks at life. Freud and Jung, for example, were themselves guilty of behaviour towards each other which, in their patients, they would have characterised as 'sick', in so far as neither appears to have been able to relate constructively to the ideas of the other. Although these two men can be regarded as pioneers in these unknown territories of freedom, it would seem that neither at least in respect of their attitudes towards each other could be described as "free."

Every individual has the ability to look within – introversion – and to look without – extraversion. However, their upbringing usually encourages them to follow one tendency almost compulsively to the exclusion of the other instead of balancing them as occasion demands. Thus the extreme extravert will hardly see himself nor the extreme introvert be able to forget himself. When these opposites meet, the outgoing individual may consider the introvert self-centred and withdrawn. The ingoing individual may disregard the extravert as shallow and unsympathetic. Each may feel misunderstood by the other and critical of him.

The extravert reacts in relation to his surroundings. They determine his actions. He is able to fit with relative ease into the circumstances in which he finds himself and he is therefore often described as well-adjusted or sociable. His main weakness lies in his tendency to be caught up too much in outward concerns and therefore perhaps to disregard his own needs for his own development.

Frieda Fordham speculates further on the extravert in *An Introduction to Jung's Psychology**:

> He meets others halfway and is interested in anything and everything. He likes organisations, groups, community gatherings, and parties, and is usually active and on the whole helpful; this is the type that keeps our business and social life going. Extraverted intellectuals have similar qualities, and are at their best working with others, teaching or passing on their knowledge in some way; their good relationship with the world helps them to do this effectively.
>
> Extraverts tend to be both optimistic and enthusiastic, though their enthusiasm does not last too well. The same is true of their rela-

* *An Introduction to Jung's Psychology* (Pelican Original, 1953). Penguin Books Ltd. Copyright © Frieda Fordham, 1953.

143

tionships with other people, which are both easily and quickly made and broken.

The weakness of extraverts lies in a tendency to superficiality and a dependence on making a good impression; they enjoy nothing more than an audience. They dislike being alone, and think reflection morbid, and this, together with a lack of self-criticism, makes them more attractive to the outer world than to their family or immediate circle where they can be seen without disguise. Since they are well adapted to society, they usually accept the morals and convictions of the day, and so tend to be somewhat more conventional in their judgment; but they are nevertheless most useful people and absolutely necessary to any communal life.

The introvert is concerned with the world within him rather than that which surrounds him. He withdraws into himself and uses himself as the yardstick by which to run his life, perhaps not giving the importance due to the circumstances in which he operates. Thus he may lay himself open to distressing and confidence-draining failures as a result of ignoring the objective facts.

Introverted adults . . . dislike society and feel lonely and lost in large gatherings. They are sensitive and afraid of looking ridiculous, but they often seem unable to learn how to behave in social situations: they are clumsy or they are too outspoken or they are scrupulously and rather ridiculously polite. They tend to be overconscientious, pessimistic, critical, and always keep their best qualities to themselves, so that naturally they are easily misunderstood.

Since they can only show their gifts in sympathetic surroundings, they tend to be overlooked, and consequently are less successful than their extraverted colleagues; yet, because they do not spend their energies trying to impress others, or dissipate it in social activities, they may often possess unusual knowledge or have developed some talent above average standards.

Introverted people are at their best when alone, or in a small and familiar group; they prefer their own thoughts to conversation and books, and quiet pursuits to noisy activities. Their own judgment is more important to them than a generally accepted opinion – an introvert will put off reading a book that is popular and depreciate anything that is widely acclaimed. This independence of judgment and lack of conventionality can be valuable if rightly understood and used, and in spite of their lack of social graces they often make loyal and sympathetic friends.

A currently fashionable introvert tendency is to apply to behaviour the criterion of 'what is right for me'. This attitude holds that if one wants to do something, the desire is enough to make the action 'right for me' – and who or what is to say it is wrong? However, to disregard objective values is to venture into an introvert world as unbalanced as Western man's past tendency to seek a guideline, standard, or scientific explanation in the outside world for every subjective emotion as well as for every objective value.

The extravert or introvert tendencies of an individual affect whichever of the four mental faculties operate most strongly within him. Thus, for example, an outgoing person may have the same degree of perception as an ingoing personality but they will see the world very differently.

Perception, called by Jung 'sensation', is the ability to observe factual surroundings and circumstances by use of the senses. Such perception goes right across the board of activity and co-ordination. It is particularly manifest in craftsmen, those adept at mechanics, sportsmen, art connoisseurs, and whosoever seeks to satisfy their senses. Sense perception operates unconsciously in animals other than man. Toss a bun to a bear at the zoo and his quickness of eye allows him to stretch out a paw and leisurely and unerringly to catch the titbit. That simple action represents immediate apprehension on the angle at which the bun was thrown and at what point in time the bun will come within reach. A perceptive person is well acquainted with the facts of a situation. The introvert is concerned with his own reaction to the circumstances around him; the extravert concentrates on the circumstances themselves. The latter has a supreme grasp of objective facts but may miss the wood for the trees. The former perceives what is important to him. He can observe what makes him happy, what makes him sad, though he may become enthralled by this subjectivity. A danger for the extravert may lie in overinsistence on the surface facts of a situation with a singular disinterest in their implications.

Thinking in the sense meant here is the ability to give meaning to facts, to relate them together in abstract concepts and build up a logical sequence which makes an assessment or judgment. The extravert brings himself into relation with the intellectual conclusions which he draws from whatever tangible, measurable characteristics he perceives. The introvert concerns himself with subjective ideas embodying concepts of experience which although intangible, in that they may concern such matters as for instance, happiness and loneliness, nevertheless remain facts. The one can provide coherence to a situation and the other can provide a new view from a situation. But reliance placed on the thinking faculty is not always justified. The extraverted thinker often has perception as a supporting faculty but he perceives so many facts – without the operation of the feeling faculty to decide which are important – that he may try to fit the worthless as well as the important into an overall frame. He may think out a scheme of things which appears rational and he may pride himself upon his logic, duty, and discipline. But as feelings and emotions are not rational, the warmth of human kindness and the frailties of human weakness may be excluded. The introvert, on the other hand, may have poor perceptive ability because of his concern with the inner rather than the outer world. Thus he might concoct theories without any regard to establishing the accuracy of the facts on which they are based. He may start out with a false assumption and continue almost absent-mindedly to build up a sequence, fitting suppositions to his ideas that bear no relation to the outside world. He might be able to construct, as M C Escher demonstrates in his engravings, a waterfall that runs uphill and a house that is structurally impossible.

The feeling faculty bestows a sense of values, an appreciation of the relative importance of the constituents of situations to the overall long-term interest and wellbeing of the individual. The use of the word 'feeling' to describe this quality has led to endless confusion since it is not the same as the capacity to experience emotion; nevertheless it is difficult to think of a better or more appropriate word. Jungian 'feeling' may on occasion be transmitted to consciousness by means of emotion but again such emotion performs some quite different function. Thus an individual who experiences a great deal of emotion cannot claim that his feeling faculty, in the Jungian sense, is working. The valuations established by feeling are different from those established by strict intellectual reasoning, since the latter is concerned primarily with what is measurable. Feeling may deal with the intangibles of future probabilities as intuitively foreseen. If thinking works upon the products of perception, feeling uses those of intuition, yet the hierarchy of values bestowed by the feeling process should appear from the outside to be logical or at least sensible. Those with extraverted feeling tend to value what are considered by the world to be correct objectives to value. They thrive in communal activities and relationships, thereby forming desirable marriages, and are often involved in social work or mediation. However, if drawn to its extreme, extraverted feeling becomes overwhelmed by the objective and is so stretched as to become artificial and insincere. The feeling introvert deals with his own wishes and inclinations in order of their importance and does not indulge in trivia at the expense of long-term objectives. He – or more commonly she – might have some vision of what is right conduct but presents a cold, undemonstrative front because of subjective factors. Such introverted feeling may find expression in religion, involvement in the arts, and a deep, if hidden, concern for the small circle that will surround such an individual. She may have an inability to cope outside that small circle and may be driven at extremes to make sacrifices for its members which are entirely to her own detriment.

Intuition is unconscious perception or instinctive apprehension, the ability to foresee the implications of a situation or make an accurate forecast without consciously knowing all the facts. Given a basic set of circumstances, the intuitive faculty weighs up unconsciously the likely results. The consequences glimpsed by intuition may be so unexpected and removed from the existing situation as to appear to have no connexion. Therefore the events intuitively foreseen may come through to consciousness as revelations from nowhere, a partial principle of so-called 'given knowledge'. They may appear to have an inexplicable prophetic quality, or may be suspected of resulting from conscious perception, feeling, or intellectual conclusion, yet cannot be directly ascribed to any of these means. Extraverted intuition can be seen in operation in the individual who can act effectively 'in the dark', be he business speculator, politician, prophet, or scientist aided to his discovery by a flash of inspiration. At his extreme, he will risk everything and gain nothing except experience in his haste to achieve the possibilities he has glimpsed. The introvert is bound up with the possibilities and visions he sees within himself. He may appear to be mystic or madman, and at his extreme can be carried away by fantasies that bombard him unless he can find a form of expression that provides him with an anchor.

*   *   *

In the earliest stages of the growth of a child's consciousness, all four faculties may well be present at least in embryo. Ideally they would grow simultaneously but the development of a synthesis is inhibited – perhaps necessarily – by methods of upbringing, styles of education and the initial difficulty of reconciling the operation of one faculty with another.

A child has enough difficulty developing the logic of thinking or the value judgment of feeling without trying to reconcile what appear to be their diametrically opposed operation. Thinking can be demonstrated as operating on logical causality, one step following upon another; whereas the operation of Jungian feeling is an instantaneous reaction, often producing conclusions apparently contradictory to logic and appearing to lack supporting evidence. Sense perception deals with what is here and now, whereas intuition deals with the future implications of the present. Each faculty on its own presents quite a different picture, different inclinations, and points out different objectives.

Thus the average child tends to develop foremost the function most compatible with his family background and the examples of behaviour set before him. A supporting faculty is usually at least partially developed but the other two remain disused at conscious level. This leads the child, and later the adult, to regard some conduct and objectives in life as acceptable or good, and others as unacceptable or bad, which he excludes from his own typical way of operating. The two faculties which have not reached conscious utilisation still influence the pattern of the individual's life but unconsciously, without recognition of the part they are playing or the extent to which they have to be taken into account in the course of daily activities, behaviour, and recognised objectives. Thus an

148

imbalance is created in most individuals' lives, and it appears to be the deepest concern of their energies and motivations to correct it. We do not know whether this relegation of some faculties to the subconscious and their subsequent attempted resuscitation is a necessary part of individual growth and development or whether it results from the limitations of our humanity, our roots in the past, or our ignorance of the most appropriate methods of education.

The different institutions of our society which teach development of the mental faculties have made provision for them in isolation but not recognised any objective involving their whole use. Traditional academic training encourages development of the thought faculty while sense perception is activated quite separately through sports and handicrafts. Religious bodies deal with the fundamental perspectives related to feeling in terms of values, though often in a ritualistic manner and directly in conflict with the scientific education given at the same time. Some modern methods of teaching the arts stimulate expression of intuitive concepts. The next step, the reconciliation and integration of such spontaneity with traditional academic standards, is lacking. Thus far society still awaits the coming of a means, instrument, or institution which will lend itself to the balanced development of the four faculties.

Among modern authorities, Jung and Howe have particularly emphasised that the result of combining four fully-developed mental faculties might transcend their sum and constitute a whole quite different from all-round acquisition of the parts. If the full development of all four faculties has rarely been achieved in the world, it is not because the process requires any high degree of intellect or learning achievement but because the reconciliation and operation of any one of the faculties appears at least at first diametrically opposed by one of the others: thinking by feeling, intuition by sensation. Thus, until any individual mind has learnt the trick of working without recourse to a polarity choice of alternatives, it has difficulty in operating simultaneously faculties which seem to negate each other and to devise paradox as the answer to be sought for solutions.

This paradoxicality of outlook is characteristic of much religious – in contrast to scientific – literature. The New Testament Jesus suggested that 'he that loveth his life shall lose it', and Laotse is reputed to have said:

> *Superior character appears like a hollow.*
> *Sheer white appears tarnished.*
> *Great character appears like insufficient.*
> *Solid character appears like infirm.*
> *Pure worth appears like contamination.*
> *Great Talent takes long to mature.*

(Tao – *Te Ching*)

The free man, we may then conclude, would be a strange, unfamiliar figure in our culture and such men in our time as may be free possibly would prefer to conceal rather than to emphasise their differences.

8

Hypothetical Man

PERFECTION OF SCIENTIFIC methodology and its ability to exercise a rational approach to problems has been the greatest achievement of our Western culture in the last two hundred years. Our greatest failure has been our inability to recognise the limitations of science and to confine its idiom to those subjects appropriate to it. Instead, time, energy, and brilliance have been misdirected on the assumption that science's objective style may equally well apply to more subjective fields where precise definition and quantitative measurement are not so practicable.

Somewhere between this triumph and this failure, we may find the clues which we need to the inability in our time to find convincing values by which we might live and die in some confidence. Somewhere in this region, the healthy security of the ongoing human expectation is undermined by the nagging anxiety of rationalism – that if we cannot conceptualise and agree on all our objectives, personal and social, we shall neither succeed in realising anything worth while nor in avoiding a thousand infinite disasters.

Intuitively we feel we should reject these implications even if it means rejecting rationality and the authoritative establishment which seems to uphold it and be founded upon it.

Different ways of expressing this unease have been found. The

151

hippie, in many ways taking on the appearance, practices, and characteristics of a more primitive age, protests in open, though often naïve attempts to discredit institutions upon which, infected as they may be, we are nevertheless still dependent. Those who operate within the established conventions, at least in their professional capacity, have a more furtive method of answering their need for a hypothesis of the purposes or at least the motivations of man. Intuitively rebelling against the overapplication of objective method, they privately dabble in strange beliefs, perhaps as contained in the myriad of irrational cults which bring some relief from the arid intellectualism that pervades the ordinary business of life.

In the best of these cults, the joys of pursuing what seems right – though not necessarily rational – in the interests of kindness, of relationships, and of our own deepest personal needs provide an absorbing satisfaction, even a happiness and contentment, no longer associated with our everyday working life where the writ of the Great Scientific Methodology runs. In the worst, those cults professing a doctrine of the *élite* or 'chosen people', adherents may at least find some security in believing that they have some special privilege and protection not accorded to others.

It would be an interesting exercise to ascertain and total the membership of such large cult-groups in the United Kingdom as the Scientologists, Jehovah's Witnesses, Spiritualists, Christian Scientists, Rosicrucians, Freemasons, Theosophists, together with the sincere participants in the older and more orthodox religious groups. The total would surely be a high proportion of the serious-minded part of the population.

Although these cults might appear to provide an escape from the limitations of a too materialistic way of life, with one or two notable exceptions they use the logical assumptions of causal processes to justify the tenets of each particular system. Perhaps therefore they are attractive to their adherents for other if uncomprehended reasons. For it is in these cults that we can keep faithfully preserved difficult facts, ideas, and symbols which cannot be incorporated into our rational, sensible world, and which we may even find too threatening to our orthodox structures and concepts on which we are so dependent.

In fact we live in a strange cultural dichotomy. In this, science and scientists are all too ready to throw out or simply ignore every fact that cannot be easily explained. Meanwhile, those who have experienced at first hand the inexplicable are perhaps too ready to abandon a science which seems as intolerant of the bizarre as the medieval church was of heresy. On both sides, too many are willing to reject, too few endeavour to integrate.

Integration of these opposites is difficult. Our conditioned minds attempt to dismiss as illusory or unreal every phenomenon which cannot be repeated in controlled conditions. We have no time or use for anything outside our own immediate experience which does not conform to the orthodox. But experiences are not deprived of reality because they do not lend themselves to the repetitious experimental requirements of orthodox science. Presumably the second and subsequent of a test series will never experientially be the same as the first and that fact must apply to anything which has to do with experience in general rather than with that special part of it which might be termed material intellectualism.

*   *   *

Since science ignores the apparently inexplicable and since the traditional faiths of our society are unwilling to reconsider their dogmas in the light of twentieth-century experience, there are no accepted standards by which cult ideas can be assessed. It is every man for himself and every man to find his own way, unguided and as best he can, to the utilisation of himself and his potential.

Thus all sorts of intuitive ideas and interpretations of experience flourish in a rash of unco-ordinated, vain experiments which endeavour to come to terms with the whole of human personality. That is not to say they should be dismissed. They may evidence mankind's determination to explain what he is and can become and to re-examine facts which have been rejected by science and misinterpreted by traditional theologians.

If some facts are particularly liable to become confused with fantasy, this in itself is not reason to neglect them. For fantasy is, in itself, a fact, and all facts need to be accounted for in any realistic hypothesis as to the nature and ends of life.

The records of the apparently miraculous compiled painstakingly and in all sincerity by the Roman Catholic Church when considering candidates for beatification are, for example, most probably factual evidence and may be relevant to our nature – even if it is not necessarily relevant to church doctrines. The interpretation put upon it by its compilers may possibly be no more than a pathetic attempt to cling to ethical structures which proved their value in the different conditions of the past, but it should be considered in relation to any hypothesis of man's potential. Openminded study of this material might fulfil many hopes, not least that even illness due to demonstrable organic damage and accepted as terminal may under appropriate conditions be healed.

The archives of the Society of Physical Research contain accounts of phenomena such as hauntings, poltergeists, telepathy, and precognition which are unlikely to be fanciful. Some were submitted by people of undoubted intelligence whose sincerity in general cannot seriously be questioned. If trickery has on occasion been apparent, the remaining material is not discredited unless one wishes to resort to excuses to dismiss it. Orthodox science too has had its charlatans.

The occurrence of extrasensory perception, investigated at length by Rhine at Duke University, has been accepted as a fact by many distinguished people. The inability of its practitioners to reproduce it at will would seem to describe one of its characteristics rather than a denial of its existence.

Firewalkers in Greece and elsewhere have demonstrated that those who follow a prescribed ritual may tread on heated stones without burning themselves. A reporter who attempted to follow the example, with prior preparation of his feet but not of his mind, was badly injured.

Anyone who has honestly investigated these and other activities such as spiritualism, fortune-telling, astrology, witchcraft, and dream-interpretation would surely surmise that, in spite of all too prevalent fraud, they contain a residue of the inexplicable.

At the same time one may also rightly feel that the conclusions of some of their practitioners are dubious. The unforseeable – such as the sinking of the Titanic – might be foreseen, and information apparently known only to someone now dead might be received via a medium. But we are not entitled to use these instances as a basis to construct theories about time or life after death, for example, unless the conclusions are reconcilable with the findings in other fields such as the laws of biology and physics. It may be enough to accept facts whose implications appear inconsistent and tolerate the uncomfortable intellectual vacuum which arises when one does not immediately attempt to place them in a causal relation to each other so as to produce some structure which can be held to contain 'truth'.

However, throughout history man has always avoided this discomfort. Those who have directly experienced that which seems different from the everyday sensation of materialistic reality have been fascinated by it and frequently sought to memorialise it in yet another cult based on some theory which accounts for too little of the overall experience of man.

What is to be done with such diversity of belief and experience? If some overall hypothesis is possible embracing the contradictions and different varieties of experience, we might have for the first time an all-inclusive view of the directions and nature of reality.

*   *   *

In his book *The Integrity of the Personality*, Anthony Storr*, a leading Jungian analyst, suggests that by whatever road one travels, the final aim is the same:

> I propose to call this final achievement self-realisation, by which I mean the fullest possible expression in life of the innate potentialities of the individual, the realisation of his own uniqueness as a personality: and I also put forward *the hypothesis that, consciously or unconsciously, every man is seeking this goal*† . . .

> The use of the word 'goal' will certainly excite critical comment from those who decry psychology as being unscientific, since such a concept has no place in the mechanical, deterministic universe which was the ideal of nineteenth-century physics. In describing the motions of the planets one need not ask what goal they are seeking; but in describing human behaviour it is, I believe, necessary to ask this question, and unscientific to omit it. Many processes in nature are only fully comprehensible in terms of the end-result or goal, and remain obscure if considered simply from the causal point of view. The concept of 'goal-seeking' is, for instance, of central importance to cybernetics . . .

---

* *The Integrity of the Personality*. Anthony Storr. William Neinemann Ltd. 1960.
† The italics are ours—M R & D S J.

It is clear that it is as legitimate to ask towards what end a process is directed, as to inquire from what cause it originated, and I believe that any psychological description of human beings must attempt to answer both questions. The highly complicated facts of human behaviour can be related to both inquiries; and whilst some facts are better explained in terms of what has happened in the individual's past, others are more easily comprehended in terms of the goal towards which the individual appears to be striving. Neither description is complete without the other.

. . . In biology, it has been found necessary to postulate 'organisers,' which, in the immature organism, regulate the processes of growth and development. Our psychological concept of an inner urge towards self-realisation is not dissimilar.

Storr presents these suggestions in so prosaic a way that their implications are likely to alude one at a casual reading. Yet if it is true – as we certainly believe and have in this book tried to produce the overall evidence supporting the belief – that consciously or unconsciously every man is seeking the goal of self-realisation, we have a valid hypothesis against which to examine the entire range of human motivation and conduct as well as the peculiarities and inconsistencies of human ideas and irrationalities.

The hypothesis, if true, throws light on so many aspects of life and makes order of so many things which are otherwise hopelessly confusing and inconsistent that it might almost be called the Ultimate Hypothesis. Once grasped in total, it is awe-inspiring and never again do our world or its inhabitants appear to be quite the same; to be quite so ill-ordered, chaotic, or confused as before.

By its implications, all actions can be interpreted as the seeking of man towards wholeness, just as, biologically speaking, the fundamental aim of every organism is that of its own physical growth and completion. All immediate superficial desires, ambitions, impulses, or mistakes can be accounted to a basic urge to bring upon their possessors that experience which he most needs at that time, to enlighten himself as regards the characteristics of his own nature in relation to those of others. And if that is so, an individual, once having discovered how to begin to perceive his own characteristics more directly than their image reflected in the consequences of his own vanities, might be expected to incorporate this insight into his life-style. In fact we find this is precisely what happens not only to mystics who have undergone some numinous and what seems to them life-shattering revelation, but also to those who have pursued the more intellectual disciplines of gradual self-discovery through the therapeutical techniques of analytical or human psychology. The age-old concept of the Wise Man has a mystic aura so that we associate wisdom with some insight different from mere knowledge. This insight, we suggest, is expressed in Storr's hypothesis; and as such explains not only our individual idiosyncrasies but those of all society and societies, the convolutions of history, and the trend of things to come; the hypothesis to which all others must be relative.

Such an ultimate hypothesis bears the same relationship to other theories about motivation as Einstein's theory of relativity bears to Newton's laws of gravity. Newtonian physics were appropriate on earth but not beyond in a greater universe where new dimensions were extended by Einstein into space and time. Similarly, an ultimate hypothesis of evolution does not prove wrong Freud's theories on sexual drives and relationships, Alder's theories on superiority and inferiority, or Jung's concepts of individuation. Their discoveries fit within circumstances of a larger scheme and most people would find, on investigation, that they had attitudes in all these fields which are in some respects undeveloped or immature.

The Ultimate Hypothesis which we then suggest – whether it is precisely what Storr had in mind or whether it is necessary to formulate it afresh – is simply that the problems of mankind, both of individuals and society, the apparent diversity of habits, motives, ventures, aspiration, nature, and characteristics, can in part be understood in the context of man as an evolving animal or perhaps one which has already evolved but has not yet become fully acquainted with his potential and the manner of its employment.

The implications are profound and tremendous. The seemingly inexplicable falls into place to make a consistent wholeness of experience and living. The processes of a purposive evolution can be seen, although not proved to be seen, everywhere in everything. Earlier theological endeavours similarly expressed the idea that the universe and all its creatures were in various stages of 'becoming' and that a particular phenomenon, described as 'God', was present in all things.

In these terms, the achievement of wholeness is inevitably and instinctively attempted by every man, regardless of whether he wants it or is aware of it. Do what he may, he is moving forward. The process is, nevertheless, for most an unconscious one and, though everybody is seeking the same goal and gradually progressing through the many different stages toward it, they do not experience the effects as such.

This is necessarily so, for it is a process begun before the advent of consciousness itself either in the individual or the species; and even after the conscious faculty had become well developed in the species, the codification of experience and the terms in which to conceptualise the conclusions to be drawn from it, did not exist. Since today we still tend automatically to screen out information which is not subject to scientific verification, the directive motive has remained unconscious. But now that the necessity of experiencing the whole of life, including its less rational elements, is insisted upon intuitively by the younger generation, such things may become subject to more understanding.

One can hardly have direct knowledge of an unconscious process because as soon as it enters consciousness, it ceases to be unconscious. Man can only be observed to behave as if the Ultimate Hypothesis were true and as if he were influenced by the forces it describes. The manifestations which individuals may see in their lives lie, for example, in their motives and desires to marry, to become wealthy, to indulge in sex, to obtain power, to pursue various forms of art or entertainment, or in the consequences of depression, illness, frustration, and synchronistic misfortune.

In any of these directions, one's own and other people's lives and the course of history can be seen always to be working restlessly as if towards greater freedom from mental conditioning and obsessional activities. The driving force in their different behaviour and stages of history can be ascribed to a similar goal, the improvement of the circumstances in which evolution can take place. Put in its widest sense, becoming is the process of the creation of the world, and the reflection of the world in each individual. Each individual and event is part of a whole wherein growth is taking place and which is the underlying pattern of everyday life, of what we do and say to each other, why we make love and why we make war.

In the Ultimate Hypothesis, everything in everyday life and in the more rarefied strata of seemingly inexplicable or disputed phenomena has its place in the business of becoming. All religions, reactions, happenings, pursuits, literature, arts, even dreams, are vehicles of evolutionary messages to consciousness concerning what is necessary to speed and facilitate development towards the completion of a phase.

Art is recognised as great, whatever the motive for its original inspiration, if it unconsciously conveys and handles consistently the language of the unconscious. Alongside works of obvious merit, such as Tolstoy's *War and Peace*, must be placed other masterpieces which attempted no such pretensions. *Alice in Wonderland* was originally published as a children's tale and Tolkien's *Fellowship of the Ring* is no more than a fairy story in the sense of that term. Yet both have far transcended their original purpose and have become widely read and known throughout the world. Away from the necessity of conforming to the rational, intuitively the authors of both have in their respective manners unconsciously expressed profound statements, symbols, and allegories universally evident and universally but perhaps unconsciously comprehended by their vast readerships.

*   *   *

The construction of the mind is such that unconsciously it continually aspires to shed its conditioning and to reach fruition. It would seem that each initial set of attitudes which constitutes an individual mind is in the course of a lifetime modified and improved to some extent, however slight.

As the consistency of attitudes within a population improves, so the culture and institutions of that populace are likely to reflect a more unified standard of acceptable behaviour. We do not seek to improve our society and our standards because it is rational to have that sort of tidiness and consistency. If man sought improvement on that account, it would leave no place for the upheavals of idealism, revolution, and heresy. We seek change in response to the shifting balance of equilibrium of what is and has been practicable and what may become practicable. We are driven towards change because, without that inherent urge, evolution would not take place. Life would continue in stagnant forms.

Indeed life would be stagnant if the healing of the inconsistent took place only when appropriate circumstances accidently coincided. In fact the process depends on our unconsciously bringing about the right extent of the right problem at the right time. Even so, nature, when left to itself, works very slowly. One or two changes of attitude may be as much as most people achieve by the end of their lifetimes. To that extent, their character can be changed; and the change which takes place in the course of a lifetime is in fact the experience of life.

The rigours involved in personality change are considerable. Whenever such change takes place, it may be felt initially as sorrow and sacrifice. The 'sacrifice' of the essence of the old personality, its attitude towards the things held most dear, is an inevitable part, possibly accounting for the emphasis placed on sacrifice by religions throughout history. This reason alone is sufficient to provide fear of the consequences by those who for reasons of self-protection are most attached to egotistical or materialistic objectives. The ridicule they may display towards the whole concept is a symptom of their fear.

The Bible tells of the law-abiding young man who asked Jesus what he must do to reach heaven:

> Jesus said unto him, If thou wilt be perfect, go and sell what thou hast, and give to the poor, and thou shalt have treasure in heaven; and come and follow me. But when the young man heard that saying, he went away sorrowful; for he had great possessions. Then said Jesus unto his disciples, Verily I say unto you that a rich man shall with difficulty enter into the kingdom of heaven.

The story does not mean he need necessarily give away his riches but rather that he should renounce the motivation which led to his acquiring the wealth. Too frequently, possessions held so dear are the result of compulsions to amass them or obsessions to retain them for reasons of greed, compensation, or basic insecurity.

Those who do stand aside nevertheless perform a necessary function; as a sort of evolution fodder, they sublimate their own potential

160

for that of children who may turn out to be more progressive and courageous than themselves. Obsessions with the desirability of large families have more to their emotional depths than can be accounted for by economic arguments. In the face of religion's placing enormous emphasis on observance of the traditional, progress may demand the pressures of the large-scale sufferings of populations. Over thousands of years, many generations have not been able themselves to achieve self-realisation. Each younger generation may make a small advance over the previous one before their attitudes, too, solidify into the stasis of the older generation. The best they can do thereafter is to multiply in the unconscious hope that their children at least may advance further in a future time.

*   *   *

We know of no facts which in themselves belie the Ultimate Hypothesis unless it is treated by the reductionist method of diminishing the idea to 'nothing but' imagination. On the other hand, many bizarre facts support it. Yet if the Ultimate Hypothesis is to prove credible, there should be some indications evident in our experience of the sort of underlying mechanisms and energies which would give effect to it. Some overall co-ordinating, even directive, principles of the sort necessary to elucidate its operation may be found in the phenomenon of telepathy and Jung's concepts of synchronicity and a collective unconscious.

Dealing first with synchronicity, consciousness believes itself to have the power of determining its own conduct – or rather that of the individual of which it is a part – and to hold itself in general responsible for the behaviour of its subject. And conscious self-determination is an effective guide for day-to-day purposes just as eye-sight is a reliable means of identifying immediate obstacles in one's path and the way around them. But sight does not warn one of the hidden trap, contrivance, or emotion; it does not predict what will be seeable around the corner. Similarly, long-term conscious plans rarely work out – in practice they are rendered either unneccesary or impracticable by the occurrence of the unforeseeable.

Few people would claim they consciously planned and successfully brought off, by their thinking capabilities alone, the most important events that have shaped the course of their lives – their marriages, such successes as they have found, or the development of their particular talents. By hindsight, everyone can look back on at least some small or perhaps large experience that appeared to be coincidence or good luck. One might marvel at the course of events, the tiny thread on which the sequence hung. Those instances which have the appearance of good luck or coincidence may be examined to see if they are meaningful, as in Jung's concept of synchronicity. By his theory, meaningful coincidence or synchronicity, activated by intuitive foresight of the implications of a situation, would put the subject in the right place at the right time to benefit from events important to his development.

At this time, the idea of telepathy is probably in much the same position as hypnosis was in the nineteenth-century; that is to say, its existence is accepted by those who have seriously looked into the matter while it is dismissed as improbable by the remainder.

No entirely satisfactory proof is likely ever to be available regarding the operation of telepathy because of the difficulty of reproducing and assessing it under test conditions; the conditions, and the place occupied by the test in a series, must influence the minds of the practitioners so that no two tests are ever the same. However it may be a more normal and usual function than we suppose. Both American and Russian Defence Departments have been sufficiently impressed by its possibilities as a means of communication to carry out extensive research.

Its importance from the viewpoint of evolutionary theory is that it offers a possible explanation as to how ideas and experience can be retained for use when opportunity, possibly after several generations, presents itself. Some such storage and communication system was necessary in prehistoric times if valuable experimental learning was to accumulate before the written word permitted its recording.

Accepting the concept of telepathy, we may then imagine ideas in the sense of observations, perceptions, even sensations, as to some degree shared, regardless as to whether they are communicated verbally or not. If I have a thought and it is subject to telepathic communication, its transference to your mind may take place under appropriate conditions, whether I will it or not or even whether it occurs in my conscious mind. In this case we should never know whether similar circumstances and stimuli have caused the thought to occur to you independently from its origins in me, or whether it has transferred itself. And, for this to happen, is it necessary that I should know you at the conscious level? In short, how far are thoughts commonly available to those minds which at least share some receptive areas of similar attitudes in common? And if this is indeed a possiblity, then thoughts may not only travel geographically in one plane of time but may also be held in storage for downwards transmittal to subsequent generations.

Individual memories and minds would thus not only serve the immediate and particular needs of their owners; they would also function as repository and supportive cells in some vast and continuing overall collective mind of the whole of humanity.

In what sets out to be a responsible work, one is hesitant to express ideas so seemingly fanciful as this. Yet one is tempted to do so not only because of the vast range of otherwise inexplicable phenomena they may bring within range of examination but because they give support to Jung's concept of a collective unconscious. This concept certainly requires such an unconscious link between each individual mind and a collective mind-bank.

Extensive research by Jung has drawn attention to the recurrence of common themes in the religions, myths, fairy stories, dreams, and fantasies of people geographically and temporally remote. While attempts can be made to explain away the common factors on rational grounds of common tribal roots and cryptomnesia, such explanations do not account for the fascination which such themes hold. Nor for the fact which Jung and his followers amply demonstrated, that these ideas occur in detailed form in the minds of uneducated individuals who are extremely unlikely to have access to their often obscure recorded sources.

Apart from individual reception of such ideas, certain themes occur widely in quite different cultures. Those concerning the striving of man for rebirth from which he can emerge anew, is a particularly interesting example in the present context. Christ said, 'Except a man be born again, he cannot see the kingdom of God.'

The words might be interpreted as referring to the change which takes place with the mind's freedom from conditioning. David Stafford-Clark* writes:

> This theme of rebirth is indeed universal. It appears in the rites of springtime celebrated in every part of the world, in the myth of the phoenix, in the hopes of every mother about her new-born child, and it forms an essential aspect of all the great religions of mankind. Jung accepted the significance of this fact and recognised that something so universally acknowledged must ultimately have an integral relationship with the whole of life itself. Nor was he surprised to discover that this same idea recurred repeatedly in the symbolised fantasies of patients with mental illness whose contact with external reality has changed, but whose preoccupations became explicable along the lines of this great central channel of human emotion and experience. From its contemplation he was led to discover that innumerable other elaborations of his theme were to be found occurring apparently spontaneously in human minds all over the world.

Jung concluded that the unanimity of common themes was due to their origins in a common reservoir of human experience and repository of human thinking to which each century added an infinitesimal amount of variation. His concept is often illustrated by analogy to a half-submerged chain of mountains or icebergs whose tips represent the conscious mentality of each individual and whose individually submerged parts represent their individual unconscious lives; but whose greater linked mass underwater represents the shared if totally unconscious mental life of humanity as a whole. Jung suggested this collective unconscious contained every hope and fear of mankind, his great and shameful capabilities, his basic thought-patterns or tendencies to apprehend life in terms of basic principals derived from universal experiences dating back over the whole of human experience. He saw the collective unconscious as an autonomous network governing all past experiences and the future potentiality of man. And, as what had not yet come about could not yet be expressed, man glimpsed his potentiality in the form of archetypes or symbolised pictures in his myths and dreams which fascinated him but were not yet understood by him.

* *Psychiatry Today* (Pelican Original, Second Edition, 1963). Penguin Books Ltd. Copyright © David Stafford-Clark, 1963.

Sir Alister Hardy* from his study of zoology has similarly been drawn to ask:

> If it is established that impression of design, form and experience . . . can occasionally be transmitted by telepathy from one human individual to another, might it not be possible for there to be in the animal kingdom as a whole not only a telepathic spread of habit changes, but a general subconscious sharing of form and behaviour-pattern – a sort of psychic 'blueprint' shared between members of a species?
>
> . . . In the scheme I am suggesting a sort of psychic pool of experience would be shared subconsciously by all members of a species by some method akin to what we are witnessing in telepathy. Individual lives, animal 'minds,' would come and go – but the psychic stream of a shared behaviour pattern in the living population would flow on in time parallel to the flow of the physical DNA material . . . it might also be supposed that the 'racial plan,' linking all the members of the race, might gradually change as the character of the population became modified both by the changing environment's external selection and by the development of new behaviour patterns due to the exploring, exploitive, nature of animal life.

Hardy, in speculating on Darwin's idea concerning the survival of the fittest, suggests that evolution may be guided by a principle of selectivity whose true nature has not yet been discovered but which might lie in the direction of that side of man which experiences spiritual feeling, curiosity, and appreciation of beauty.

The evidence for a blueprint begins with animal behaviour. Animals live by instinct or intuition which is triggered off unconsciously because the alternative – a conscious mind – does not appear to exist in animals. They are not taught how to eat, hunt, swim, or reproduce. Humans exhibit similar promptings of instinct and intuition but our unconscious guiding force appears to have wider objectives than merely the provision of the immediate necessities for physical survival and reproduction. It seems to aim at bringing about a natural order of things and developing intuitive ideas regarding ethics and ideals possibly of future forms of society and relationships between individuals and groups to which we may one day realistically aspire. Certainly, humanity as a species seems to have an inbuilt regard for its future – the more remarkably so in that for the

* The Living Stream. Sir Alister Hardy. Collins, 1965.

165

first forty thousand years of its existence, the conditions of its known history and foreseeable future were almost unchanging.

Thus the Ultimate Hypothesis that consciously or unconsciously every man is seeking the goal of self-realisation, appears to involve the corollary that in doing so he may enjoy the support of the collective mind of mankind itself with all its relative omniscience and omnipotence.

Relying upon the concern of this fundamental guiding force to develop its own realisation in the welfare of its units, the future, individual or social, is seen no longer to be dependent upon conscious contrivance but to be aided by acting in concert with, as it were, that bigger mind containing the blueprint for the future course of mankind. The individual mind, when freed from a sufficient degree of conditioning, may even gain conscious access to this collective force and receive knowledge, thoughts, a sense of destiny, and one-ness with the world. Once contact is made with this universal guiding force, the large unconscious chunk of mentality beneath the surface is seen as more responsible for motivating actions than the conscious tip of the iceberg.

This is a similar vision to that of the mystics; it is interesting, however, that we have reached it by a different route from theirs. Whereas they glorify intuitive vision, we have endeavoured to follow the odd factual clues, observations, and reports, to relate them afresh and to piece together from these a picture of life which would make sense of our hopes, our despairs, and the inconsistencies with which we are surrounded in our everyday world.

Today man has reached the point of knowledge of himself where he may see an unconscious drive taking place towards release of mental processes from compulsive attitudes. He would presumably find life easier and happier if he was conscious of what was happening to him, if he could make sense of everyday experience rather than find himself the helpless victim of unconscious forces. Evolution happens whether he helps it or not. The unconscious movement will not be controlled any more than physical healing forces can be prevented from mending a broken limb.

But, one may ask, is mankind as a whole condemned to carry on in a state of conditioned imprisonment until slowly, remorselessly, and over the centuries, his mind evolves into freedom by the normal course of evolution? Or can an individual by his own efforts speed up the operation in respect of himself if not the whole of society? If the latter is indeed feasible, the answer may well be found in a 'natural theology' representing a reconciliation of old religious insights with modern objective observation.

With appreciation of the nature of the problem and the inadequacies of traditional routes of achieving freedom, release will probably become easier in the future for anyone who wishes to undertake the adventure. Furthermore, new inspiration is afforded to life by the realisation that a force is at work outside one's control which is entirely benign.

A potential way to freedom might be constructed by knowing the nature of the objective and the obstacles to be overcome, knowing man and his motives. Thus a natural theology could be formed, as opposed to an intuitive theology filled with mythical and personified figures.

Up to now, man's information about God has come from the subjective revelations of a handful of people whose claims had either to be accepted at face value by the remainder or ignored. However, if the will of God can be equated with the drive of the unconscious towards completion, then access to the mind and will of God can be achieved by methods other than subjective revelation. The rewards hitherto believed to be restricted to the religious in their afterlife might become available to whomever observed himself and his experience of life.

In the course of evolving psychotherapeutic techniques, psychiatrists would appear to have tumbled upon the elements of such a potential route. Conflicting attitudes can demonstratively be changed by methods which bring to consciousness the hidden motives that activate one's way of life. The subject can cease to distort his personality, connive at his own defeats. Development of these techniques has been hampered thus far by their near exclusive professional use for those severely disorientated or wealthy enough to pay for expensive treatment. Extension beyond this sphere has been largely neglected, or where such attempts have been made, lack of professional guidance has often led to the practice of a 'black psychiatry' which may destroy more of an individual's way of life than it constructs. However, the knowledge developed primarily in helping disordered mentalities has thrown light on the normal psychology of everyday living. It can be adapted to assist the 'normal' individual to improve his performance and enjoyment of life, to realise aims and aspirations from which conditioning as a necessary factor in our survival has hitherto held us all in bondage.

In respect of these matters, the Ultimate Hypothesis is a hypothesis of becoming.

9

Religious Man

THE MAJOR RELIGIONS of the world – Christianity, Buddhism, Hinduism, the Islamic and Jewish faiths – cannot all be literally true. Nor is this book concerned with their basis, or otherwise, in 'truth'. The question is irrelevant to our view that they have traditionally provided a means of aiding man's growth towards maturity. We wish to maintain only that forms of faith have become intuitively expressed in words and ritual which are highly symbolic of the later stages of an evolutionary process and provide a vehicle whereby some of its aspirations and destinations can be communicated to man's conscious mind.

Such a view may go far to explain why man regards the 'truth' of religions as important, why he should hold in awe and respect a providence which, while esteemed as omnipotent and omniscient, is still apparently compatible with appalling suffering, terror, and misery, even of innocent children. The matter goes still further. Man may hold a volcano or an atomic explosion in awe. But the more cruel yet sentient being of God should, he urges, not only be held in veneration but actually loved. Recognition of religions as an aid to man's growth may help to put this problem into perspective. For if

169

this is so, and if 'love' is held to mean that which fascinates, then religion and the concept of God may engage the fascination of an individual in the sense that he is apt to become preoccupied with the experiences and emotions they evoke.

In respect of their evolutionary function as vehicles of transmission of certain ideas, the many different religions of the world may well be reconcilable with each other. All are effective and well-adapted instruments to this end, relative to the cultures and times in which they have flourished. The more primitive religions can be seen to perform a similar function at a more elementary level of self-realisation.

Theologians have justified religions on every ground except that of assisting the evolutionary development of man, yet their disciplines may contribute towards this objective even where their followers have no conscious awareness that the content concerns the achievement of freedom.

Interpreted thus, the many different religions of the world become current guides to living, relevant and revealing to the course of everyday life. One religion is not seen as right and the others wrong, but each as a statement related to the same subject in terms of a greater or lesser degree of sophistication. One may imagine a theoretical possibility of arranging them in an ascending order of subtlety.

Besides their original task of helping man identify himself, those of an elementary type can create at least a transient freedom from conditioned reflexes by such means as drugs, fasting, sensory deprivation, and ritualistic dancing. The hallucinations produced by physical or mental stress as well as by drugs appear to break conditioning temporarily and to release mentality to experience events other than those directly attributable to causality. Similarly the so-called miracle-cults open the mind to entertain a wider spectrum through phenomena such as firewalking, handling of poisonous snakes, self-mutilation without apparent pain, and other well authenticated feats that lack explanations of how the normal physical effects are avoided.

More sophisticated religions encourage the gaining of insight. The principle of 'know thyself', a central theme of higher religions, leads directly towards self-realisation by uncovering the causes of one's attitudes. But the usefulness of these religions as a means of assisting an intuitive process has become overlaid by the dogmatic assertions of devotees in their search for truth. Religion perhaps is not so much a revelation of truth in itself as a way to obtain a revelation of truth. Christ said: 'The kingdom of heaven is within you and whosoever knoweth himself shall find it. And, having found it, ye shall know yourselves that ye are sons and heirs of the Father, the Almighty, and shall know yourselves that ye are in God and God in you.' The Roman Catholic practice of confession would lead to a high order of self-knowledge if sincerely conducted on both sides with conscious recognition of its aims. Judaism alone of the higher religions does not emphasise 'know thyself'. But its code of conduct may lead to the same concept of free mind. The mystical religions of the east, far from being esoteric cults, are similar guides. They lay great stress on emptying – or deconditioning – the mind, and see salvation as a release into an unconditioned form of existence. The Islamic faith prescribes 'submission' to the will of Allah, which may be consistent with following the will of the unconscious drive to self-realisation.

Only Taoism, among the oldest of the known religions, stands out in a category separate from the others in so far as its language, if difficult to understand, is nevertheless more directly to the point – and therefore proportionately less comprehensible to the mind of twentieth-century man. This exception points to the necessity for the shape or guise of the other religions. For the Taoist doctrines in their purest forms apparently had a short life of a century or two before deteriorating into Confucianism not unlike the ineffective humanism of today and later, owing to their potency, into forms of black magic. The direct statement can be very ambiguous. Taoism has suffered from this and in consequence one of the earliest and surely one of the greatest religious statements has been described as 'a most beautiful poem but a quite effete and impractical doctrine'. The contrary view might be maintained today; that Taoism is in fact a most effective communication between the unconscious and individual consciousness. What statement could be more practical, more mystical, more disturbing, than this one?

A good fighter does not become angry.
Who well vanquishes the foe does not contend.
Who well uses others renders himself lowly.
This is called the Te of non-contending.
This is called using the strength of man.
The highest goal of antiquity.

Since space does not permit detailed study of more than one religion to illustrate the relevance of its content to the hypothesis that every man is seeking the goal of self-realisation, the central ideas of Christianity will be taken. This is not to regard Christianity as more or less true than other religions or to exclude other interpretations. Christianity is chosen simply because its details are likely to be best known to English readers. From the point of view of the hypothesis, Christianity arose when the mind of man became too sophisticated to accept easily the simpler doctrines of his forebears. Those doctrines had been sufficient to help him part of the way towards self-realisation. But, as he became more and more aware of the apparent inconsistencies in life which they failed to reconcile, he needed a more advanced system of beliefs. Yet the language, terminology, and concepts of mental functioning which he had acquired by two thousand years ago were still hopelessly inadequate to express the goal of the unconscious processes, or, put another way, the will of God.

He had two difficulties at this point to contend with:

1. That of casting off the encumbrance of beliefs and superstitions which had served their purpose in the past but which had nothing to contribute to the future. It has been said that the god of one age becomes the devil of the next; and the inability to discard dream-aspirations beyond their period of validity can, as the Jewish nation has illustrated so terribly, lead only to death and disaster.

2. That of constructing an adequate guide to assist the development of man far beyond his existing state into centuries ahead, the circumstances of which his consciousness could have no comprehension.

No conscious invention could have helped in such a crisis. But evolutionary drives, under sufficient tension and longing, could utilise unconscious intuition. Under sufficient stress the individual mind will break and its perception of the manifestations of reality will disintegrate to reveal other systems and relationships, of relevance to a more ephemeral but possibly more enduring world of ideas and attitudes. Such states of schizoid madness are not apparently as disorientated or as chaotically isolated as they first appeared to observers.

The Jewish nation – under material subjugation by a tyrannical Rome and spiritually dominated by a self-centred deity jealous on the subject of his own attributes to an extent equalled only by a Victorian parent – was perhaps suitably conditioned to undergo a sort of revelation of unleashed intuition on a collective scale.

For centuries there had been current ambiguous prophecies of the coming of the Messiah and, in those circumstances and pressures, what better medium could exist than such a beneficent being upon whom to reflect the contents of expanding, maturing attitudes?

If man's attitudes had benefited by some centuries of civilising experience and growth, the ability to express the new ideas required to bring them to consciousness still did not exist. Ideas which cannot be expressed can, however, be acted out. The action may, in due course, be interpreted in much the same way as the essential significance of other symbolic stories. Such acting out should never be taken literally. Perception of reality has its place. Imagination in all its forms in an essential part of life, but confusion results where one is treated as an experience of the other. If Christianity is breaking down today, it is because before and as well as all else, Christianity is an imaginative intuitive truth which the churches have insisted on treating as historical experience.

Perhaps Christ was a historical fact and perhaps the Gospels are largely an accurate account of the events surrounding him, including the somewhat ambiguous and confusing stories of the miracles and finally the resurrection.

However, it seems unlikely. Apart from anything else, the significance of the overall story is greatly enhanced by the inclusion of certain incidents – the Annunciation, the conversation between Christ and the Devil, the Agony in the Garden – to which by their nature there could have been no witnessing reporters. Although records survive today of many administrative transactions of these and earlier times, none corroborate the Gospel accounts of Christ or connect a living man who may have been named Jesus of Nazareth with the qualities and miracles of a Christ. The existence of some of the disciples is, of course, confirmed. This in itself is quite unsufficient to support the historical authenticity of the events which the Christian churches have always claimed took place. Yet if there is insufficient proof of historical events for the basis of Christian doctrines, there is more than enough support for its intuitive validity. And this latter may be far and away the more important type of evidence in this field.

Christianity is concerned above all to extol the spiritual rather than the materialistic experience of being. How then does it rely so much upon material evidence of its origin?

The story of the birth, life, death, and resurrection of Christ does not accord in any way with our daily experience of the behaviour of material or historical events. Can the story have some other meaning, that is to say, is it true in some other context which is compatible with our experience? Because, if so, it may well be worth while to give up the ideas of its literal accuracy, which add nothing to it but an aura of incredibility, and to accept a more relevant account which is capable of communicating its content on many levels. The content would be interpreted, not so much by the discredited doctrines of theology, necessary only to make a God-in-the-sky plausible, but by the same sort of disciplines as have proved themselves useful in producing order from everyday experience.

The Gospel story as literal truth is inconsistent, confusing, and incompatible with experience. From this point of view, in fact, the new testament has one merit only: it promises possibilities transcending materialism and refers to a state of being different from that with which we are familiar, a state of being which we may hope to attain in due course. This important insight has always been accepted to be bound up implicitly with the historical truth of the Gospels. If the events were true, it is implied, so may be the promises. Therefore, in order not to lose the promises, let us cling desperately to the absurdities of the literal interpretation.

However, we have now reached an age where this course is no

longer acceptable. Rather than swallow the slender indications supporting the Gospels as fact, the present generation would forgo the potentiality of the whole thing. The promises become as impossible as its origin. It is then abandoned and a vain search for a better interpretation of life begins.

Let us abandon instead the idea that the Gospels in the main ever had foundation in fact. After all, the Gospels themselves state that Christ was conceived by a virgin – the claim made of founders of some other religions. We speak commonly enough of the conception of an idea, an inspiration or a poem. By definition, no material being could be conceived by a virgin. But a virgin mind, one which had not accepted the current dogmas of its time, might indeed form a concept of the Christ, the prototype of fully evolved man: man whole. In this event, we could expect the life story to be analogous to the process of realising the innate potentialities in man. In fact the Gospel story lends itself precisely to such an interpretation. It becomes a precise communication from the deepest levels of the basic unconscious mind to the conscious understanding of every individual. The scriptures then tell us not of the life of an historical man or God, but of the present existence of a psychological process for fulfilling the nature of man. They describe a way of liberation, personifying one of the principal elements in it as Jesus Christ. Here is a transitional process, set out in figurative but faithful language, to assist man to his next evolutionary destination. Far from losing the promise contained in the traditional interpretation, this approach brings the Gospel story alive in the present with a reality hitherto lacking. Here the possibilities of the factual equal the mystical in wonder.

Certain sorts of ideas – Jung called them archetypal ideas – have a peculiar fascination for man's imagination. They recur in many variations in his dreams, his legends, and literature. One may speculate that they correspond to certain concepts held by the unconscious mind which have not yet been commonly accepted into consciousness. But the nature of mind structure, by the device of fascination, holds such ideas embodied in some symbol to the forefront until such time as they may be understood.

The legend of Christ is just such an archetypal idea. Fathered by the intuitive process contained in the deepest levels of unconsciousness, the potential of every individual is projected upon a figure – probably by a number of minds simultaneously affected by stresses of the times which could be relieved only by the healing revelation of ultimate truth – so that paradoxically ultimate truth was contained in a present fiction. Yet the authors of this fiction were themselves in all probability unaware of its extent. The story seemed true in that age and in those circumstances; it was said to be true, and it had a fascination which other legends lacked. Jesus of Nazareth may have existed; upon him the concept of Christ was projected. Thus the idea was taken up by other minds – including St Paul's among the first – where it could dwell until its true meaning and significance could become apparent and interpreted for individual guidance.

Thus the integration process was described in the Christian legend not only because it could not be described more directly but also because man had not the tools of thinking to develop a direct statement further and so get full value from it. The Christian legend marked the fruition of processes of intuition and feeling which had been developing for centuries prior to the Christian era. Before the legend could finally come to be seen in all its relevance, the faculty of thought had to develop its techniques of science and objective thinking, without which its significance could not be fully comprehended. For two thousand years, then, the legend lay fallow. Yet because of unconscious awareness of its significance for him, Western man valued it above all other legends, and paid it not only lip-service but built for its glory magnificent monuments, cathedrals, and churches over all the civilised world.

Acceptance of this view is not to denigrate religion, God, or the life hereafter, but to bring them or at least some aspects of them within the range of understanding. Nor does acceptance mean that ideas venerated by the religious are 'nothing but' some sort of psychologising. On the contrary, it is to say that a study of psychology leads us to understand that the basic motivating power of human conduct is an unconscious mental activity bent on piloting our mind-style from one *modus operandi* to a more advanced one, a preliminary to which is a modification of certain attitudes necessary to us in the earlier stages of our evolution and now archaic. The final

176

form cannot be deducted but might be, perhaps, no less than the emergence of consciousness as a life-form in its own right. Material to spiritual life is no greater jump than that already taken by evolution in the production of plants and free-moving animals from inorganic chemicals.

*   *   *

What, by accepting this view, does the Christ legend tell us concerning the psychological processes of becoming, whatever it is mankind's destiny to become?

The essence of the Christ figure is its ability to think in terms and concepts freed from traditional thought patterns. It can take what is useful and discard what has become outmoded to construct an 'action pattern' of behaviour which is adaptable and appropriate to whatever circumstances and environment in which it may find itself situated. The egotistical concerns of vanity and possession, necessary to the immature personality as a stage in its development, are discarded. They are superseded by a wider, more mature outlook in which the opposing interests of self and community are transcended so that one is seen merely as an aspect of the other. The important aspect of this transformation – important because it has been so rarely realised in the past – is that it progresses not by suppression or mere sublimation of the immature attitudes but by transcending them.

The adolescent does not have to make an effort to suppress his earlier childish interests. At a certain stage he simply outgrows them. The same growth occurs in relation to more sophisticated derivatives as the personality passes from the early state of development so typical of *homo sapiens* to a different, more balanced stage of a complete development. If this point is emphasised, it is because so much of value with regard to the symbolic significance of the Christian legend has been lost by the churches' insistence on the practice of suppression of what they have styled 'sin' and what more accurately could be termed immature ego pursuits.

The birth of Christ symbolises the coming to consciousness of the 'concept' of the whole or reborn man, the coming into operation in one mind of the four faculties of perception, intuition, feeling, and thinking. The life of Christ is symbolic of the process of learning to live with the action of these four faculties, which, in the end destroy or mentally crucify the previous way of living and the attitudinal structure on which it was based. The 'concept' as such must give way to something more realistic. It must in its turn die so that the warring faculties may be reconciled and transcended in a resurrection of the final personality. The journey out and return will have been completed.

The deconditioning which allows the four faculties to come simultaneously into operation arises primarily from insights gained through self-knowledge. Such insight occurs when fears of personal inadequacy are overcome sufficiently to permit the subject to see himself in relation to others with some objective accuracy. In seemingly few, this ability occurs at least to some degree naturally. More often it is cultivated by following a discipline consciously expected to lead to some other goal. Nevertheless, however the insight comes about, the ideas of the personality concerned are 'reborn' and the new personality emerging is symbolised by the Christ child.

At first the difference between this new personality and the 'once-born' must necessarily be concealed. Animals which are born conspicuously different from their fellows, even if superior in some respect, are frequently killed by them. *Homo sapiens* will tolerate some types of difference but positive evolutionary changes are not likely to be acceptable. Herod set out to kill the Christ child, who had to be removed to Egypt, a land of more primitive religion that would presumably not fear or interfere with him. The reborn personality which does not conceal its changed outlook is likely at best to be ridiculed; at worst, to be put away as deranged.

In the early stages, then, the new-born personality must, like the Christ child, hide its new identity and proceed quietly about its business in the former way while learning to operate inconspicuously but effectively in harmony with the once-born. All the time it is tempted to reveal the power of its liberated mind, its ability to perceive the relationships between things and people accurately, to foresee and prophesy future events by means of its insight into the implications of present circumstances. Knowing the motivation and

178

direction of the unconscious urges of others, it has little difficulty in fascinating and persuading them to follow it into enterprises of its choosing. Since it sheds only slowly the remnants of its original motivations of vanity and possessiveness, such enterprises are, at least in the early stages, more likely to be concerned with these things than with the general advancement of humanity.

Influential figures of history – Hitler, Napoleon, Joan of Arc, some of the saints and martyrs – may be interpreted in terms of the reborn personality which has gone awry and failed to withstand the temptations mythically offered to Christ by the devil on the mountain.

As time goes on, the Christ figure sheds the remnants of its predeliction for vain gain and profit. It discovers instead in the midst of plenty, a barren wilderness of isolation. Essentially alone, it has few concerns or interests in common with those of its former friends or relations. It sees the world and its inhabitants in the process of becoming – as it has itself by now partially become – pursuing an endless variety of activities, occupations, games, entertainments, arts, so-called vices and virtues. These activities have one deep and constant motivation only, the conveyance of some needed particle of unconscious realisation which may modify an attitude out of harmony with other attitudes.

From this universal pattern the future stretches forward as distinct as the path lies behind. As acceptance of the new condition grows and previous identity is at last forgotten, the absorbing ability to be taken up in the trivial fades into the scale of the eternal. A new interest and motivation arises. Henceforward one may act in furtherance of the unconscious and its aims. One may aid the Becoming, and, in so doing, achieve a degree of peace and quietness of mind.

The art of such aiding is something to be learnt. This sort of learning and the digesting of the experience from which the learning derives, is the true business of the reborn personality. Henceforth the Christ figure must be preoccupied with the evolution of others. But how is this precisely to be done? Its mind has the capacity for thought, feeling, perception, and intuition, and the fruits of any of these faculties are available – if the inclination was there. But since God, or the unconscious, has by this time revealed itself, normal human inclinations which originate from the process of becoming are no longer active. The overriding concern is for others.

The first idea that may occur to the initiate is that the communication from the unconscious to contemporary consciousness might be conveyed in words. The Word, that is, can be preached. That would seem a pleasant solution. The comfortable existence of surrounding, respectful disciples has something gratifying to the remnants of former tastes for vanity or tycoonery. Inevitably, that appears to be a solution compatible with the tastes of all parties. Yet preaching is not the answer. Words result in an intellectual understanding which is different from, and by no means so important as, the emotional acceptance derived from experiential learning. The way to integration cannot be taught by anything less than example. The well-founded initiate is not slow to realise this. Unfortunately the temptations to remain a preacher are considerable, and the majority of those who reach this stage would seem to have insufficient integrity to pass to the next.

The Christ legend, however, illustrates the setting of a particular example. The example is not confined to the throwing-down of temples and the flouting of the establishment as the present generation seems intuitively to believe. Rather, the example is: firstly, of following motives dictated by the deepest levels of unconsciousness and serving its purpose, selflessly content to risk the consequences, which is quite different from following out obsessional conduct arising from compulsions; secondly, of acting in accordance with a perspective and viewpoint which owes little to previous thought.

These two qualities are likely always to be present at this stage in the initiate's action, though the type of action itself is likely to be very different according to the period of history, its needs, customs, difficulties, and circumstances.

The following of Christ today is not likely to entail repetition of a literal crucifixion if that gesture is recognised as having filled its purpose once and for all. The sequence of events which led to the crucifixion and the agony on the cross did more than bring the Christ legend to the forefront of human attention and hold it there for two thousand years. They also serve as a warning to the initiate, one who has come so far as the rebirth but not yet undergone the symbolic crucifixion and resurrection, the outward journey but not the return, that the matter is not so simple as the relinquishing of conduct to the Unconscious, or to God. Examples may be negative as well as positive.

For God and/or the unconscious forces have their own purpose to fulfil and will happily sacrifice the individual to their ends. Humanity's business is to reconcile God and man, consciousness with unconsciousness, and to give to each only its just rights in relation to the other. The following of the dictates of the unconscious wholly and uncritically is as lopsided and disastrous a commitment as to follow out the Messianic, materialistic, and isolationist behests of the ego. Both are to be harnessed and used in tandem by a self which, at some point, transcends conscious forces, by a personality which in due course supersedes the original once-born personality.

This interpretation of the Christ legend has referred to the symbolic crucifixion as a stage through which the initiate must pass on his way to complete fulfilment of the new or resurrected personality. For the individual in the process of becoming needs to pass on from the comparatively comfortable status of the master of respectful disciples to that of leader or exemplar and to do so in unprecedented ways which, although they may satisfy conscious criteria, owe nothing to conscious processes of analysis, contrivance, and prescription for their formulation.

The crucifixion is a recurring symbol because it lends itself to interpretation in so many ways: as the destruction of the personality's former ideals and aspirations; as the polarisation of the welfare of his ego as opposed to community interests; and of the preservation of traditional roots as opposed to the needs of future man. Thus the crucifixion further represents the stretching of the victim as a result of the material weight of his body and its obedience to gravitational force, between diametrically opposite limbs of the cross. Such too is the distressing labour of the initiate as he tries to reconcile, in his conduct and way of life, the capabilities he has recently acquired of thought and perception on the one hand and feeling and intuition on the other. A move towards one inevitably brings sharp reminder of offence towards the other. Frustration and bewilderment prevail for months, perhaps years. The urgency of the life-force dictates

181

Vanity
possessiveness = defeat

movement, struggle, the outcome of vanity and possessiveness always ending in humiliations and defeat. After so much promise, so much endeavour, progress and exhilaration, and at length having arrived at the ultimate testing point of his convictions, could all his aspirations in the end be crucified? Must the materialism of common sense after all enjoy its dreary mundane triumph? Why has the unconscious force which supported him for so long with so much display of superhuman synchronicity, now deserted him? And at this point the initiate's ideas of himself must be sacrificed. The concepts most dear to him are given up; all secret pride in achievement is over. That is the business known in mystic literature as the Long Night of the Soul.

Long
Night
of
The Soul

Afterwards a stillness comes down and, the death of every ego motivation and appetite accomplished, the resurrection can take place. The New Man can go his way; his teaching, his intervention in affairs, is not by the former methods. His potential is in every man and therein lies the old intuition of equality, for in this all are equal. His existence is perhaps consciously unknown to the world at large. Nevertheless, he in some degree activates that potential and brings a little nearer the completion of the evolution of the species.

evolution
of
the species
of
man

Such then is the briefest outline of that interpretation of the Christ legend, which stands in no need of the possibility of historic truth and holds out no less promise than the orthodox.

Christ remains the Son of God, the product of the unconscious acting upon the Virgin, i.e. uncommitted, mind. He is the Son of Man, the descendant of *homo sapiens*, the next form of life to emerge. He is the Saviour, for without this concept we are nothing but the outcome of a random process of chance events with no satisfactions except those of material appetites and with no better alternative to the present than the oblivion of sleep and death. If such were the case, it would indeed be better, even for the richest and happiest of us, if he had never been born.

At the present time, the extinction of desire for that which we normally consider pleasurable may not be regarded as a reasonable incentive to undertake the process of becoming, Nevertheless, it is only when the self is no longer driven by wants and desires that its tensions are resolved and freedom from suffering gained. The change is in fact worthwhile and has attractions of its own, but these are difficult to comprehend from the starting point. Should a currant in the baking then perceive the final cake? The pursuits and interests of elders are incomprehensible to a child; in the same manner the satisfaction of a different state of life may be incomprehensible to the normal adult. *"Through a glass, dimly"*

* * *

It has taken two thousand years of development of language and the mechanics of thinking, to say nothing of the growths of such *language thinking* disciplines as anthropology, biology, physics, and paleontology, before a formulation of any interpretation such as this could become possible. And if the original story of Christ was not historically true, who was its author? The answer surely is that the story emanated from the collective unconscious as soon as the state of civilisation was ripe for it, as it was needed and as the beauty of its terms could be appreciated. Whoever the author or authors were, they owe more to this collective phenomena than to their own individual imaginations. Mechanically, the concept of Christ grew up, like a rumour, put together by hearsay, and maybe attached to a suitable subject such as Jesus of Nazareth who, like so many others, succeeded in getting himself condemned to death. And if that man fell far short of the divinity of the Christ, at least he provided a channel for intuitive processes to project upon him their knowledge of the future destiny of man and the way of his next steps up the ladder of evolving life.

The Jews were right in rejecting him as the promised Messiah; the Christians were right in worshipping the subject of the legend as something more than human, in persisting in their acceptance of him in spite of the irrationality and inconsistencies of their doctrine. But the Jewish Messiah and the Christian Jesus will in the long run be seen as one and the same – the intuitive message from the unconscious understanding regarding the future of man.

* * *

To what extent do the implications of such an interpretation affect

183

existing church ritual, symbolism, and forms of worship? The acceptance of a symbolic rather than a historic Christ may affect them little if at all. Many aspects of the Christian faith, at least as propounded by the Church, have existed long before the date put upon the birth of Christ. They arose and persisted because they are symbols which the unconscious tries to convey to the conscious mind: the cross, the duality of bread and wine, the figure of Judas Iscariot, twelve disciples, and the sacrifice of the God King. These become more meaningful, not less, because they are constituents of mind as opposed to accidental, isolated historical facts. The New Testament story, by this interpretation, is not something which happened once, two thousand years ago, but the essence of a drama waiting to take place in the life of every living person on his or her way to the full realisation of individuality. It is a long, isolated, incommunicable transition to which few consolations will be found outside the ritual serenity and music of the churches. The fact that prayer is offered not so much to the individual's personification of an unpredictable God figure as to an unconscious mind which can be felt at work deep within oneself, does not lessen the numinous quality of worship nor remove the fact that its basic essential is our relationship to an unfolding evolutionary pattern, pre-existent to humanity and unchanging in its nature. Leaving aside the mawkish triviality of the themes of Victorian hymns, the ritual of the different churches is well designed to give expression to the growth of this relationship and to our understanding and acceptance of Christ's teaching, as indeed one would expect since so much has necessarily been owed to intuition.

On the other hand, the literal interpretation of the Christ story inevitably leads to inconsistency and disagreement between different churches. J S Bezzant*, Dean of St John's College, Cambridge, outlines as the literal interpretation of Christian belief:

> Traditional Christianity has what was known as the scheme of salvation. It was based on scripture regarded as the verbally inspired record of Divine revelation; and the scheme as a whole, but by no means all included in it, stands or falls with that view of the Bible. The Pauline teaching on sin and salvation was elaborated into a science containing

* *Objections to Christian Belief.* J S Bezzant (One of four authors). Constable. 1963.

elements of Aristotelian science and the theology of St Augustine. It began with an alleged rebellion of Satan against God in which angels fell. By direct acts of God, Adam and Eve were created, apparently as adults, not only innocent but fully righteous. Their descendants were intended to restore the number of angels depleted by heavenly revolt. Moved by envy, Satan persuaded our first parents to disobey one absolute command of God, that they were not to obtain knowledge, and so brought about their fall from original righteousness, in consequence of which they transmitted to all their offspring, by natural generation, a corrupted nature wholly inclined to evil, an enfeebled will, and also the guilt of their sin. Thus all mankind lay under the curse of sin, both original and actual, justly the object of Divine wrath and destined to damnation. In order to restore his thwarted purpose, God sent his Son, who, assuming human nature, was born on earth, whereon was wrought the drama of his death and resurrection. Jesus, pure from all defect of original and actual sin, alone fulfilled the conditions of a perfect sacrifice for human sin.

By this God's legitimate anger with guilty mankind was appeased and his honour satisfied; he was graciously pleased to accept his Son's sacrifice, enabled to forgive sin, and man was potentially redeemed. The Christian church, a Divine corporation, came into being; those baptised into it who by grace persevered in the fulfilment of its commands would be secure in life to come. From the supernatural life of the church, the world and history derived their meaning and without it would at the last day perish by fire. This would happen when the unknown number of souls required to replace the fallen angels was complete. The Anglican Prayer-book office for the burial of dead still prays that God may be pleased shortly to accomplish the number of the elect and to hasten his kingdom. The dead would be raised from their graves in their bodies despite St Paul's clear assertion that flesh and blood cannot inherit the kingdom of God nor corruption incorruption. The saved were destined to their salvation by an inscrutable decree of God, not by any merits of their own, but solely for those of Christ. As to the fate of the rest, there were differences of opinion, but it was generally held that they would suffer endless torment in the flames of hell, by which climax not only would God's power and justice be finally vindicated but heaven's bliss intensified.

*   *   *

Our hypothesis implies that one may teach primarily by example, for, although precepts have their place, they are in vain unless illustrated by the conduct of the preacher in the essence of his

185

freedom to
become

Imitation
of virtue
before
TRUE
motivation
exists

everyday life. There is no virtue in virtue in so far as it is adopted as part of a socially acceptable or envied *persona*. Virtue is descriptive of the conduct of the mature man who is free to act in any way he pleases, who has grown out of childish things yet become as a child. The liberated man has more absorbing interests than the pursuit of vicious habits. This is a truth the churches have hardly appreciated. Because virtue is a characteristic of integration, they assume the adoption of virtuous behaviour will bring the subject a stage nearer to integration. When a car travels at 50 miles per hour, the speedometer points to the '50' mark. But if the car is standing still, it is obviously futile to try to make the wheels move by adjusting the speedometer so that the finger points to 50 mph. Imitation of virtue before a true motivation towards virtue exists is no less futile. Probably this vain endeavour more than any other single aspect of their disciplines is reducing the churches to impotence.

Finally, tempting as it may be to churchmen and laity alike, there can be no maturing, at least past the elementary induction stages, by retreating from the normalities of life as it has to be lived by those who contribute to and perpetuate the existence of their species. The celebate life of good works, austerity, acceptance, and self-sacrifice lived in a community pridefully or even ambitiously pledged to these things has little in common with the suffering of experience of living. Mortification, deprivation of instinct, and meditation upon saints may in the best circumstances only create a state of psychic tension where the subject meets face to face his particular god. There he may realise that his cherished illusions and delusions are imaginative and symbolic rather than factual. There he may defeat all the teachings he has formerly so eagerly absorbed. The *Bhagavad Gita* says that those who feel the need to renounce wordly actions are still inwardly attached to them. Anyone genuinely unattached to the fruits of actions may mix in the world with equanimity.

Religion has provided the major traditional channel whereby the subject might hope to establish communication between the two isolated functions of conscious mind and collective unconscious. If it has not been a very effective channel, it has been the best available pending the development of language and thought concepts which would permit the construction of a better one. If the subject matter of religion is not historically based, it is nevertheless still and always symbolic of a reality of a deeper, more wonderful, and indeed even more miraculous nature than the limited insights which can be contained in theological language. Expressed in this idiom, the second coming of Christ is indeed imminent. And as before, he will appear in the least expected place in the least expected guise. As the Son of Man he is the potential in every man, even in his own lifetime. Wherever the seed falls on fertile ground, each man may come sooner or later to rebirth, crucifixion, and resurrection.

10

Travelling
Man

THE EXPANSION OF consciousness may reasonably be supposed to be one, if not the principal, objective of a continuing stream of evolution. The possessor of the 'most expanded' consciousness is not likely, however, to prove the fittest to survive. The extent of expansion is probably less important than the ability to integrate its accompanying insights with existing modes of life, thereby avoiding any of the sharp deviations abhorred by nature.

Thus the expansion of consciousness, if it is to serve any useful purpose, will take place in distinct or discrete stages – no development of individual potential into actuality occuring until the insights have been taken up and incorporated into the habitual behaviour pattern of the individual concerned. The problems of landing a man on the moon were not simply those of transporting him there but of training him and bringing him back. The expansion of human potential likewise appears to entail a training or initiation, an outward journey and a return.

Many legends of earlier times, particularly those of the Greeks, may be accepted as intuitive statements of an instinctive urge which their authors sensed within themselves, to undertake some outstanding feat. They depicted this urge in many and various ways which could be understood in terms of the circumstances of their times – even though these ways lay outside the boundaries of their day-to-day experiences. Their common theme was a journey outwards, the Odyssey, the quest for the Golden Fleece, later to become the Holy Grail or precious object; and the journey home. The preparation was itself difficult; the journey outwards more so; and the journey home most difficult of all.

Of what do these legends speak? Our Ultimate Hypothesis suggests that man's fundamental preoccupation underlying all else he does impels his imagination to reflect the development of both himself as an individual and his species as an evolving life-form. We might then expect that unconsciously he would be led to relate stories analogous of the evolutionary journey on which he is always engaged. If such legends do in fact reflect the processes involved in the expansion of consciousness and the subsequent integration into the whole personality of this new content, representing it as a picaresque journey, we may learn a good deal about it from the nature of the incidents occurring on the way. From these clues and other observations, we are possibly for the first time in history able to describe the journey of travelling man – or the realisation of human potential – in terms more direct than those of religion, myth, and allegory. We may also experiment with and explore possible means of expediting the journey.

The preparation stage consists of comprehending the origins of personal motivation. While one ostensibly possesses some socially acceptable and rational objective, it comes as a revelation to find that in some cases this immediate objective conceals a deeper need with which the subject may have some difficulty in coming to terms.

The outward journey starts when the initiate has developed effective ways of observing himself and his behaviour in a detached manner. The journey continues as the attitudes constituting the personality are gradually dismembered, freeing the underlying unconscious energies to go to work to bring about fresh points of view.

The distance of the journey will vary enormously, depending on how far the subject wants and feels the need to go, how great his capacity for courage, curiosity, and detachment. He may venture only far enough to throw light on a particular problem, or sufficiently along the way to reform his whole life, or indeed to see visions of a

190

new universe which could transform the lives and thinking of others, perhaps of all mankind.

Whatever the means used as a vehicle for the journey, the individual must unlearn much of the universal, social, and personal conditioning which formed a necessary but temporary structure in his preceding years: the suggestions and habitual thought-patterns inevitably imposed upon him by living in the human condition; the social ideals of the community in which he was brought up; and the conduct examples and attitudes displayed towards him by his immediate family.

The difficulties of the undertaking lie in initiating the start and recognising the furthest point of the journey where the turn must be made and where inflationary urges are especially experienced. So long as the energies thereby set free can be held and controlled, they may continue to exercise their stimulus on whatever comes within their orbit. But if the personality and stability of the subject are insufficient to contain his own reactions to insights and thoughts unfamiliar to him in their range, power, and potential, he may become inflated and disorientated. For he can digest only as much as his capacity and humility permit.

The situation is analogous to that of the man who all his life has subsisted at the lower end of the income range and suddenly finds himself possessor of a fortune. When choice in ways of life is open for him, luxuries from yachts to mansions may be had for the asking. Nevertheless, most of us, in such circumstances, would find the greatest difficulty in adjusting our conduct to a manner appropriate to the privilege and authority so newly acquired. Not uncommonly, initial good fortune brings about ultimate disaster. Similarly the sudden capacity of an unschooled, undisciplined ego to exercise abilities hitherto unknown to it, may lead to its being carried away in an excess of ill-chosen and ill-directed projects. Although these often have the ostensible purpose of helping others, they are likely in fact to be motivated by a subconscious desire for self-glorification to compensate for previous obscurity. This state of inflation sometimes is accompanied by a limited amount of recognition so that the subject lives out his new career happy in the thought that he has been a fulfilled and successful man. However it may be that had he res-

191

trained his initial impulse and modified his motivations sufficiently to
penetrate further to the next stage, he would have realised how far
he had still to travel before he could account himself successful in
any overall sense. More often, to act on early impulse brings frustration and failure, a lesson hard learnt. The subject must wearily
extricate himself as best he may before he can go forward to the
realisation of dreams more wonderful than any associated with the
trivialities of the ego-glorification of kings and dictators, film and
pop-stars, and other such heroes of the adulation of a publicity-
absorbing, adolescent public.

Beyond this point and as the mind is emptied of its compulsive or
obsessional ideas and preoccupations with its own satisfactions, the
zenith of the journey may be reached. Firstly, the mind becomes able
to use its capacity to develop ideas hitherto unacceptable to it, to
examine them with interest and curiosity, to appreciate their quality
and relationships with other ideas. This becomes possible when the
mind has overcome its adolescent concern to classify ideas in a system
of familiar categories such as favourable or destructive to one's
particular way of life. Secondly, the mind becomes receptive to
concepts so different from the familiar that it seems they must
originate from sources other than those of immediate sensory perception or forgotten memory. The mind, when devoid of personal
preoccupations, appears to act much as a radio-receiver, picking up
thoughts and images unrelated to the immediate circumstances and
experience of the thinker.

The source of these insights, fantasies, and visions could be
theorised to be the accumulated library of experience in the collective
unconscious. In this view, the sum of the experience of mankind has
amassed there, accounting for the survival of progress before written
records came into existence. Imitation and example are responsible
certainly in part but perhaps not in total for the handing on of
progress among man's primitive ancestors over thousands of years.
An idea, once held in one mind, may be transmitted to the unconscious memory store of others so that experience is never lost but
passed down from one generation to another. From unconscious
storage, the fund's products may flow out again to produce ideas,
dreams, fantasies, and often great imaginative inspiration in the

192

minds of those freed to a sufficient degree from conditioning and self-centred drives.

The possibility of the existence of such a fund beyond awareness is evidenced by the many demonstrations that memories inaccessible to consciousness do endure somewhere in the unconscious mind of the individual because they can be retrieved under hypnosis and under certain drugs. Further evidence is provided by the manner that dreams, fantasies, and disordered mentality throw up mythologic images of which the subject has no apparent conscious fore-knowledge. Among the cases cited by Jung, as quoted by Josef Goldbrunner in *Individuation**:

> A man in his thirties suffered a good deal from hallucinations. In his quiet hours he was allowed to walk around freely in the corridor. Jung once met him there, blinking out of the window at the sun and moving his head backwards and forwards in a curious fashion. He at once took the doctor by the arm and said he wanted to show him something: if he blinked and looked into the sun he would be able to see the sun's penis. Whenever he moved his head backwards and forwards, the sun's penis moved too and that was the origin of the wind. Jung noted this in 1906. During the year 1910 he was pursuing mythological studies. There chanced to fall into his hands an edition of the so-called Paris Magic Papyrus, which is thought to be a liturgy of the cult of Mithras. It contains a series of directions, invocations and visions. One of these visions is as follows: 'In a similar way the pipes become visible, which are the origin of the serviceable wind. For you will see what looks like a tube hanging down from the orb of the sun, towards the Western regions, as though it were an endless East wind. But when the die is cast to the other wind that blows in the Eastern regions, the vision will turn that way too.' Obviously this is based on the idea that the windstream blows through pipes from the sun. The patient's vision in 1906 and the text that was first published in 1910 are, Jung argues, sufficiently distinct in time for even the possibility of cryptomnesia on the part of the patient or thought transference on the part of the doctor to be quite out of the question. The evident parallelism between the two visions is undeniable. But Jung is also able to refute the assertion that the similarity is purely accidental. If this were in fact the case it would be impossible to establish connexions with analogous conceptions or an inner meaning in the vision. Jung is able, however, to point to quite similar representations in medieval paintings.

* *Individuation*. Josef Goldbrunner. Erich Wewel Verlag, Munich, Germany.

At the stage of the journey where archaic imagery and symbolic drives are presented to the subject's conscious mind by unfolding unconscious, it is important he succeeds in relating them to the tangible reality of his circumstances before they become so powerful as to pass forever beyond his control. One may surmise that minds open to the reception of too much power have over the centuries been eliminated by hazards peculiar to their state. Hence the realisation of potentials accompanied by unfamiliar sensations of omnipotence and omniscience, at this stage so likely to be misconstrued, is best limited to the comparatively small doses which can be tolerated by the average run of mortals. Thus the expression of man is limited by the bounds of individual vanity.

Once a subject can comprehend the relationship between these insights and the circumstances of his own situation, then he will be content to embark on the return journey. This understanding is the end, aim, and object of the outward journey. When he started out, though, he did not pause to ask what he would do with the visions of the kingdom, the sensations of omnipotence and omniscience, which he had associated with the expansion of consciousness. The business of how to obtain these insights seemed more important than the other questions of how to interpret their fruits into suitable activities in his everyday life. Yet this can be the only valid reason for which such a journey is made.

The understanding of these insights and their use must be complete. An undertaking of this sort cannot be carried out in the manner in which the facts of an academic subject are intellectually grasped but the emotions left untouched. One must dually experience and accept the process emotionally and intellectually for any real change to take place. We may know something is 'true' but we can remain unconvinced still. We know that one day we shall die. Yet few of us act consistently with that knowledge even at an age when the matter would logically be an urgent one. Intellectual without emotional knowledge of the existence of something hitherto known as God can still be as meaningless in influencing our emotional behaviour as the twelve-times table. Any doctrine, to become part of our lives, must be capable of complying not with intellect alone but also with the mind's other three mental faculties: feeling, perception,

194

Absolute Truth must satisfy
4 sets of criteria – feeling, perception, thought,
intuition.

TRAVELLING MAN

and intuition. This satisfaction of all four separate sets of criteria is
in fact the acid test of 'truth' in the absolute sense.

ought

ought not

The final stage of the return journey consists in reassembling the
type of logical and emotional structure once with such difficulty
broken down. On the outward journey, the conditioned code of
'ought' and 'ought not' was necessarily unlearned. The structure of
society and its educational processes have mostly been built up in
order to contain the free, untrammelled activities and instincts of
uncivilised man in civilised, conventional channels where he can
operate together in large bodies. These conventions have, however,
frozen man's development. Their overthrow sets energy free. The
way out therefore demands he forget them. But having drawn fresh
nourishment from the atavistic state which is experienced at the
zenith of the outward journey, he must again harness his intellect
and use it to relate to everyday life in order to make sense of the
chaos of potential he has encountered. He must find how these
insights apply to the circumstances of his life. Which are important?
How can they be brought out of chaos and usefully employed in the
present context? A new stable structure and standard – for the
individual or the larger view of society – must be built up, but with
a difference. Attitudes are reconstellated. A new system of freedoms
and sanctions comes to prevail, superseding the previous one and
acting as a guide to others who may need to work in this field
without having to repeat once again all the hazards of the earlier
journey for themselves.

Journey
Back

The journey back is on the whole more perilous than the journey
out. Indeed we simply do not know if anybody has been to the limits
of expanded consciousness and got back safely to integrate this
experience in the course of normal human operations. Unless one is
careful, it is soon apparent that one may be carried away by misin-
terpretation of the insights or led into a split existence where part of
the personality carries on a dreary everyday round while the other
part is off somewhere in a detached fantasy. In such instances, the
two worlds fail to meet.

schizophrenia

The states of enlightenment and ecstasy described in mystic
literature may be the experience of coming into contact with the
universal force of the collective unconscious. But the authors use a

self-defeating amount of exaggeration and obscurity – for instance, describing the experience as granted by divine intervention – that they destroy the credibility of their case. Since they have some knowledge of religious teachings, they believe that they have undergone a religious experience. Yet the experience might not in fact be of religion but of unfettered unconsciousness which is both exhilarating and terrifying. The unaccountable sensations of power and enlightenment, being different from anything hitherto known to the personality, would naturally be felt as derived from outside and might be expressed as establishing communion with gods, devils, angels, and saints, for want of other terms.

Many of the delays and difficulties met with in the outward journey provide experience which will be essential if the return is to be accomplished safely. The instant enlightenment provided by drugs and some other techniques yield insight of a sort, but such insight is highly difficult or even impossible to relate to reality. Tourist trips may provide entertainment but rarely give more than a superficial view of a country.

Return requires capacity for limitation, the ability to sacrifice one's immediate aggrandizement to attend to the needs of others. Return takes every ounce of the sort of moral self discipline which it was so necessary to shed on the outward way. It calls for the ability to adapt to different circumstances so that what was appropriate before is inappropriate now; what was death before now brings light and growth.

The further an individual has gone, the less can anyone else's experience help to guide him on his return. Whereas before he was concerned to satisfy himself, now he may feel a mission to sacrifice himself for the common good. A balance must be arrived at where one's own welfare is given at least the same value as, and is impartially related to, the welfare of others. As self-centred drives which represented a compensation for what was feared to be inadequacy gradually disappear, so too do the differences between 'I' and 'thou.' Since there is no longer a need to safeguard myself at your expense, a basic tenderness for others and an urge to work for the overcoming of the obstacles impeding their progress surges up and demands satisfaction as urgently as sexual craving and physical hunger.

196

A sufficient change of attitudes to achieve at least a partial degree *integrating* *wisdom* of self-realisation takes place sometimes, but by no means predictably, *+* under great emotional stress where strong enough to initiate a review *behaviour* of past outlooks. It may also occur as a result of self-knowledge arising from prolonged psychotherapy or following philosophical or religious doctrines with sufficient sincerity to involve the sacrifice of former ideals, opinions, or ambitions.

Much exploration and groundwork remains to be done to discover a safe, complete, and objectively directed system to speed up the process of integrating wisdom with behaviour.

The undertaking is necessarily an open-ended one. Not the least difficulty is that of coupling it to any objective sufficiently explicit to be useful in specifying an approach. Whatever method in the long run proves most effective, we believe it will rely mainly on the enhancement of self-knowledge and self-recognition. The varieties at present in use include psychotherapeutic techniques, group methods derived from them, yoga, meditation, Zen Buddhism, and certain other religious practices. The importance, sequence, combination, or futility of such techniques will vary tremendously according to the backgrounds, needs and present personality development of the individual. Indication of mental disorder might well increase both the potential and the dangers. The collaboration of an experienced psychiatrist might afford, but by no means ensure, some mitigation of the perils.

The question of one's identity – the personal implications of the age-old philosophical question 'Who am I' – is far more complex on examination than one might at first suppose:

> Court examiner: First we'd like you to tell us who you are.
> Witness: My name is Hall, Rodney Hall.
> Examiner: I didn't ask your name. Listen to my questions carefully. Who are you?
> Witness: I am a doctor.
> Examiner: No. No. Try again. I don't want to know your profession. Who are you?
> Witness: Very well, I am a man, aged 40 years, brown hair, brown eyes . . .
> Examiner: No. I don't want a description of you. Try again. Who

197

are you? Do you know what I mean by the question? What does it mean?

Witness: It means you want to know about me.

Examiner: Right! Splendid! And what should I want to know about you?

Witness: My name, my profession, my description.

Examiner: Nothing else?

Witness: I don't see what else I can answer.

Examiner: Are you exactly the same, in every way, as many other beings?

Witness: No, not exactly.

Examiner: Certainly you are not. So tell us, in what way are you different? In what is your own unique identity?*

The main features which initially distinguish one personality from another are his characteristic attitudes which have resulted from his particular upbringing and circumstances. If he becomes aware of these and their causes, he will know the reasons for his particularity: why he pursues his particular activities, where his behaviour is leading to, how and why he will react to particular situations. He escapes from the subjective approach to problems – I see this as such – to the objective where he sees himself reacting to a problem in a particular way because he is a particular sort of person. Given this self knowledge, he becomes free from his one particular approach to life and open to many others.

Reflection and distortion

The difficulty of getting a true estimation of oneself is that a large area of self-knowledge is distasteful in the light of the sort of person one hopes or pretends to be. Wishfully one blanks out such knowledge. Consciousness cannot criticise itself any more than a man can see his own face except in a mirror. Neither can consciousness experience itself except as reflected in its own actions and attitudes. The reflection is liable to distortion and a technique is essential in order to obtain a clear view as from outside oneself.

For example, Gerald was brought up by a stern father after his mother died when he was three. The father was a difficult man, isolated to a degree and unwilling to display emotion. When the mother had made a suicide attempt, the father's chief concern was not so much for her but to protect himself from professional disgrace

* *Kraepelin's Patient.* David S. Jeans. 1973.

which he feared would ensue. It may be surmised that Gerald was deprived of the normal attention and kindness of both parents. In the only years when his mother was alive, she was unable in the circumstances to give Gerald his due because of her own problems, including the lack of reassurance from her husband.

Gerald, in adult life, was asked as an exercise in self-knowledge how far he recognised those characteristics which differentiated him from the next man. He acknowledged that he had broken up his marriage. He felt he had an appreciation of the arts and a certain urbanity in company.

It was pointed out to him that although he had always known the facts of his childhood, he had not realised their importance nor how they had influenced his behaviour and made him the sort of man he was. His apparently commonplace observations about himself regarding the arts and his behaviour in company provided keys to unravelling his particularity.

Under objective examination, his admiration for the arts appeared to be limited to superficial exclamations of approval rather than critical appraisal related to a system of standards. His talkativeness in company appeared obsessive. He could not abide sitting through a silence. He behaved in fact as if unwittingly he was still trying to attract attention to himself – the attention which was his right as a child and of which he was deprived, leaving him emotionally unsatisfied and seeking ever more to correct the imbalance. Exclamations about the arts and animated talking are more socially acceptable than direct attention-getting and table-thumping. Once Gerald started observing his reactions to inattention on the part of others, how much he hated silence for instance, he was able to see how his early experience had created his particular character. His inability to make the normal concessions to others because they were never made to him in childhood can be dispersed by the realisation of the causes for their absence. It is not that he is in some way an inferior being but that those who should have given him their love and confidence were unable to do so. No longer need he exist in isolation or seek attention as a substitute for the give and take of relationships.

This type of analysis of oneself is hazardous and hard of

honest
witness

achievement without the aid of what, for want of a better term, we shall call an 'honest witness' in preference to master, guru, teacher, instructor, or guide. An 'honest witness' is one who can be trusted by the explorer to provide a stable-reference-point for him; to offer reassurance when it is needed on the journey; to encourage the receptivity and balance that enables the subject to contain self-knowledge; to demonstrate the procedure of gaining self-knowledge in order that it may be understood; to report the outward manifestation of change which the traveller is inwardly undergoing.

The prerequisite of the 'honest witness' is that he should have a genuine concern for the welfare of the explorer. Ideally, he should have some knowledge of the objectives of the project and of depth psychology, including dream theory and the analysis of motivation. To the extent that he does not have the qualifying, first-hand experience of travel and exploration himself, the experiment will be that much more hazardous. And the hazards must not be underestimated. If the dangers of embarking on the journey were truly appreciated, few would attempt it alone.

The subject will at the outset dismiss the idea that he may have constructed his life in such a way that, unknown to himself, the immediate effects of his deficiences and inconsistencies are camouflaged and rendered as unimportant as possible, yet govern the shape of his life. Other people, yes; oneself, no. As soon as he begins to overcome his reluctance to accept the idea, he receives inevitably a series of emotional shocks. The tortoise without its shell is a common simile. Since he has depended on all sorts of compensatory devices for self-defence of what are felt to be vulnerable aspects of his character and way of life, he may well experience deep alarm and depression at learning unpalatable truths about himself. At other times the danger arises from exactly the opposite cause, inflation at the discovery of more pleasant truths and expanding abilities. Therefore the two extremes must be kept in balance. An overconceited view of oneself in one area cannot be dismantled without building up the feelings of inadequacy in another. Neither can the underestimation be built up while the superior is left standing. As one side is added to, the other must be subtracted from. An 'honest witness' is essential at this point to direct the journey onwards; to

Middle course (minimap)

prevent an inflated ego-drive from gratifying its early immature wishes and longings; to overcome the despondent, denigrating fears of inadequacy. The middle course is difficult indeed to steer.

But where is an 'honest witness' to be found? Those who talk do not know. Those who know have no need to talk. There is no qualification or diploma for the teacher in this field. Every charlatan can claim his knowledge and achievement since only the fact of his claim identifies him as the charlatan. Your friend may have been there or he may not. If in fact he has been there he will know. It he has not succeeded in getting there he may nevertheless honestly and sincerely believe he has. In the first case he will know too much to have interest or vanity in proclaiming his achievement. In the second case, his readiness to take pride in his experience, in his ability to act as a teacher to others, makes his claim suspect. There are many in the field of becoming who claim special knowledge or experience: psychiatrists and gurus, professors and priests, the Pope and the soap-box orator at Speakers' Corner. The validity of their claims can be assessed only by their reactions to the experience which they claim; that is, do they themselves live in accordance with their teachings – and does their way of life imply an example to be followed?

Don Yott
Patty Grant

Actions speak loudest.

One does not learn business methods from a bankrupt, music from someone who is tone deaf, ethics from a criminal, nor logic from a fool. Neither can guidance in the process of becoming be learnt from a person vain enough to proclaim his ability, shallow enough to describe the depth of his experience, ignorant enough to expound his knowledge, misguided enough to believe himself under divine direction, avaricious enough to ask high payment for what should be given from love.

There is said to be safety in numbers, and if there is any protection to be had from misguidance by others, it may be found by working in groups. Recently, groups have sprung up, particularly in the United States, to experiment with sensory perceptions and artificially-induced forms of relationship. These groups, as operated at present, provide a valuable if often shallow start to the business of relating to oneself through the eyes of others, and may spark off interest in the deeper subtleties of the journey. But they are the starting point, not the complete means. Nor can we definitely say

Group work

where the complete way lies, though it may be developed by taking current group techniques to deeper levels with the participants pledged to the specific aim of undertaking the journey.

The common basis to most group work is the breaking down of conditioning so that one does not always react mentally or physically to situations in the way in which one has been conditioned to react. Those groups using awareness technique derived from the older methods of psychoanalysis deal more directly with childhood conditioning and its effects on relationships. These older methods have been updated, added to, and experimented with, particularly at centres like the Esalen Institute in California. Another group of techniques dealing with posture and sensory awareness, which remind one of Western adaptations of yoga practices and Zen Buddhism, have particular appeal to other psychological types whose conditioning has taken different forms.

Although a logic or rationale is often presented behind whatever methods a group uses, in fact like many experimental processes their validity often depends upon the intuition of their originator. The rationale is adopted afterwards, as evidenced in the bizarre theory offered to account for the whys and wherefores of many practices. Those methods which have not gone through systematic development tend not to be transmissible to other practitioners and imitators because, although effective, they rely upon the intuition of their original author.

Groups are increasing in number although there are not yet sufficient which are responsibly conducted. Nevertheless, they provide a useful vehicle whereby one can speed up the attainment of self-knowledge in the mirror proffered by the other members of the group. They offer a laboratory situation where one can act out experience without the disadvantage of suffering its consequences as in real life.

In the normal course of social contacts, one may get a hint as to how others view one and some suggestion that their opinion is in some ways different from one's own. But it is none of the casual acquaintance's business to voice precisely what he thinks of you. Society, in order to shield itself from undue change and enable the transaction of its daily affairs with the minimum of emotional upheaval, has built up terms of conventions in which we can operate and communicate without impinging on others. But the protection which enables us to carry on our day-to-day conduct and relationships also keeps us from the insight which brings about progress. The techniques practised by groups using, for example, dream-watching or encounter methods are deliberately devised to suspend those conventions which preserve roles and thus obscure new views of oneself and the world.

In groups specifically formed for the purpose of abandoning social roles and where members may discuss feelings and reactions to each other with complete candour, experiences of relationships that would normally take place over a very long period can be condensed into a comparatively short time in such isolated laboratory or workshop conditions. The members can take their problems to the group and gain its help; they can act out their fantasies, dreams, fears, and emotional inclinations; they can track down their conflicts of attitudes by focussing on what they try to avoid or have a resistance against – the tell-tale signs of hidden neurosis.

By dispensing with the niceties of social behaviour and defensive mechanisms, group members can give free rein to the reactions which others provoke – reactions about which they might normally have kept silent in case they were hurtful when in fact they are often received as helpful. They are thereby enabled to learn a great deal about themselves and each other, how they tend to react in the wider society outside, how to avoid collusion with the roles of others, and how in relationships to avoid assuming problems which belong to the other.

Initially it is obviously disconcerting to step outside the protective conventions of well-mannered society. To do so is to risk exposure to the other's candid view of oneself. To be able to accept such a view as a fact – encouraging or distressing as it may be – in a detached manner without wishing either to disguise or to justify oneself is a prerequisite in the acceptance of oneself.

For effective group work, two conditions must be fulfilled: the leader must have overcome that fascination and preoccupation with his own personality and personal affairs which could cause him to react with strong emotion towards members of the group; the composition of the group needs to be relatively balanced in respect of psychological types and stages of development. The more stable their dispositions, the more effective and subtle will be the reflection given back to each individual. Those who are intensely unbalanced and wrapped up in themselves often can only give back reflections distorted beyond recognition by their own problems.

Talking out a problem or a reaction with a group may help to give a clue to its origins because of the associations raised. Examinations and evaluation of the problematic experience itself is usually self-defeating in terms of trying to discover one's motivations but analysis of the reactions it provokes may be more profitable. If one discovers one's reactions to an experience are in any way different to the reactions of others, this might uncover that the difference is due not to the inherent nature of the experience but to one's conditioned way of viewing it. Any strong reaction to an experience is worthy of examination because of the reasons underlying its strength to make the subject feel this or act thus. This is the best method of placing subjective experience on an objective basis as far as it is possible to do so.

The aim of groups to encourage their members to be themselves – in the sense of dropping subconscious pretences – may be compared with the Stanislavsky acting techniques which aim at enabling actors to find themselves before taking on the role of other characters. A man is unlikely to become or have the ability to act what he would like to be until he can admit to himself what he already is.

As regards the acting out and analysis of dreams in group work, dreams form the subject of the succeeding chapter. Suffice to say here that while those who have not experienced their usefulness might believe them to be meaningless phenomena, records of progress in self-knowledge achieved purely by dream analysis imply otherwise. On translation, the cartoon-like characters, symbols and imagery of dreams appear to be deeply meaningful. On the whole, the unconscious mechanism which produces them provides a far more objective and complete view of the motivations of the dreamer than can any mere account given by his conscious mind.

But dream analysis by itself is not enough. There must be a certain amount of movement, of contact with people and circumstances, to generate the emotional reactions which betray, and therefore allow identification of, inconsistent motivations. In this respect, groups provide a unique opportunity for contact without the consequences that experiences entail in real life.

The value of experience lies in what can be learnt from it. The disadvantage of experience is that it takes time and alters our personal circumstances, not always for the better. The man who undertakes to rob a bank may learn from the experience that, whether the police catch him or not, the raid does not in fact settle his problems except perhaps in a very temporary sense. However, had he stopped short of the actual experience and instead examined his preceding fantasy that robbing a bank offered a solution to something, he might have gained the benefits without the disadvantages of becoming associated with any irrevocable consequences the act might entail. One might wish to marry a particular though unsuitable person, to murder one's wife or husband, to drive faster, climb higher, achieve fame, fortune, glory, at whatever cost. Although one might be wiser in the end, the result of some of these experiences will be uncomfortable. The value of fantasies – as with entertainment as second-hand or simulated experience – is that they can be time-savers, substitutes for actual experience. If they can be acted out in a group situation with the necessary reactions gained, the subject reaps the benefit of uncovering his motivations and is thereby saved the penalties of acting out his wishful thinking in the world of reality.

Group exercises which are based on sensory awareness – on making one look around more, feel more, sense more – are akin to Westernised yoga practices and Zen Buddhism. Yogis and Zen Buddhists have long regarded varying systems of awareness, exercise, diet, posture, breathing, and intellectual concentration as training in insight. Again, their basic value is in breaking down habitual or conditioned reactions. Much of mentality and daily routine is purely a matter of how one is accustomed or brought up to act and perceive. One falls into the habit of breathing in a particular way, sitting in a particular way, seeing in a particular way. Yet sensory awareness demonstrates that these patterns can be changed. Once the structure of automatic reflexes is broken down in one area, the freedom tends to spread to other areas of conditioning. Thus although sensory awareness may deal in the physical rather than the mental field and is not in itself enough, it helps to break down the vicious circle of false perceptions accepted as true. Because most of our actions are conditioned, we accept the conditioning. Because we accept the conditioning, we continue the reflex actions and compulsive habits. A person without any means of questioning his habits has the utmost difficulty in observing these objectively. Those most pronounced – such as obsessional handwashing, treading on the lines between paving stones – are grosser indications that attract the attention of others. The more insidious habits – compulsive working, hurry, compulsive punctuality or lateness, a million different worries – pass unquestioned or are all too easily accepted as one's lot.

The mystic's technique of meditation, extolled in such exaggerated terms as easy of attainment, is unlikely to provide a starting point for self-awareness. In meditation one empties the mind of day-to-day preoccupations, of sensual reactions to immediate surroundings, in order to let something else come in. But so long as mind remains subject to heavy conditioning, any attempt at meditation is likely to result in overdue attention to and justification of personal fixations with the danger of reinforcing resistance to relaxation. Only in later stages when the mind has already achieved some degree of the principles of self-recognition, may the so-called 'given-knowledge' of meditation have a validity and reality upon which the subject can act.

*   *   *

Group techniques – even when conducted by the best of academically qualified practitioners – may have their hazards. There are almost insuperable difficulties in assessing their results over periods sufficiently long to be significant. Those who are formally qualified by some cognitive criteria to conduct groups may lack the necessary intuition to do so; the many group leaders who have no formal qualifications are often the subject of misguided, sometimes megalomanic, motivation with little intellectual awareness of the possible dangers.

As soon as one moves outside the conventions of society, inevitably one is at risk. To live entirely within those conventions in sure sterility and the choice between both discomforts can only be one's own.

As the channels by which society has traditionally conducted relationships close down, as entertainment becomes mechanised and reaction increasingly orientated towards competitive games, the appeal of group work will grow. One may predict that within the foreseeable future it will become an established feature of life throughout our community. If the rate of growth is high, so may be the casualty rate. Yet that in itself would not be grounds for abandoning the method. In the past, man's ignorance regarding the conduct of relationships has resulted in other sources of casualty – wars, revolutions, the rule of despots, the cruelty of the Inquisition, and the concentration-camps. But out of this, progress has come. If groups also bring their toll of hazards, it is not likely to be greater than those of the past. Therefore the venture may be worthwhile, although the participant must realise he is at risk.

One may surmise that it is the instinctive urge to escape from the stifling effects of society's rigid structure of conventional conduct and concepts, which provides the attraction of drugs for the younger generation. If a less safe way than that of groups for expanding consciousness, any method which provides insight into the clichés on which our culture is based must have some value. Those who have fallen victim to the drug cult may be regarded not so much as weak drop-outs congenitally deficient but rather as casualties of the unbalanced structure of the acquisitive, competitive, manic-progressive society of our time.

Setting aside the dangers of addiction, what value has the vision of the drugged mind? Is it really an expanded view – or merely a twisted, selective one?

At best, certain drugs seem to afford a sort of ready-made excursion into the state of expanded consciousness. But they do not provide first-hand experience of the journey out. Thus to short-circuit the natural process is to risk a vision of reality which may thereafter seem eternally unobtainable or inaccessible to the would-be traveller.

The visions on his trip have been the attractive part, just as exciting as a journey to another planet. How much duller is the business of getting back, and since he has not bothered with the tedious groundwork and disciplines for the return, he is unable to bring what he has seen back to earth. Unguided drug-takers rarely ever succeed in adapting to their everyday lives the insights they have glimpsed. They have no way of connecting the revelations back to their lives and therefore they attribute this different view of life to the effect of the drug and cut it off from reality. They begin to believe there are two worlds: one lived in everyday routine, and the other, a completely different and artificial state attainable only on a drug trip. They never bridge the two. The insights are therefore dismissed, wasted, or forgotten.

However, on the rare occasions when similar states appear to have been achieved without drugs, it can fairly be stated that the subject feels he is looking beyond normal into a deeper reality. Realising some sort of breakthrough which gives him further sight, like putting a telescope to his eye, he can have faith in the 'truth' of an experience which is not attributable to drugs. Even so, too much insight too soon brings danger of disorientation. For such reasons the mystics of all denominations have always urged that exploration of this sort should be undertaken only with the help of a guide or guru.

The journey is a continuing process. It would be easy for the enlightened traveller to sit back and luxuriate in his wider view of life, as does the drug-taker who wants to be high all the time. Yet unless he wants to make himself a complete outcast and withdraw from society, the traveller on the road to integration must be sufficiently balanced to bring back this wider view to his more mundane pursuits.

Dr Richard Blum, in *Utopiates, The Use and Users of LSD**, says that the users of the drug

> .... see in these drugs a tool for bringing about changes which they deem desirable. The emphasis is on the enhancement of inner experience and on the development of hidden personal resources. It is an optimistic doctrine, for it holds that there are power and greatness concealed within everyone. It is an intellectual doctrine for it values experience and understanding more than action and visible change. It

* *Utopiates, The Use and Users of* LSD. R Blum & Associates. Atherton. New York, 1964.

concerns itself with areas dear to the thinker: art, philosophy, religion, and the nature and potentials of man. It is a mystic doctrine, for it prizes illumination and a unified world view with meaning beyond that drawn from empirical reality. It is a realistic doctrine as well, for it counsels compromise and accommodation between the inner and outer worlds. 'Play the game', it advises, 'don't let the Pied Piper lead you out of town.'

Conversely, R E L Masters and his wife, Jean Houston, point out in *The Varieties of Psychedelic Experience** that those who take LSD without guidance tend to get led into introspective spiritual pursuits and neglect the rest of life. They say:

> The Pied Piper does lead many such persons out of town; and he leads them into small cultish units of fellow true-believers where the interior pursuits are followed to the exclusion of almost everything else.

The authors state that eleven out of 206 subjects who took psychedelic drugs under controlled conditions reached a deep experience of a sense of fundamental personality transformation. Afterwards they said the experience had been so satisfying that they felt no inclination to repeat it or take drugs again. There was furthermore some evidence in their subsequent life-style that a positive change had taken place.

A five per cent success rate is not, however, high and special circumstances applied to these cases. Prior to the change, each had already acquired exceptional self-understanding through long, hard effort using various means, including analysis, yoga, and mysticism. Their descriptions of the voyage outwards during controlled drug sessions were similar to those found in psychotherapy. The authors state:

> Abreactive release of unconscious materials frequently occurs, especially if aimed for in a session predefined as therapeutic. Insight is added to insight as the subject typically announced that 'the scales are falling away from my eyes and at last I am seeing myself and the world without self-deceit or illusion' – a view that may liberate the subject from guilt, enhance self-esteem, and effect other changes desirable in themselves and prerequisite to still more important experience of growth and self-fulfilment. Of course, not all of this occurs in every

The Varieties of Psychedelic Experience by R E L Masters & Jean Houston. Turnstone Books. London. 1973.

case; but on the recollective-analytic level these are the characteristic phenomena and some or all occur with variations as well as to the neurotic patient.

If we have not described an ideal recipe for a conscious way to integration, we may have indicated some of the features which such a procedure, when it is perfected, may possess. In summary, these are methods of self-knowledge as may be aided by an 'honest witness' and group experience of analysis of motivations, reactions, dreams, fantasies, and sensory awareness. If the goal has been correctly identified, the mental techniques and at least some of the necessary concepts are available for a more direct approach than the intuitive methods of the last several thousand years.

Who will undertake the journey? Perhaps the neurotic personality needs the process more than the stable at least for the sake of his own immediate welfare. But his instability is due in part to his sensitivity to the pressures imposed by society and his intuitive awareness of his own potential. The additional pressures generated from integration procedures may in such a case constitute an overdose.

The neurotic personality has this advantage: since his sensibility has already disrupted his life, he may as well go forward to try to turn misfortune to positive ends. The successful personality, on the other hand, would do well to ask himself this question before setting out to see the face of what for thousands of years mankind has referred to as God: Is he ready to undergo a wild voyage from which, although he may not have to venture far from his armchair, he may never quite return?

He should reflect that he has found some temporary relief from those exigencies of life of which the more farsighted complain. Should he be so restlessly ambitious, then, to jeopardise the comforts he enjoys to gain some indefinable goal? He might believe himself to have too much common sense or too strong a grasp of 'reality' to allow his mind to be affected by the wonderful or terrible that may become apparent. But once the adventure is embarked upon, the subject, although aware of what is happening, may be virtually powerless to control the sequence of events for some time thereafter, and only then with the strongest of characters and in domestic and surrounding circumstances of reasonable stability.

By every common-sense standard the undertaking is absurd. The exploration of the New World was an equally crazy venture in Columbus' day. Voyages to the moon are equally offensive to the criterion of sensible security. Elderly gentlemen sail round the world, spending months in isolated peril, to prove that the voyage can be done and that they are the ones who can do it. For similar reasons, driven by similar motivations, there will be no shortage of those who will attempt to open up their inner worlds to easier access.

11

Dreaming Man

So-called rationalists are particularly prone to dismiss dreams as meaningless or superficial phenomena caused by indigestion or similar physical sensations. More openminded people might occasionally wonder why they dream but, lacking any positive indication, leave the matter aside as one of the more puzzling aspects of their existence. Yet dreams are powerful stuff. Some are so disturbing or frightening that they create a mood which lingers until well into the day. Their bizarre quality, their vividness, have special power to distract even the most materialistically preoccupied person. The least fanciful man can journey in the night through otherworld dramas and plots far beyond the scope of his waking imagination. That piece of cheese last thing at night might have given rise to the dream but cannot account for or control its subject matter.

Dreams are not consciously constructed. Such an obvious statement leads on to the less obvious conclusion that they must be unconsciously produced, and in a world where a purpose can be affixed to other everyday occurrences, it would be very curious and untidy of nature for dreams to have none. An understanding of dreams, their language and meaning is essential to any appreciation of the subject of self-fulfilment because they appear to be, when properly used, the best single instrument of self-knowledge. Without exception, everyone has some experience of the unconscious process of maturing which takes place in dreaming. Dream interpretation also gives essential clues to the part played in integration by superstitions, cults, fantasies, legends, myths, literature, and religious belief because they seek to convey their message from the unconscious to the conscious mentality in similarly coded terms. They use symbolic imagery very different from the logical thought-sequence of waking life and their true meaning is lost unless deciphered in a symbolical light.

The meaning of dreams is beyond the scope of science to investigate. So nothing said in this chapter can be regarded as definitive and one has to tread warily to avoid arriving at unduly dogmatic conclusions. But science has indicated dreams to be essential to life. Experiments to prevent dreaming have produced the death of otherwise healthy animals and alarming psychotic symptoms in humans. Dreams appear to be as necessary to life as food and oxygen. The implications are that if they are essential, they must have an important role to play.

The old world paid profound attention to dreams. The ancient Egyptian, Hebrew, Greek, and Roman civilisations believed that the gods communicated with men through dreams. In the Bible, they are one of the chief means by which God imparts his will. But in the West, understanding of the use of dreams as a means of communication had to await re-discovery centuries later. The pioneer work performed by Freud and Jung uncovered that dreams are like parables, carrying a meaning but in a sort of code. They have been found to express in symbolic terms man's inner journey through life, what is really going on in his mind, the truths he may unknowingly try to hide from himself, the underlying causes of the problems that he meets in life, the potentialities he has within him, the destihy he might achieve. In short, dreams are a guide to his nature.

From observations made to date, the behaviour of dreams is consistent with the hypothesis that consciously or unconsciously, every man is seeking the goal of self-realisation.

Since Freud published *The Interpretation of Dreams* at the turn of the century, they have been used for therapeutic purposes to seek out the causes of the complexes and conflicts in psychiatric patients. But dreams and the benefits to be gained from them are not limited to sufferers from the more severe neuroses. Everyone is hampered to a greater or lesser extent by the fallacies imposed on them in childhood and everybody dreams an accurate pictorial reflection of the causes and effects of this conditioning. The purpose of dreams is to help them lead a fuller life, not to hinder or frighten them. Jung* said: 'The dream is a natural event, and there is no reason under the sun why we should assume that it is a crafty device to lead us astray. The dream occurs when consciousness and will are to a great extent extinguished. It seems to be a natural product which is also found in people who are neurotic.'

Dreams take place as if they are concocted by an impartial outsider who sees one's problems and attitudes in perspective and is concerned with solving them and restoring basic human nature wherever it has been distorted by imposed ideas and illusions. 'Within each of us,' said Jung, 'there is another whom we do not know. He speaks to us in dreams and tells us how differently he sees us from the way we see ourselves. When, therefore, we find ourselves in a difficult situation to which there is no solution, he can sometimes kindle a light that radically alters our attitude – the very attitude that led us into the difficult situation.'

Thus dreams are a constant guide to everyday life. They give early warning of personal disasters which inevitably arise from inconsistent attitudes towards life. If they can be heeded in time, bitter experience may sometimes be averted. J A Hadfield writes in *Dreams and Nightmares**:

> Behind their fantastic visions they are full of shrewd common sense even dealing with the practical affairs of everyday life; they contain flashes of insight which enable us to solve problems even more effectively than our lumbering reason, and reveal to us characteristics in ourselves which surprise and sometimes shock us. Indeed we discover that, unknown to us, dreams are busying themselves throughout the night with those problems of our lives which in the day we find too much for us, and by recapitulating the events of the day help towards a solution of those problems. Dreams rightly interpreted may thus act as a guide when we are lost in bewilderment in those trackless forests of the imagination, and help us to overcome difficulties even when we have abandoned them as insurmountable.

* *The Collected Works of C G Jung*. Routledge & Kegan Paul.
* *Dreams and Nightmares* (Pelican Original. 1954). Penguin Books Ltd. Copyright © the Estate of J A Hadfield. 1954.

The method of dream interpretation can be understood only by realising that it is like a system of decoding. Dreams do not speak in the plain language of everyday conversation or the reasoned sequence of abstract thought. They draw symbolic or pictorial images to express such thoughts. They use analogy, simile, appallingly mixed metaphors, the most awful puns. For example, if a man dreams of going to Piccadilly, it could signify for him the reaching of a landmark in his life, or could represent London to him as the centre of his world or civilisation. Again Piccadilly could also mean to him the heart of the matter currently on his mind or, with Eros as its centre, the focal point of that which fascinates him, mentally or sexually. As one of those awful puns, Piccadilly becomes to pick a dilly of a subject to consider.

Dreams are visual imagery, using symbols all the time to present ideas, just as cartoon strips tell stories. The dream sequence usually appears illogical and absurd but, on interpretation, can be found to have a valid connexion. Every scrap of the dream has a meaning, not in the rational logic of conscious thought but through perceptions and emotions that carry deeper significance and are expressed sym-bolically because words rarely can define them accurately. A piano concerto cannot be translated effectively into words but can be set down in the symbols of music. Neither, apparently, does the un-conscious usually choose to translate its meaning into words but uses symbols and pictures moulded into a drama or scene. Dream lan-guage might take the abstract idea of progress and express it in visual form as a train or plane journey. Difficulties might be expressed as concrete obstacles – a rockfall in front of the train. Values might be presented pictorially as gold and pearls.

Perhaps the idea can be grasped readily by comparing dream symbology with day-dreams because both arise through a similar unconscious mental process. An individual does not consciously, logically, and rationally construct a day-dream. In a moment of relaxation, he lets his mind wander where it wants, out of reality into fantasy where he visualises himself playing out certain situations or roles. The images in the day-dreams are entirely symbolic. A man might visualise himself as the big boss. This could signify that at work he functions below his potential because of a feeling of inferiority but that he does have the capability to be the boss. Equally, such a day-dream could mean he is not giving his family the leadership that might be required from him as its head. Or else he might already be the holder of a 'bossy' outlook. A plain girl might day-dream that she is pretty and admired by the most handsome man – symbolising the admirable qualities within herself that she has not yet recognised, or perhaps an overestimation she has made of herself to compensate for her underestimation. A day-dream might conjure up a situation, such as a need to stop a factory from polluting the atmosphere. That might mean an attitude towards work or more generally manufactured ideas, represented by the factory, are poisoning the individual's enjoyment of life.

Such multiple meanings can be found not only in day-dreams but in literature, because all products of the imagination appear to have symbolic reference to progress through life, though some are much clearer than others. As a speculative thought, the total scope of our imagination may be currently tied up with trying to tell us in figurative language what our problems are and what needs to be done to escape from them. Works of fiction are often far more closely related to personal or general problems than the authors realise. It may well turn out that the full force of imagination cannot be set to other ends than dealing with conditioning problems until they have been resolved. The first paragraph of John Lennon's *In His Own Write** – a pun as good as in any dream – reads:

> There once upon a time was a man who was partly Dave – he had a mission in life. 'I'm partly Dave', he would growm in the morning which was half the battle. Over breakfast he would again say, 'I am partly Dave' which always unnerved Betty. 'You're in a rut Dave', a voice would say on his way to work, which turned out to be a coloured conductor! 'It's alright for you,' Dave used to think, little realising the coloured problems.

Translating this passage as a dream, Dave's problem is indeed that he is only partly himself, only partly able to follow his true nature. He has won half the battle by realising his lack of freedom but is in a rut because the reasons for his frustration are still unconscious. An unconscious problem might be symbolised in dream language as

* *In His Own Write.* John Lennon. Jonathan Cape. 1964.

217

coloured. A message from the unconscious could ideally be delivered by a coloured conductor.

Various theories have been voiced to explain why dreams incorporate symbolic images and are therefore complicated to interpret. Not only are they obscure in this respect but often they depict long and involved incidents which seem to defy any hope of making sense. On the other hand, some speak out in plain words. We therefore must assume that when necessary the dream mechanism can and does function in plain language, automatically raising the question that if dreams can do so, why do they not regularly do so. The reason appears to be two-fold:

1. Words are very ambiguous and closely related to the logical materialism of the outer world rather than to the emotions of the inner. Conveyance of an unambiguous message in words requires the weighty phraseology of a legal document, which even then is not guaranteed against loopholes. Dreams could probably avoid ambiguity only by using the emotionless phraseology of an act of parliament. However, symbols are not as ambiguous as they at first might seem. Relative to the circumstances or the life of the dreamer at that particular moment, they are likely to have only one very relevant comment.

2. Dreams could present the simplest messages in precise terms but continual direct communication might make the recipient too lazy to seek out the full range and significance of the more profound messages. If a dream tried to convey a complicated truth, the dreamer would not bother with its unravelling. However, if both the easy and difficult are set out in cartoon characters, he is induced to grasp the meaning of both.

There are, of course, exceptions to the rule of ambiguity and some ideas are easier to convey in words than images. For example, the subject dreamed he was told in plain language: 'If you tell a man he is God, he will either not believe you or he will become inflated.' This meant to the dreamer that he could not believe he possessed that which he worshipped, i.e. his full potential. Or if he did believe, he would become inflated with his own importance because he could not place what he possessed in its correct context in the circumstances of his own everyday life. In plain language, the meaning is clear, if profound. It is difficult to visualise how such a thought could be depicted in symbolic images. On the other hand, dreams can and do convey abstract thought in terms of cartoon images to an amazing degree. The abstract idea must always be sought. Thus a dream of a father must be examined to see if the figure represents a personal father or God the Father. A dream of a mother might refer to a personal mother or Mother Nature in the creative sense.

In another example of an abstract idea expressed symbolically in a dream, 'a shaking, trembling dog is trying to remove a scrap of paper off its nose.' Such an image may seem meaningless at first glance but interpretation summed up a major problem for the dreamer. The dreamer associated the dog with its faithful attribute and it is interesting to note that God, an object of faith, is dog spelled backwards. The dreamer's faith in himself and life was pinned to that piece of paper, which represented worthless scraps of instructions, always going through life doing what he was told to do, instead of being free to make his own decisions. On such a false foundation, faith and confidence were bound to be shaken and the ties must be removed.

Whereas the meaning of dreams is not ambiguous once their symbols have been interpreted, they often are ambiguous in a different sort of way. They might be giving a picture of how the dreamer wants to regard himself, how he ought to regard himself, or how he used to regard himself; they might be depicting what is happening, what has happened in the past in order to comment on it, or what will happen in the future; they might be symbolizing his personal desires, ambitions, problems, or the desires and problems of humanity as a whole in relation to some basic unchanging blueprint of the fully integrated man.

A number of interpretations can be suggested from the subject matter of each dream situation. The key to discovering the relevant interpretation will be found in the context of what the person has been preoccupied with lately. There is very little chance of giving a meaningful interpretation to a dream in isolation without recognising from the dreamer's background and current preoccupations the essential context of where he is at any one time.

The different possibilities should be tried until one interpretation is found which feels as though it leads to a relevant comment. This feeling on the dreamer's part is particularly characteristic of a correct solution since it brings a sense of relief, acceptance, and release of energy.

There is no general vocabulary or hard and fast rule for translating dream-images. The various objects that appear in dreams mean different things to different people, and the dreamer must always be asked for personal associations. Some symbols do appear to be regarded by people generally in a particular light and thus have a universal meaning but even these must not be interpreted arbitrarily, for the dreamer's personal associations can still be different from the universal association.

Among the approaches to dreams, they can be considered for angles related to the past, present and future. Dreams not only state current problems but sometimes may recapitulate past aspects of one's personal history in potted form to enable useful comment on the present situation to become apparent. The historical review points to the root cause. Thus dreams skip about in time, darting back to an event in early childhood, then suddenly changing to a different scene. They appear to muddle up actual events, dates, locations, but in fact are producing condensed statements connecting the experience of the past with the problems of the present by this method.

They might on the other hand be a depiction of the possible consequences of the present situation, an enactment of the implications. At first acquaintance with dream technology, when one is largely ignorant of the full possibilities of dream usage, a prophetic dream may occur perhaps with a view to fascinating the subject with the whole topic. In the further course of interpretation, dreams sometimes appear to provide advance warning of the consequences of one's actions, and an unhappy outcome can be avoided if the warning is heeded. Again, perhaps in any lull when the pressures of immediate problems or self-examination have been released, the mind may still ramble on with dreams and produce prophetic ones at this point. The time-range of prophetic dreams varies considerably. A person may dream six months or even a year ahead of the actual events which occur to him. At another time in his life, he may dream a few weeks or days ahead.

In interpreting any dreams, all the figures should be reviewed in the first instance to ascertain whether they depict some aspect of the dreamer himself or objective circumstances. From time to time, one's way of life might be influenced by outside forces to which one has to relate. The dream may picture the relationship between the dreamer and the outside circumstances, between self and other. More often, all the figures in the dream are aspects of oneself. The dream about one's best friend or worst enemy is rarely about them but about one's own attitude towards them or the attitude in oneself that they have been chosen to represent in the dream. One's own thoughts or feelings are depicted in dreams by suitable strangers or acquaintances on whom these traits are projected and personified. Thus the cast of characters in the dream are all likely to be oneself, the kindly side, the striving side, the impatient side, the false side, the intellectual side, the childish side. A conflict between the characters may signify a conflict between one's own attitudes. A marriage could symbolise unity and an end to the conflict. Jung* emphasised:

> One should never forget that one dreams in the first place, and almost to the exclusion of all else, of oneself . . . the 'other' person we dream of is not our friend and neighbour, but the other in us, of whom we prefer to say: 'I thank thee, Lord, that I am not as this publican and sinner.'

Dreams of a nightmarish nature usually refer to an unsolved and pressing problem, often relating to a situation in childhood that was too terrifying to face and has remained unsolved years since. The effects might be grossly distorting the individual's life, hindering his relationships, causing him distress and fear, giving him a sense of inferiority or failure, or producing unsociable traits such as anger or aggression. He cannot help himself consciously because he does not know what is wrong. His emotions in this field will be repressed, doubly imprisoning him by holding down potentials within him which would otherwise be enlarging and enriching his life in the problem area. Dreams keep trying to chisel away at the problem to force awareness of the warring attitudes, however painful the process

* *Memories, Dreams, Reflections*, C G Jung, Collins, 1963.

might be. For a problem is almost a continuing matter fed by the inconsistencies of our attitudes and will refuse to be thrust out of conscious or unconscious mind. It will keep intruding on dream life or conscious concentration until the situation is faced. If the incon-sistency is removed the problem may remain for a time but is no longer generated by the emotional turmoil and will die away in its own due course. Hadfield* sums up the therapeutic functions of dreaming as:

> First, it makes us aware of the causes of conflict by reviving the experiences which originally gave rise to the neurosis. It tries to do this, but commonly succeeds only in bringing up fragments of the original experience, so deeply are these experiences repressed and so unwilling are we to encourage their recall. That is why the dream has to return time after time to the same experience, and why we have recurrent dreams and nightmares, sometimes in the same, and some-times in different forms. It takes a long time for the dream to convince us, or to put it more accurately, for us to acknowledge the cause of the trouble.

> Secondly, dreams have a therapeutic effect in acting as a safety valve for the release of repressed emotions. Therein lies the value of the patient himself reliving the experience as he does both in dreams and in analysis . . .

> The third therapeutic value of dreams is that they show us up for what we are, for in a neurosis, as we have seen, we repress our natural selves and impose on ourselves a false personality, a persona more pleasing and ingratiating, one more acceptable. The dream calls our bluff. The woman prides herself on being the 'perfect mother'; the dream shows her strangling her child from jealousy. It is as well that she recognises her jealousy. The war-shocked man bluffs himself that he is still a brave man; the dream shows him terrified out of his wits.

An individual is unlikely to be able to interpret his dreams without help at least at first. In order to find the accurate meaning, one would have to see oneself perfectly objectively as if an outside observer of one's attitudes instead of the holder of them. Such detachment is very difficult to achieve.

Quite apart from this obstacle, self-interpretation is unwise in the early stages for a vital reason. Either self-interpretation will lead nowhere after preliminary success or it will lead to inflation and

* *Dreams and Nightmares* (Pelican Original 1954), Penguin Books Ltd. Copyright © the Estate of J A Hadfield 1954.

disaster. The first few dreams are often quite easy to decipher as a means of drawing attention to themselves, but help is needed when they become more complicated or their path will be lost. Should the individual have the knack of explaining even the more complicated ones to himself to a certain extent, he faces a practically impossible task in digesting them on his own. He could always interpret them in the most favourable, optimistic light, believing the more wishful interpretation and neglecting the counteracting one, so he takes in only half the content. Over a period he may acquire a completely false and grandiose view of himself. Or he could listen only to the dreams which tell him truths about himself which might come as shocking, difficult to accept, and hurtful. He could build up an equally disastrous system of self-denigration and incapacitate himself. He must have the balanced view of another person to interpret and encourage, to hold his hand, to help him understand that these skeletons in his cupboard are not his fault. Again and again, he will need to be reminded that no blame is attached to him, and that he too should accept himself for what he is, like every other human, a system of dynamic attitudes. All of us overvalue qualities to compensate for what has been impressed upon us regarding our deficiencies; and undervalue ourselves to balance out the excessive opinions held in other directions. The process of self-knowledge requires recognition of the balance until, in the end, no quality is seen as favourable or unfavourable but entirely relative. Each has its opposing advantages or disadvantages.

Freud's suggestion that dreams originate in wish fulfilment seems less probable than the idea that it may be the interpretation, not the dream, which represents wish fulfilment. A person who leads a very disciplined life might dream of a situation where he indulges in irresponsibility. The dream is not so much wish fulfilment as a clear indication the problem is lack of freedom to relax from that discipline. Freudian interpretation of a dream of being the boss would be that the subject was carrying on this private fantasy to make life tolerable for himself. However, it could be said to be doubtful that the subject would dream of leadership unless he had the potential within himself.

An individual needs help not only in understanding his dreams but in overcoming the natural resistance to entertaining modes of thought which break down his old way of life. Only the guidance given by the dreams from an unconscious level can point out which attitudes need to be examined and from what angle.

The subject of the following dream was baulked at the start from getting rid of old ideas and might never have become free of them, had the dream not occurred as a guide out of the impasse:

> I was investigating an organisation and trying to find the head. Outwardly it was legitimate but in fact it was a front for a criminal organisation. The building housing it was huge. At one point I climbed down the outside with a rope to see what was going on in a room where the people of this organisation were asleep. Elsewhere during Red Indian wars in which people were getting killed, I was on the beach with a machine we had found which was a constant source of fun. It talked and could make sense like a robot computer. It posed questions and whoever was at the steering-wheel had to push the right button for the right answer or be told in a funny way where they were going wrong. In the dream I went to sleep and when I awoke the machine was still there. The tide had gone back a long way and a cow was out at the water's edge. Then an Indian appeared, saying he was a messenger and delivered a message to end the war, but the whites were hesitant to go in case they got massacred.

The first part of the dream states the problem. The subject is up to something. Outwardly, everything is right and proper. But the inward structure is riddled with inconsistencies. The problem will be recognised only by getting outside oneself while the 'criminal' attitudes are asleep, i.e. not putting up resistance. The next section of the dream is more specific. The Red Indian wars represent unconscious conflicts over the machine, which turns out to be the way the subject regarded dream interpretation and the interpreter who was helping him. Instead of the dreams being trusted as a help and guide to the solution of problems, they were not taken seriously. The machine is a source of fun, not real and relevant, but like a robot computer, impersonal and automatic. Realisation of this now causes relaxation (the sleep in the dream) and, on awakening, the tide of unconsciousness is found to have gone back, and the former attitude towards dream analysis is recognised as stupid and bovine, like a cow. The unconscious, in the guise of the Indian messenger, proposes an end to the conflict now the problem is understood but the conscious personality, i.e. the whites, is still hesitant in case acceptance of the interpretation means too much modification (or massacre) of its normal way of living.

In fact, the dreamer faced the situation, accepted the need for change, and subsequently came up with a dream that indicated a deeper area of problems:

> I dreamt I had no choice over with whom I shared my life. It was a fixed cycle of people. Then I was walking down a very steep slippery slope with my parents to reach Richmond Park. One had to go very slowly and carefully not to lose one's footing.

The opening indicates that the dreamer is not free to form relationships and can only get on with a few fixed types of people. A vast area of living is cut off because of false impressions gained in childhood by some unknowing action of the parents. The steep, slippery slope indicates the subject might feel removed from, or even superior to, many people and must descend from these opinions to reach Richmond Park, which could be an Anglo-French pun for *Riche monde,* or rich world. The journey would be slow for the subject not to lose understanding – a pun on footing as feet stand under one – of the complex causes of the block on relationships; and also footing in the sense of status or self-esteem. This dream was the start of a lengthy series that unravelled childhood misconceptions which prevented trust in others, feelings not only of superiority in some areas but inferiority in others because the two always balance each other out. Eventually the subject dreamed of leaving home to go to live in a pretty cottage surrounded by cornfields, which signified a breakaway to a more independent life from the parent's attitudes.

The symbolism of dreams has an added advantage besides explicitness. Dreams elucidate problems which the conscious mind is unwilling to face, including those which the conscious personality might be ashamed of. They might be related to sex, burning ambition, greed, hate, selfishness. The obscurity of the symbols allows the subject to take the dreams to an interpreter without the same censorship operating that would if he was talking consciously about the same problems. The symbols allow him to smuggle through in disguise what he cannot otherwise disclose, as much to himself as anyone else.

There has been a great deal of controversy as to whether Freud was correct in the way he interpreted dreams in terms of sexuality, Adler in terms of power, or Jung in terms of the collective unconscious. Many schools of psychiatry have interpreted dreams in various ways. We know dreams have been used prophetically in history and many of them seem to have been comprehensible when interpreted this way. The question arises which of these various schools of dream interpretation is correct. The answer appears to be that the unconscious adapts itself in advance to dream in terms which will be meaningful to the person or method likely to be consulted, thus the dreamer who goes to a Freudian interpreter would get that part of the message right which could be interpreted in terms of sexuality. Personal difficulties most commonly encountered first are those concerning relationships, which is probably why Freud became convinced that the entire drive in life was connected with sex. But once these sexual problems have been solved, dreams go on to deal with other attitudes. This is why Freudian patients never really finish analysis. By using a fixed Freudian vocabulary, the other areas of work, religion, and creativity might not be able to receive attention because the meaning of the symbols can be found only by personal association except in the cases of those with universal connotations. Attempts by Freudians to define all long, thin objects as masculine symbols and all large containing objects as female symbols are of doubtful use because such a dreambook mentality might aid translation of sexual dreams but be meaningless for those about other problems.

Free association makes sense of the most absurd-sounding dreams. For instance, a dreamer experiences the following: 'I am going in search of a pot of shellac. At that moment I see coming from the distance a row of silver planes built for the sole purpose of carrying very large quantities of shellac. I reflect this is quite ridiculous. I only want a small pot.' By personal association, shellac turned out to have been used in his father's factory and therefore identified with the manufacturing process on which the family fortune was based. The subject at the time of the dream was at an indecisive point in his career and ready to settle for a job beneath his capabilities, represented by the small pot of shellac, which would nevertheless yield a fairly secure income. The excessive quantities of shellac carried in valuable silver planes indicate a potential far greater than the subject was consciously recognising in himself, and that he was setting his sights too low.

Animals are among the symbols which, while having personal associations, also appear to carry universal meanings in that they often represent in dreams the embodiment of human attitudes. The tiger, for example, is so commonly recognised as symbolising ferocity that advertisements cash in on its power. However, should someone dream of a tiger, they must first be asked if they have particular associations with a tiger before assuming that it symbolises for them a ruthless attitude. They might have been scared by a tiger on a childhood visit to the zoo, or known someone who had been on a tiger-hunt, serving to remind them of specific incidents.

Animals appear so frequently, however, as having a universal meaning in dreams that interesting speculation can be made about their role in the greater scheme of evolution. The many different life-forms of the animal kingdom appear to be not so much haphazard creations but each distinctively as a physical embodiment of a different attitude or way of life, and it is this attitude that they depict in dreams. The sum total of these attitudes is found in the most complex and sophisticated animal, man. For example, a tortoise is the essence of the defensive attitude. Its answer to every problem is to put its head and legs behind its hard defensive shell and retreat. The mouse's way of life is to hide itself, to be very timid, to keep out of view as much as possible. The tiger's answer is to live in isolation and attack, whereas the lion at least cooperates in packs. The tiger is like a ferocious man but with all the other attributes of man eliminated. The remaining attitude or energy is ferocity which is well embodied in a tiger shape.

The symbol of the Tree of Life, found not only in the Bible but in other religions and recreated in the Christmas Tree, may hold an important key to the pattern of evolution. The Persian weavers who often portray the tree in their carpets show the members of the animal kingdom spread out along its branches. By interpreting the animals as embodiments of attitudes, the tree becomes the symbolic picture of life evolving. The foot of the tree where the trunk is thickest contains all the attitudes possible towards life, towards other beings, towards one's own development. Branching off the trunk are attitudes which have split off individually and borne fruit. The mouse has evolved a way of life that is well adapted for the life of a mouse, but can go no further. The mouse must necessarily be small and inconspicuous, for it cannot be the size of an elephant and still be afraid of everything. Nevertheless, the mouse maintains itself and prevents itself from slipping backwards.

Whereas these individual attitudes split off the trunk and come to the dead end of each branch, the attitudes as a whole are sustained together up the main trunk and evolve into man. Beneath him, all the different attitudes possible that went to produce man are depicted singly and put on record in different life-forms. In man, they are reproduced as a whole. Higher up the tree, man himself begins to diversify and specialise. Certain men are very able athletes, scientists, or administrators. They have carried their specialisation to its extreme, but, in effect, have gone up a dead end in their own profession by failing to enlarge their other capacities. They have developed as far as they can go in the life-span allotted to them and there is nothing much else they can do unless they lop off their speciality and rejoin the mainstream, perhaps combining their physical fitness with mental fitness, their science with theology, their administration with creativity. Their most important quest must be to find out where the main trunk is leading. That is the business of becoming.

It is in fact from the examination of a large number of dreams that useful clues regarding the nature of whole man and his ultimate destination can be obtained. When an individual first begins to study dreams, a fairly grandiose introductory dream of a general prognostic nature is apt to take place. The dream often sums up the person's key problems and indicates the course of his inner development, whether the problems will be resolved or not. From this introduction, dreams tend to go into the detailed matters of personal attitudes obstructed by conditioning.

If interpretation is persisted with for long enough to rectify these, the dreams of a strictly personal nature are likely to give way to the more general social problems or at least personal attitudes that have a universal dimension, such as the conflict between the needs of each self and the community. Such dreams are often similar to the legends of antiquity, taking archetypal symbols from the fund of ideas which fascinates all humanity.

To make this concept clearer by example:

> I dreamt I was following a path that twisted and wound until I came to the River Styx, on the other side of which was Christ in sackcloth asking for help. The river was not so much a river as a rectangular shape like a huge Roman bath. As I watched, I saw someone who, trying to cross the river for his own ends, was attacked by mythical figures which arose from the mud in the pool and destroyed him. I think there were four – minataur, centaur, winged man, and griffin.

The dreamer is following the twisting, winding journey along the path of life to the River Styx, symbolically the crossing point between life and death, the preliminary to rebirth and new life. On the side of new life is Christ, signifying ultimate man, asking for help and dressed in the clothes of humility. The river is not a natural obstacle because it has arisen only by reason of artificial conditioning. It is like a bath, a cleansing process washing away misconceptions and returning to first innocence. The crossing must be undertaken in humility, not for selfish gain. The self-seeking individual is destroyed by figures representing his own shortsighted materialistic ambitions. These beasts appear not only in various mythologies but in the New Testament as the guardians of the throne in heaven, where they probably represent man's own limitations or motivations which prevent his ascending to a higher state.

The figures of Christ and the mythological creatures are typical of the universal symbols or archetypes which constantly recur in the dream life of human beings of different cultural groups and at different periods of history. They may be regarded as symbolised clues to the destiny of man. Many religious and mythical symbols probably gained their conception from the unconscious through dreams. These archetypal ideas attract the conscious mind even when they are not consciously understood, and that is why they survive where logic might cast them off. Such archetypal legends as Cinderella, St George and the dragon, hold appeal for successive generations because of the inner satisfaction they instil. Any child who feels neglected and unloved, as many do at some stage or other, is reassured by hearing that Cinderella – with whom unconsciously he can identify – comes at last to be wanted by someone, no less than 'the prince'. St George, the more advanced side of oneself, triumphs in combat over the retrogressive side. King Arthur orientates his knights or diverse attitudes around a round table, symbolising their integration into a whole. The Holy Grail again signifies completion in the wholeness and receptivity of a challice. Such myths can all be translated in evolutionary terms. Primitive forces symbolised as giants are overcome. Petrified feelings are brought to life with the kiss of love and attention. The admonitory fables warn of the dire consequence of deviation.

The words and reasoning of the myths are not so important as the feeling and emotion they arouse. For they must fascinate by arousing emotions until their meaning can be generally understood and, as yet, the words are insufficient to convey this understanding. The myths that survive from the earliest of man's literature are those which still constantly recur in dreams and hallucinations: myths of creation, heroes, paradise and fall, avenging goddesses, light and darkness, quests, cycles of nature, human relations. They are not dead stories concocted in a flight of fancy long ago but appear to symbolise the universal drama that man is presently involved in.

In the course of sufficient dream analysis, an archetypal image of the self eventually emerges in the form of a newborn child, or a mandala, or anything related to the number four. These signify the progress of the subject's striving towards self-realisation. The number four appears to represent the four faculties of whole mind, so anything counted in less than four would indicate the partial or unconscious operation of them.

Christ and other avatars appear in dreams as the archetype of man's potential, the epitome of what he could become. He is his own saviour or deliverer. The Terrible Mother, witch, or avenging goddess is the destructive process of the materialistic earth, the fact that one comes into existence and in due course has to die, or the materialistic side of us has to die, which appears as a terrible fact to one's ego-structure. One's being is also derived from the mother earth, so the two go hand in hand. The doctor is the archetype of the healing power present in mankind, and the wise old man, sage, or teacher is his intuitive wisdom. The *persona* is the façade or social mask that one presents to the outside world and oneself because of the attitudes, faults, and fears imposed by conditioning.

More difficult to explain are the *animus* and *anima* archetypes; the 'perfect man and woman'. If one talks of completion in terms of the soul, these idealised figures are the 'soulmates' whose properties must be understood and incorporated to achieve mental wholeness. The *anima* might appear in dreams as Helen of Troy or Venus or another beautiful woman, perhaps of one's acquaintance, perhaps not. The *animus* might appear as the hero figure or a handsome man.

These *animus* and *anima* figures of unconscious life get interminably mixed up with conscious life. When a person falls in love, they confuse the person of their conscious fascination with the figure of their unconscious life which also fascinates them and represents their inner potential. In the outer materialistic life, the ideal mate is presumably everybody's hope and need. Virtually all people hold in common this very strong urge. This is why the ideal mate is so often used as a symbol for the *anima* and *animus* and why the need for the *anima* or *animus* is projected upon the woman or man who represents the ideal sexual partner. The mate represents the completion of physical life; the *anima* or *animus* represents that which is most necessary for the completion of psychic life; and the two become confused.

Henry F. Ellenberger says in *The Discovery of The Unconscious*:*

> The existence of the anima is manifested in the manner in which a man distorts the representation of the real women in his life: his mother, sisters, friends, love-objects, and spouse. The anima is also personified in dreams, visions, and fantasies, in many myths of all populations, and has been a rich source of inspiration for novelists and poets. Sometimes the anima is projected from the unconscious in a dramatic way such as love at first sight, or incomprehensible infatuation, with disastrous results. . . . Because there is in man a feminine and in woman a masculine component, man and woman are attracted also to the complementary personality element they find in each other. It belongs

* *The Discovery of the Unconscious* (Allen Lane, The Penguin Press 1970). © Henry F Ellenberger.

in the nature of the anima that a man can project her image upon the woman with whom he is in love, and he then sees her differently from what she really is. . . . The animus is often a plurality of male figures. In a very young woman it will appear as an infatuation for an older man or a paternal figure; in a mature woman the object could be a sports champion or, in negative cases, a playboy or even a criminal; and with an older woman more like a physician, an ecclesiastic, or a supposedly misunderstood genius. . . . The projection of the animus on to a real man can have effects as disastrous as those of a man's projection of the anima on an 'anima figure'. More commonly the animus can manifest itself in a woman's distorted perception of her husband or other male figures in her life. It may also give rise to fixed ideas and stubborn, irrational opinions which are the source of irritating discussions.

These projections must be worked through and dissolved in order to gain their benefit. Whereas the *anima* and *animus* are universal archetypes, the choice of person on whom they are projected is very varied, depending on individual needs. Otherwise everyone would fall in love with or dream of the same person: the best, the most integrated man or woman in the world, to the neglect of all other men or women.

The infinite variety of psychic needs of different personalities gives rise to the infinite variety of dreams. It takes all sorts of dreams to fulfil man's psychic requirements. While this is the basic reason for the dangers inherent in generalising about dreams, they nevertheless remain probably the most revealing mechanism keeping us in touch with our inner lives and development.

12

Whole
Man

THE THESIS OF this book holds that many phenomena have been observed – and are still to be observed in the context of personal life – which are at first sight strangely inconsistent with the greater part of everyday experience.

Certain claims are well authenticated that 'miracles' have occurred and continue to occur, always without warning and unrepeatable under controlled conditions. Diseases which are well founded in terms of infection and cell destruction disappear almost overnight for no accountable physical reason. Feats of endurance, fire-walking and deprivation of oxygen and food for prolonged periods, are demonstrated regularly by practitioners of various cults. Instances of telepathy and precognition are both plentiful and established beyond reasonable doubt. Coincidences which are significant enough to change the course of the person concerned, involving odds of millions to one, happen not once but often several times in a lifetime.

Many individuals feel they experience processes within them which encourage them to act in particular ways and strongly inhibit them from following other directions. Certain accounts of historical matters and explanations of the world in which we live and the universe at large, however improbable, are found in some extraordinary way to be satisfying as if they contained an element of truth important to conserve. Other accounts, much more probable and even more pleasant in their implications for the comfort and security of mankind, are far less acceptable. Certain codes of ethics and behaviour, often restrictive and arduous to observe, are respected by communities and believed by them to emanate from divine sources; that is, to have origins outside the terms with which man is familiar.

Finally, throughout the ages and in many very different cultures, a conviction recurs that the special sort of consciousness found only in man exists or potentially exists in its own right and although obviously highly dependent upon the host body might survive its death in certain circumstances.

However we may regard these specific examples, few educated people would deny today that strange and unaccountable phenomena do occur from time to time. Different types of mentality have quite different ways of attempting to reconcile the inexplicable with everyday causitive circumstances. They break down into three main categories of attitudes towards acausal matters:

1. They are the work, manifestation, or consequence of a deity who is usually considered to be omniscient and omnipotent.

2. They do not exist and most of the evidence concerning them is overimaginative. To the extent that evidence is incontestable, then it can be explained away in terms of familiar physical laws.

3. They do for the most part exist and will eventually be found to be explicable in terms of a scientific discipline in much the same way as lightning became comprehensible with the discovery of electricity.

The mind's polarising habit of selecting one alternative and excluding others makes it difficult at first to accept our claim that none of these three possibilities is correct and none entirely false if viewed from a particular angle. In literal terms each can be demonstrated to be unsatisfactory but, by accepting the preoccupation with reality underlying each, the differences are minimised. This transcendence has been our object. To the extent that the attempt may have succeeded, a bridge becomes available between the material and the spiritual, between the tangible world of matter and that of abstract thought. Eventually one end of the bridge is seen to be an aspect of the other end.

In summary, the hypothesis set out in this book proposes that:

1. Life is purposeful in that it is programmed so as to produce a particular life-form and, in so doing, throws out a number of byproducts or offshoots, including the lower animals. Man as we know him may not be the completed life-form but merely an intermediate one. The end product may be a creature identical to man but having more consistently orientated attitudes towards circumstances and his fellows. Or, maybe, even such a creation would be an intermediate stage, the matrix from which consciousness could emerge as a life-form in its own right, rather as a butterfly emerges from a chrysalis. Such a view of evolution runs counter to the random processes described by neo-Darwinism. Even the most respectable biologists are now uneasily aware of the idea that creation is dependent on the occurrence of the one useful chance mutation at each stage in a necessary series of several billion is as fraught with wishful thinking as any other explanation to date. It seems that the organic material present on earth may be just as capable of gradually orientating itself into a predestined form of life as the cells of an acorn allocate functions between themselves to produce eventually an oak tree.

2. Man has a sense precisely of such a destiny which arises from the action of a part of his mind which takes place outside his awareness. The presence of unconscious mind has been amply demonstrated and its existence need no longer surprise us. On the contrary, the more surprising fact is that we are conscious of as much of our mental activity as we seem to be. We can reasonably expect a good deal of motivation and decision-making to take place outside the discretion of consciousness, just as our livers and spleens fulfil their specific tasks without requiring instructions from our conscious minds. Since we cannot, by definition, be directly aware of what is going on in our unconscious minds, we can deduce a great deal by analysing the activities and motivations of these mechanisms with the aid of mirroring techniques.

3. Many people will not admit the fallibility of their conscious minds and thinking processes. If their minds worked as freely and accurately as they would lead us to believe, observation of the unconscious mechanisms should be easy. That is not the case. Consequently, one should be constantly distrustful of one's deepest

convictions and unsupported conclusions. The initial experiences of the individual mind imprints upon it false information and associations. Moreover, social conditions and the course of evolution have left habit patterns on the community at large which have formed mental channels along which thought processes flow in comparatively elementary shapes. For this reason we have great difficulty in perceiving objects, phenomena and abstract ideas in a realistic relationship to each other. Archaic views regarding intangible phenomena still persist – archaic because they were formulated before man had sufficiently sophisticated concepts in which to explain them. He was therefore forced to use analogous descriptions and to personify energies as gods, angels, and devils.

4. Man as we have shown him is not a stable species yet. He is and always has been gradually increasing his consciousness. The day is foreseeable when he will succeed in aligning far more compatibly than at present his attitudes towards his fellows, his work, his relationship to life and death, and original thought. He will then cease to be driven by unconscious urges towards experiences which might have a correcting effect on his misconceptions. He will then be free – free to exercise choice without the constant intervention of unconscious corrective motivation.

5. The line of investigation indicated to follow up the hypothesis appears to be very fruitful. The hypothesis accords with many observed phenomena, the history of human thought and beliefs, and the products of art, dreams, and the objects of human fascination.

*   *   *

We have offered some facts and arguments in support of this hypothesis. Proof in the scientific sense is never likely to be forthcoming even if every detail is correct because few components of life are subject to quantitative measurement and repetition under laboratory conditions. The best supporting evidence is that it accounts for more of history and observable events in a manner more consistent with everyday experience than does any other hypothesis. But there is still a need, even at this point, to indicate the implications of points raised in earlier chapters, particularly concerning the concept of God. Only through these implications can the answers to some of the fundamental questions asked by man be provided in an idiom which satisfies modern mentality as much as theology satisfied medieval mind. Man has a deep-rooted need to recognise forces outside of himself, essentially and at least in the long run benign, which propel him both towards his own destiny and that of the species to which he belongs. If our hypothesis is correct, religions are not empty myths owing their origin to wishful thinking but analogous statements regarding the nature and destiny of man, formulated intuitively in the absence of thought concepts in which they could be expressed. Though reality may be very different from the analogy, it promises equivalent wonder in the prospect of ultimate 'salvation' or, more accurately, destination.

We have argued that all three currently accepted attitudes towards phenomena are not contradictory in essence. They appear so only because of the mind's habit of considering things to be either this or that and because we see them from a particular aspect which causes them to appear as isolated propositions.

St Paul said: 'God was in Christ reconciling the world to himself, not counting their trespasses against them.' A primary aim of un-conscious activity is to bring about reconciling of these divergent views so that each has its proper place in an overall view of life and its purpose, and in the attitudes of man made whole. But to bring about this reconciliation, some misconceptions must be examined to clear the way to the essence of the matter. On the concept of God, two main divergent views exist; one that God is a sort of super-personality; the other, on the lines suggested by the former Bishop of Woolwich in *Honest to God*, that God is some sort of force like electricity, not quite inanimate or 'thinglike' but more resembling a field of energy which yet possesses some sort of consciousness. Often associated with either of these views is the ardently upheld proposition that God – person or field of energy – is good, just and merciful.

Now there are many arguments in favour of the existence of God; the necessity for a first cause behind creation, for instance; another undeniable one is that there is a system of relationships between life, matter, time, and energy and that these relationships themselves, since they possess the energy to assert their existence and influence our destinies, may collectively be termed God. God may also be defined as that which a man, by his actions, may be seen as worshipping. One dedicates his life towards the pursuit of making money, another to gambling, a third towards his children, a fourth towards an art. In this sense a man's God is that for which he sacrifices the time he spends on earth, i.e. his life. And in this sense there are many Gods. The supreme, the reality perhaps, is when a man realises that the underlying motivation behind any of these activities is essentially a step on the way to becoming, and the process of becoming is, in itself, the highest form of knowable God.

In spite of all the arguments for the existence of God, none would seem to bear out the associated contention that God is necessarily good, just, and merciful as we understand these terms. Indeed an impartial intellect has difficulty understanding how God – person, process, or field of energy – should ever have become associated with goodness or justice. Water is 'good' if needed to quench thirst, extinguish a fire, moisten parched ground. Water is 'bad' if leaking into a ship or flooding towns. In view of these varieties of circumstances, water can hardly be classified as inherently good or bad. One can only maintain that water is necessary to life. If one cannot argue that water is good, let alone just, how can one possibly argue that God – person, process, or field of energy – is good? Good and bad, just and unjust, in fact any adjective descriptions, are purely relative terms. Theologians assure us their concept of God is absolute. Therefore, if he is in some characteristics personal, are his qualities likely to be relative to the beholder? Processes of becoming or fields of energy are even less likely to be relative. The importance of this digression is simply this. The church, presumably in its mistaken endeavours to persuade us to believe in a particular interpretation of the person, process, or field of energy which it terms God, has assured us that God is good and just in a personalised way. By so doing, the church has not persuaded us of anything, but has confused us by presenting the conflict of a beneficient being permitting appalling sacrifices.

If God cannot be 'good' relative to man – and if he was, then he would surely be a creature rather than a creator of man – man would do well to be 'good' relative to God, the field of energy, or the complex of phenomena from which he has sprung. In this sense of good, we mean aligned with the energy so that his behaviour and attitudes conform to some universal process of growth and becoming which, so far, can only be discerned mistily through the fogs and confusions of our relatively inefficient mentalities.

What concept of God could comply, then, with the human condition as our senses record it, as our intellects know it to be? For there certainly exists, if only in human minds, a complex of phenomena which accounts for the concept of God. How can the concentration-camp, the starvation of the helpless and the rape of the innocent be consistent with the existence of a purpose, a beneficience – in short of any sort of God however different from any previous concepts of him or it?

For here is the final confrontation. If creator there is, then he or it is responsible for these horrors as much as he or it created the lark in the clear blue sky of the spring morning. How far can we hold both these extremes in our minds at the same moment, confront the one with the other and let the vision fade, leaving us with nothing save the clear conviction that all is resolved, reconciled and that the way ahead is clear.

Is it possible because, in fact, you and I are ourselves that which we have conceived as God?

The conscious part of mentality, like the tip of the ice-berg, shows above the surface of the sea and this we are aware of as 'us'. This tip as me, that one as you, and apparently different and isolated; each drifting southerly on its own course from the Arctic towards the tropical seas – melting and dying a little as it emerges into the greater ocean – and never to return to the cold unknown regions of its creation and birth. Is the Ultimate Hypothesis stating that our entire life and experience is geared towards bringing about not only the intellectual but also the emotional recognition of this fact? As Christ was in Jesus – and so unconsciously recognised as indeed to be wholly identified with him – so Christ is in me and in you. The difference then between you and me is only one of the degree of recognition; the recognition demanding not only a review of intellectual ideas but a shift of attention from the tip of the ice-berg apparent above the waves to every beholder, to the whole ice-berg and to the sea itself.

Thus far we have made a suggestion only. More is needed to demonstrate its consistency with observed facts, with the possibilities it opens up for a reconciliation between opposites.

*   *   *

In the meantime we see the affairs of nations become more rather than less confused. Perhaps we have suspended major wars, but genocide is still practised and minor wars abound. Perhaps the objectives of legislatures are more humane, but the atmosphere and environment, do what we will, become daily more polluted, less congenial. Perhaps we have succeeded in suppressing the locust plague that would have deprived a hundred thousand of their daily bread, but the hundred thousand have taken this opportunity of relative affluence to become two hundred thousand and there is a limit to the space and the natural resources of the earth.

Yet that, God help us – for whether we believe in him or it we can hardly refrain from automatically conceiving him – is only the beginning. In our own lives we may, if we are lucky, see the maturing of ambitions and the realisation of dreams. We may count ourselves among the privileged and fortunate ones of this earth, but we have to be blind indeed to attribute these blessings to our virtue in the sight of a God, field of energy, or complex of phenomena. At every stage personal energy has combined with luck and, however we conceive virtue, others more virtuous that we have met with fates less fortunate. And there is no security or permanence in these blessings. Day by day we grow older. Our strength begins to fail, our looks to fade. Our ideals long since gone are supplanted only by a determination to hang on as long as possible.

Confronted with this evidence, can we maintain enough faith in ourselves, in the universe, in pleasure, or in purpose to carry on the day's work with a light heart?

There is no intellectual answer. And emotionally we go on to live for the sake of those we love. To have behind us children who may restlessly seek for an answer where we have failed. We see nothing but the process of evolution using us as its fodder. Those who went before us endured this that we might live and we endure to live and die in our time that others may one day rejoice. Only we do not feel that way, we do not believe it and we are far from taking consolation in it. We are still trapped on our left hand by the deity determining in an inscrutable, obsessive, irresponsible, inhumane manner the moment when each sparrow shall fall. On our other hand we have blind chance, with its apologists Messrs. Freud and Darwin, hitting out in every possible direction so that our future depends not only on the right blow in the right place but at the right instance of time – the chance in a billion endlessly coming off.

Who shall rid us of these mighty Gods? Are these mockeries the best alternative possibilities which the intellect of man can, after fifty thousand years, conceive? They cannot be. The answer cannot lie in either extreme.

'Who sees with equal eye, as God of all, a hero perish, or a sparrow fall,' wrote Pope. But the fall of the sparrow is not willed as such by an odious deity. Nor is it shot down by a blind destiny playing an infinite game of Russian roulette – in which at every turn all the chambers save one are loaded.

The complex of phenomena determining the fall of the sparrow is more likely to be found in the laws of enantiodromia, entelechy, and synchronicity, principles little recognised in our intellectually planned world of the twentieth century. Whether these laws operate within the mind of an all-embracive deity and conform to the rules of statistical random activity is neither here nor there, save that both are possibly true and, if so, their reconciliation may be brought about.

The deist can surely accept that God the Creator is content to create the context and the rules within which the process takes place. Does he personally have to determine the exact moment of the sparrow's fall before we can accept him? And if he did, would he not be devil rather than God? The scientist can hardly deny much longer that some principles besides the random event at the random moment shape our destiny. An explanation of man, his origin and his destiny in terms of enantiodromia, entelechy, and synchronicity may at this moment be incomplete and be seen only darkly through the

proverbial glass. But such an explanation is infinitely more intelligent and intelligible than the other two which it so manifestly
transcends. Here is a way through. Here springs hope. Here we may
discern a little of the truth, enough to restore order – order of a
different kind from that conceived in the past – and from the
reorientation of attitudes which it may offer can our salvation come.

* * *

Enantiodromia, a concept first used by Heraclitus, is a running
towards the opposite. If man will not or more accurately cannot yet
act consciously in accordance with the complex of phenomena which
has brought about his existence and continues to bear him onwards,
then he will act in contradiction to it. Since growth took place long
before consciousness and will continue inexorably in spite of consciousness misused, man as a whole or in separate communities or
individually encounters precisely the effects of conscious will in
conflict with the creative complex of phenomena. The creative wins
the encounter every time for indeed it can succeed in more than one
way. One may progress directly from a starting point to a destination
ten miles to the west with a minimum of trouble. But if travel
towards the west is for some reason ruled out, then the destination
can still be reached by travelling east in precisely the opposite
direction. The journey will be much longer and harder but eventually, having circumscribed the earth, one will arrive. What appears
to delay evolution at any particular time only tends to dam the river
until the weight of water builds up to sweep away the obstruction
or carve a channel round it. And as it is with man the animal, the
race, the nation, the town, the village, the family, so it is with every
individual. In the short term he can create a diversion, cause strife,
build up misery for himself by running counter to his destiny and
trying to stem the tide. But each in his lifetime progresses a little –
or his misfortunes point the way for the benefit of others.

Progress is not a matter of conscious thought or life would hardly
have evolved to the point where consciousness itself first developed
from life. Nor does progress cease because there is no conscious
contribution to it. If our hopes depended on such conscious efforts,

242

they would be small indeed. The directors of even the smallest company sitting round their boardroom table have difficulty agreeing their policy. Many politicians are less concerned to give objective examination to facts and prescribe the remedies than they are to air their opinions. Scientists disagree within their own fields, often acrimoniously. And man's ability to foretell the future by conscious reasoning is so pitifully inadequate that few attempt it and none agree on it. In fact, since consciousness has hitherto had no idea as to the destination of the development process, its restless efforts have been confined more to bringing about change as distinct from planned progress.

But change, even as distinct from progress, can be valuable. Movement allows the elements of life to form and reform their relationships one with another until they conform to one of the parts of a structure at which evolution may be seen to have been aiming. Once this relationship is made, that part at least crystalises whilst other less satisfactory experiments continue in the chaos of the matrix which embodies it.

If man will not, or cannot, move in the direction of his destiny by acting consistently with reason, feeling, sensation, and the implications of the circumstances in which he finds himself at every turn of history, then he will be propelled forward willy-nilly by his misfortunes through the action of enantiodromia. Each excess will produce its remedy, probably also, but not quite, as unfortunate as the excess to which it was itself a reaction. Life goes forward as if every aspect was governed by the swing of the pendulum. Gradually, the swing will become less and less until, one day, the pendulum will hang motionless and man will have arrived, arrived in the sense of having completed his evolution. He will have become a stable species, man whole at last.

In the meantime, in every age, one sees improvement achieved not by conscious action but by the reaction against excess. Mankind staggers from crisis to crisis, letting situations develop to such a pitch that either society must break down or the excess become self-evident. Thus, before progress, we are likely to have to suffer the abuse which unites us all in the conviction that action is necessary to correct that abuse. Society is not easily moved to action. Only extreme circumstances bring unity of purpose.

Wars increased in scale until the great nations could no longer resort to them without destroying the world. So the H-bomb, long and loudly declared as the ultimate horror of our civilisation, may be seen by history as its salvation.

There are few exceptions to the rule of enantiodromia and when its gradual but inexorable operation comes into play, many innocents are carried away. In earlier times, the population needed to expand and grow. Man implemented this need by conditioning his mind with certain ethical and religious ideas, myths, legends, and taboos. Today a large proportion of mankind still multiply in the continuing blind belief that there is personal and social merit in having many children – even though the experts already warn that eventually the planet will not support them all. It is within the realm of possibilities that certain natural disasters or social disturbances are the result of enantiodromia in areas that cling ignorantly to blind belief.

It might be argued on nature's behalf that the victims have for the most part cut themselves off from the mainstream of evolving humanity and, by preserving practices far beyond the time when they have served a useful purpose, are intent on blocking the course of the very complex of phenomena to which they owe their creation. By man's logic and man's sense of justice, the holding of anachronistic convictions is the worst charge of which they could stand accused. Does that justify the terrible fate of their thousands, their children who have no convictions and those among them who hold different beliefs? But nature is not governed by man's logic or his sense of justice. And so long as man wishfully clings to the proposition that if nature is not thus governed, it ought to be, then he is not likely to form by unbiased observations a concept of nature's logic or nature's sense of justice. To his cost, he will be unable to live in any conformity with the inexorable. He will not discover the purpose behind a God, field of energy, or complex of phenomena if he insists that its actions or reactions are inappropriate to what he considers befitting to an 'it' of this order.

If man cannot focus his mind upon such 'unworldly' activities as tolerance or concern for others, then he will enantiodromically

244

entertain himself by contemplation of their opposites in plays, novels and films of crime, ego-aggrandizement and the consequences of acting out the impulses of inconsistent attitudes. He may, in short, progress positively and consciously or negatively and blindly. One way is beset with pain and shame by contrast with his potential. The other requires a wisdom he has not yet learnt to apply throughout his affairs. But progress is inherent in both.

The pendulum swings of enantiodromia mean that man's present discomforts signify little or nothing regarding the shape which society will ultimately adopt or the features which will be present. Things do not go from bad to worse – though often they go so far as to be intolerable. At this point a mechanism deep inside humanity is triggered off, and the reaction to the intolerable sets in. The major perils, afflictions, and dangers of mankind are averted in this way, by the unconscious actions of those who, if questioned, would in all probability attribute their actions to wholly other motives than those they are in fact serving.

George Orwell's *1984* drew attention to the inherent evils in the bureaucracy which makes life possible for enormous numbers of people who today congregate together in mutually organised dependence upon one another. The administrative machinery which runs such communities is itself a miraculous creation, as man is not by his nature a thoroughgoing, methodical animal and agreement with his fellows is extremely hard to obtain. The machinery requires him to impose artificial rules and restraint of normal inclinations upon himself and his family. As the load upon the bureaucracy increases, the system endeavours to meet it by a proliferation of tortuous rules and taxes. The blessing of the ability to organise which enabled man for a while to speed up his progress is pushed to a degree which threatens to stifle further growth. And youth, quite inarticulate and unaware that it has sensed the implications, nevertheless indicates unmistakably that the establishment is confronted with stagnation by regulations at one extreme and chaos by breakdown of order at the other. From this point of view, the very phenomenon which is generally deplored in modern society as being symptomatic of its decadence might in fact be foreseen as pointing the way to freedom from abuses of conscious planning which cater only for a part of man's need.

So far, so good, yet perhaps the most important principle of all, entelechy, remains unaccounted for. Entelechy is the revelation of potential, the transformation of that which after countless changes is to emerge as evolution's end product.

The scant evidence available indicates reassuringly that entelechy is irreversible and no ultimate disaster can prevent it. In this instance, the acorn cannot go rotten or man malform.

The progress of entelechy is experienced in the life of every individual although it defies description. One might meet a man who says in all sincerity that he has seen a ghost or had a vision. To the listener the account is interesting but essentially meaningless. The real or imaginary experience of the one cannot be communicated to the other. Yet should the same listener himself undergo even the slightest direct experience of this type, he is likely to be deeply impressed and it may well change his entire outlook on life. Such is the difference in impact between direct experience and a related account. Nevertheless, an attempt will be made to describe entelechy so that at least the reader, like the listener to the vision, may have his attention drawn to the possibilities and may seek out the experience for himself.

The first type of evidence is the seeming inexplicability of the life-pattern of each individual. One does not live one's life by consciously planning it. It is rather as if one is lived by one's life – for the destiny of any individual, looking back, can be seen to have hung upon a number of events trivial and fortuitous in themselves, often incredible coincidences which, however, have led to results very different from any reasonable conscious expectation.

Valuable as plans may be, they rarely work out for more than a few weeks ahead or more precisely than along very general lines, making impractical any attempt to plan consciously the long-term conduct of one's life. A hundred minor incidents or accidents which could not have been foreseen intrude at every turn. One's motivating drives themselves unaccountably change almost overnight. One cannot easily comprehend just how far unconscious drives and motivations may underlie one's day-to-day activities, revealing themselves and their intended destination only to the impartial analysis of a disinterested spectator who can point out the pattern of development revealing itself. The subject may find the pattern to his liking and therefore regard himself as 'lucky' or consider it runs counter to his conscious plans and therefore do his best to resist it.

Once the subject has had his life-pattern analysed and pointed out to him, he becomes sharply aware of it and of just how far his life is lived according to the dictates of something other than his conscious will. Thereafter he will recognise the difference between events brought about by his own efforts and planning, and those which occur apparently by chance and yet conform to some overall pattern. As he recognises the latter, he will feel that sense of the numinous which in less sophisticated times man attributed to the presence of God. Now he can be no less astonished at the power and ability of his unconscious mechanisms to cause him to be at the right place at the right time doing the right thing to bring about the billion-to-one chance result which alone could further the pattern of his life.

One may or may not believe in fortune-tellers. Nevertheless, one has usually witnessed or heard reliable accounts of their abilities. It might be suggested that behind fortune-telling lies an intuitive ability to pick out a subject's life-pattern – as dictated by his constellation of attitudes at any given time – and to project it into the future and the sort of events it will inevitably entail.

If an individual – in the sense of a constellation of attitudes – has a life-pattern which inexorably unrolls itself before his conscious passive eyes, can it be that society itself, in the sense of mankind supporting a collective complex of attitudes, has a pattern of history and destiny which is proceeding slowly to reveal itself? If this is so, the mechanism possessing such power and ability is unlikely to direct itself finally into some awful chaos of complete self-destruction.

The second type of evidence which points towards a purposeful destiny is that derived from history both before and since the arrival of man.

Throughout the history of the past fifty thousand years, man has survived every sort of natural peril which might have exterminated him and he has continued to develop. Whether his way of life is better at any given moment than at some point in the past is always debatable, but nowhere in history has he gone backwards without a step forwards as well. In some respects he progresses. In other directions the necessity for progress activates the process of enantiodromia to pull him back into a situation which will stimulate him to react.

If man has indeed evolved by random mutation, then he has arrived as the result of a billion billion coincidences piled up one by one upon the other, the odds against which are an equally great number of billions to one against. More likely some unconscious part of his mechanism, seeing the larger requirements of the individual and the species as a whole at any one time, has engineered the appropriate action for the purposeful outcome of survival and evolution at each stage. If random mutation and survival of the fittest alone determined the course of events on earth, their laws could best be satisfied by a form of life which multiplied most rapidly and would endure in the widest variety of territorial climatic conditions. Life need not have proceeded beyond a higher state than bacteria. But life did not take that course. Why? And it survived countless hazards to arrive in the twentieth century. How? If some other factor – the fulfilment of a destiny so far only dimly discernible from past events projected into the future – was involved, then the reasons why life has taken human shape might be deduced. This is circumstantial evidence certainly, and as such far from conclusive, but at least more convincing than the alternative of the whimsical creator or the blind randomness of chance.

The third type of evidence is that which offers some explanation, however unproven and unprecise, of how an unconscious mind could operate and achieve results. In the case of the individual, such an unconscious ability would have access to his memory and aptitude channels and would use them to override consciousness as occasion demanded to fulfil its decisions – decisions, motivations, and destinies of which the individual might be unaware. But the matter is more difficult than that. The process of entelechy either of the individual or the species requires more than the cooperation of a number of isolated intelligences, however powerful these might be. Jung, in his work on synchronicity or meaningful coincidences, has given instances of events which cannot be accounted for except by supposing that one mind has access to the knowledge and memories of other minds.

Theories of past evolution will contribute to present dilemmas only if we postulate that what is evolving is not a number of isolated separate mind-cells, each with its own survival motivations, memory stocks, and individual aptitudes, but rather the development of collective attitudes. The first step in this direction was Jung's concept of a collective unconscious which presumably individual experience both contributes to and draws upon. The conscious mind belongs to the individual but the more important part of the individual, his unconscious mind, is not his at all. It is perhaps ours. In this sense I am you and you are me. That part of me or you has been – when this phenomenon was first dimly perceived – described and personified as Christ.

St Paul said: 'I live, yet not I, but Christ lives in me.' He said it as though this had been true only after the crucifixion. More probably it had always been true, but after the crucifixion, real or mythical, there existed an image which could carry the projection of the intuitive truth.

The existence of evidence regarding telepathy as a serious possibility has already been pointed out. Let us speculate that some degree of telepathy takes place at the unconscious level. One is then occasionally aware of it as a sort of leak through to consciousness of a process which may be continually and constantly in operation. Individual survival would indeed demand that only occasional leakage occured. Otherwise the distraction from immediate pursuits necessary to individual survival would be too great and the individual would become incapacitated. Indeed, some forms of madness appear to have such origins and the empathy reported in certain other states of mind seems to be based on sensations of mutual mind sharing. But conscious awareness of this phenomenon is not important. It is the implications of telepathy as a common and perhaps essential phenomenon at the unconscious level which are exciting. Communities of ants and bees behave as if directed by a central mind emanating from the queen. If the queen is destroyed, chaos immediately prevails. So long as she exists in the middle of the colony, activities take place in a co-ordinated manner as though each individual insect was one of a number of cells performing a function in a biological organ or as a single life species in its own right.

Let us further suppose that mind, as already suggested, has access to the memory store in the collective unconscious. Thus it may be that my – or rather, our shared – unconscious memory bank has virtually held every event since the evolution of mind.

This hypothesis would go some way to account for the curious phenomenon whereby individuals are convinced they are reincarnations of historic personalities. A particular complex of attitudes, coinciding in some respects with those of a particular individual known in history, acts as a sort of filter allowing some memories from the common stock to leak through to the individual's conscious, which is usually disturbed or temporarily enlarged. In so far as the present day subject has a similar constellation of attitudes to the historic personality involved, it would be correct to say at least in one sense that he is, in fact, a reincarnation of the person he claims to be.

*   *   *

We may conclude from these three types of evidence that mankind has survived thus far not by accident but because his form of life has an inbuilt protective mechanism. Some individual men already hold the power to release atomic or germ warfare that would contaminate life on earth. We may say or choose to believe that we exist at the theory of the whims and tempers of a few such men. Yet there is an alternative belief. He and you and I are one, in so far as we share some aspects of a living, motivating, collective unconscious mentality. On this account we have greater power than we know for restraining him or anyone else from the act of ultimate destruction.

If this hypothesis is true and acceptable to modern mind, how do we live in accordance with it? Conscious actions to further a doctrine that conscious action is not nearly so potent as it seems to be, would be inconsistent. Therefore we can only refrain as far as possible from acts which would run counter to the course of the evolutionary trends which we find going on around us. We may accept the fact of our circumstances rather than some idealistic notion as to how they ought to be. And maybe we can assist the process of the reconciliation of life and suffering. Suffering is the attendant of consciousness, the disadvantage of a particular sort of blessing. The legends of the Fall of Man and the casting out of Lucifer express this as the unity of God broken. Evil was cast out. God ceased to love his enemy. History has been the gradual reconciliation of good and evil; of seeing the usefulness of evil and the stagnation inherent in what we think of as good. So long as some things are regarded as good and some as evil and therefore to be avoided and cast out, just that long will they recur time and again demanding our acceptance, our recognition of their function in our universe. So long as we heed the terrible example set us by the odious deity – whom we are told condemned his enemy and threw him into torment – so we shall be tortured by the dichotomy in ourselves. Our present task is the reconciliation of so-called and so relative 'good' and so-called and again relative 'evil', the reconciliation of life and of suffering, of our limited consciousness and our fantastic potential both as a species and as individuals.

ACKNOWLEDGEMENTS

Virginia Axline	*Dibs: In Search of Self.* Penguin Books, 1960.
R Blum & Associates	*Utopiates, The Use and Users of LSD.* Atherton, New York, 1964.
J A C Brown	*Freud and the Post-Freudians,* Penguin Books, 1961.
Chekhov	*Three Sisters.*
C D Darlington	*The Evolution of Man and Society.* George Allen & Unwin, 1969.
Charles Darwin	The Origin of Species.
	The Voyage of the Beagle.
Bernard Delfgaauw	*Evolution, The Theory of Teilhard de Chardin.* Fontana Library, 1970.
Henry F Ellenberger	*The Discovery of the Unconscious: The History and Evolution of Dynamic Psychiatry.* Allen Lane, The Penguin Press, 1970.
Eduard Erkes	Ho-Shang-Kung's *Commentary on Lao-Tse.* (ed.). Artibus Asiae, Ascona, Switzerland.
W Y Evans-Wentz	*The Tibetan Book of the Great Liberation.* (ed.). Commentary by C G Jung. Oxford University Press.
Ann Faraday	*Dream Power.* Hodder and Stoughton, 1972.
Frieda Fordham	*An Introduction to Jung's Psychology.* Penguin Books, 1953.
S H Foulkes & E J Anthony	*Group Psychotherapy: The Psychoanalytic Approach.* Penguin Books, 1965.
Eric Fromm	*The Art of Loving (I-Thou Relationship).* Unwin Books.
	Psychoanalysis and Religion. Bantam Books, 1967.

George Gamow & Martynas Ycas	*Mr Tompkins Inside Himself.* George Allen & Unwin, 1967.
Kenneth W Gatland & Derek D Dempster	*The Inhabited Universe.* Allan Wingate, 1957.
Josef Goldbrunner	*Individuation.* Hollis & Carter, 1955.
R L Gregory	*The Intelligent Eye.* Weidenfeld & Nicolson, 1970.
Rasa Gustaitis	*Turning On.* Weidenfeld & Nicolson, 1969.
J A Hadfield	*Dreams and Nightmares.* Penguin Books, 1954.
M Esther Harding	*The Way of All Women.* David McKay, New York, 1933.
Sir Alister Hardy	*The Divine Flame.* Collins, 1966. *The Living Stream.* Collins, 1965.
Dr E Graham Howe	*To Cure Or To Heal.* Allen & Unwin, 1965.
David Hume	*A Treatise Of Human Nature.* Pelican Books, 1969.
Christmas Humphreys	*Concentration and Meditation. Manual of Mind Development.* John M. Watkins, 1935.
Francis Huxley	*The Invisibles.* Rupert Hart-Davis, 1966.
Aniela Jaffe	*The Myth of Meaning in the Work of C G Jung.* Hodder and Stoughton, 1970.
William James	*The Varieties of Religious Experience.* Fontana Library, 1960.
C G Jung	*The Collected Works,* published by Routledge & Kegan Paul. In total, 18 volumes; specific interest in:

Vol. Six: *Psychological Types*
Vol. Eight: *The Structure and Dynamics of the Psyche*
Vol. Nine: *The Archetypes and the Collective Unconscious*
Vol. Ten: *Civilisation in Transition*
Vol. Sixteen: *The Practise of Psychotherapy*

	Vol. Seventeen: *The Development of Personality, Memories, Dreams, Reflections.* Collins and Routledge & Kegan Paul, 1963.
R D Laing	*The Divided Self.* Penguin Books, 1960.
John Lennon	*In His Own Write.* Jonathan Cape, 1964.
Lin Yutang	*The Wisdom of China.* (ed.), Michael Joseph.
Arthur Koestler	*The Act of Creation.* Hutchinson, 1964. *The Roots of Coincidence.* Hutchinson, 1972.
Arthur Koestler & J H Smythies	*The Alpbach Symposium. Beyond Reductionism.* (ed.). Hutchinson, 1969.
Norman Mackenzie	*Dreams and Dreaming.* Aldus Books, 1965.
P W Martin	*Experiment in Depth.* Routledge & Kegan Paul, 1955.
R E L Masters & Jean Houstin	*The Varieties of Psychedelic Experience.* Turnstone Books, 1973.
D N McKinnon H A Williams	*Objections to Christian Belief.* Four Lectures. Constable & Co. Ltd. 1963.
Desmond Morris	*The Naked Ape.* Jonathan Cape. 1967.
Hugh Odishaw	*The Earth in Space.* Routledge & Kegan Paul, 1967.
J B Priestley	*Man and Time.* Aldus Books Ltd. 1964.
John A T Robinson as Bishop of Woolwich	*Honest to God.* SCM Press, 1963.
Carl R Rogers	*On Becoming a Person.* Houghton Miffin, Boston, 1961. *On Encounter Groups.* Harper & Row, 1970.
Bertrand Russell	*History of Western Philosophy.* George Allen & Unwin Ltd. 1961.
William C Schultz	*Joy - Expanding Human Awareness.* Grove Press, 1969.
Bernard Shaw	*Back to Methuselah.* Penguin Books Ltd. 1939. *Man and Superman.* Penguin Books Ltd. 1946.

David Stafford-Clark	*Psychiatry Today.* Penguin Books Ltd. 1963.
	What Freud Really Said. Penguin Books Ltd. 1965.
Anthony Storr	*The Integrity of the Personality.* William Heinemann Ltd. 1960.
	Sexual Deviation. Pelican Books, 1964.
	The Dynamics of Creation. Martin Secker & Warburg Ltd. 1972.
	Jung. Fontana/Collins, 1973.
Robert Thompson	*The Pelican History of Psychology.* Penguin Books Ltd. 1968.
Tolstoy	*My Confession.*
Arnold Toynbee	*An Historian's Approach to Religion.* Oxford University Press, 1953.
C H Waddington	*Villa Serbelloni Symposia: Toward a Theoretical Biology, in three parts: 1. Prologomena. 2. Sketches. 3. Drafts.* (ed.). Edinburgh University Press, 1968-70.
Alan W Watts	*The Wisdom of Insecurity.* Vintage Books, 1954.
Leslie D Weatherhead	*The Christian Agnostic.* Hodder & Stoughton, 1965.
G A Wells	*The Jesus of the Early Christians.* Pemberton Books, 1971.
H G Wells	*Mind at the End of its Tether.* Heinemann Ltd. 1945.
	Outline of History. Cassel, 1920.
Roger W Westcott	*The Divine Animal (An Exploration of Human Potentiality).* Funk & Wagnalls, New York, 1969.
Victor White	*God and the Unconscious.* Fontana Library, 1952.
Richard Wilhelm	The I Ching or Book of Changes (trans.) Routledge & Kegan Paul, 1950.
Colin Wilson	*The Outsider.* Victor Gollancz, 1956.
Ernest Wood	*Yoga.* Penguin Books, 1959.

perception
intuition
feeling
thinking
} = one mind